COMPUTER APPLICATIONS IN MANAGEMENT

COMPUTER APPLICATIONS IN MANAGEMENT

Harsh Marwah

ANMOL PUBLICATIONS PVT. LTD.
NEW DELHI-110 002 (INDIA)

ANMOL PUBLICATIONS PVT. LTD.
Regd. Office: 4360/4, Ansari Road, Daryaganj,
New Delhi-110002 (India)
Tel.: 23278000, 23261597, 23286875, 23255577
Fax: 91-11-23280289
Email: anmolpub@gmail.com
Visit us at: www.anmolpublications.com

Branch Office: No. 1015, Ist Main Road, BSK IIIrd Stage
IIIrd Phase, IIIrd Block, Bangalore-560 085 (India)
Tel.: 080-41723429 • Fax: 080-26723604
Email: anmolpublicationsbangalore@gmail.com

Computer Applications in Management

First Edition, 2011

ISBN 978-81-261-4478-5

PRINTED IN INDIA

Printed at Mehra Offset Press, Delhi.

Contents

Preface

This textbook has been designed specially to cater the needs of first year students of MBA and PGDBM. It covers comprehensively the latest syllabus as prescribed by the UPTU, along with the syllabi of many other universities. This book will be helpful for the majority of students and faculties because of its simple presentation in a simple manner. It is also observed while planning this book that updated in the terms of textbook so far.

The focus of the book is not merely on theoretical explanation of various concepts but relating them with the real life business situations thereby facilitating the business processes. The book therefore aims to serve a wide array of students of under-graduate and post-graduate courses in business management, computer applications and other related streams. It will also come in handy for business managers, computer professionals, and almost all categories of end users, etc. Overall this book is written for those who wants to learn the basic and new technologies of computer so that they can implements them to serve their purposes.

Author

Chapter 1

Basic of Computers

INTRODUCTION AND DEFINITION

The development of the modern day computer was the result of advances in technologies and man's need to quantify. Papyrus helped early man to record language and numbers. The abacus was one of the first counting machines. Some of the earlier mechanical counting machines lacked the technology to make the design work. For instance, some had parts made of wood prior to metal manipulation and manufacturing. Imagine the wear on wooden gears. The history of computers includes the names of early pioneers of math and computing.

The first computers were people. That is, electronic computers (and the earlier mechanical computers) were given this name because they performed the work that had previously been assigned to people. "Computer" was originally a job title: it was used to describe those human beings (predominantly women) whose job it was to perform the repetitive calculations required to compute such things as navigational tables, tide charts, and planetary positions for astronomical almanacs.

Imagine you had a job where hour after hour, day after day, you were to do nothing but compute multiplications. Boredom would quickly set in, leading to carelessness, leading to mistakes. And even on your best days you wouldn't be producing answers very fast. Therefore, inventors have been searching for hundreds of years for a way to mechanize (that is, find a mechanism that can perform) this task. The *abacus* was an early aid for mathematical computations. Its only value is that it aids the memory of the human performing the calculation. A skilled abacus operator can work on addition and subtraction problems at the speed of a person equipped with a hand calculator (multiplication and division are slower).

The abacus is often wrongly attributed to China. In fact, the oldest surviving abacus was used in 300 B.C. by the Babylonians. The abacus is still in use today, principally in the far east. A modern abacus consists of rings that slide over rods, but the older one pictured below dates from the time when pebbles were used for counting (the word "calculus" comes from the Latin word for pebble).

ABACUS

This is a brief history of the abacus and a Bibliography follows. The earliest counting devices known to man were his own hands and fingers. If that wasn't enough, things in nature were used like shells, twigs, pebbles, stones, and so forth. It is a good idea to think about the history of arithmetic, mathematics, writing and recorded information. Man's invention of the computer resulted from man's need to quantify, to count and to do mathematic calculations. Long before the computer, in the Roman Empire, Ancient Asia, and other parts of the World, man was inventing easier and faster ways of counting and calculating.

Definition

The abacus is a device, usually of wood (plastic, in recent times), having a frame that holds rods with freely-sliding beads mounted on them. The use of the abacus was pre-dated by the use of counting boards. A counting board had grooves along which one could slide beads or stones. The beads or stones did not have holes in them but only grooves along which they moved on the counting board. "The oldest surviving counting board is the Salamis tablet (originally thought to be a gaming board), used by the Babylonians circa 300 B.C., discovered in 1846 on the island of Salamis." The oldest surviving counting board is the Salamis tablet (originally thought to be a gaming board), used by the Babylonians circa 300 B.C., discovered in 1846 on the island of Salamis.

Around 1000 AD the Aztec peoples invented a device similar to an abacus which used corn kernels threaded through wooden frames. This was known as a Nepohualtzitzin. An Aztec abacus would have seven "beads" by thirteen columns.

NAPIER

John Napier's father, Archibald Napier, was an important man in late 16th century Scotland. His family had owned the Merchiston estate from the 1430s when one of his ancestors acquired the estate, becoming the first Napare of Merchiston. The family also owned estates at Lennox and at Menteith and a residence at Gartness. Archibald Napier married Janet Bothwell, the sister of the Bishop of Orkney, in 1549 when he was only 15 years old. Their son John Napier was born the following year. Archibald Napier was a justice-depute and was knighted in 1565. He was appointed Master of the Mint in 1582.

Before continuing we should comment on the spelling of John Napier. The name John is most easily dealt with as John Napier, and almost everyone else around his time, used the old spelling "Jhone". His surname appears in a large variety of different spellings. The forms Napeir, Nepair, Nepeir, Neper, Napare, Naper, Naipper are all seen but John Napier would most commonly have been written Jhone Neper at that time. The only form of Napier that we are sure would not have been used in Napier's lifetime was the present modern spelling "Napier"!

Napier was educated at St Andrews University, entering the university in 1563 at the age of 13. His mother arranged for him to live in St Salvator's College and special arrangements were made for the Principal of the University, John Rutherford, to take care of him personally. Napier's name appears on the matriculation roll of St Salvator's College for 1563. Shortly after Napier matriculated his mother died. We know that Napier spent some time at St Andrews University and he wrote himself many years later that it was in St Andrews that he first became passionately interested in theology. However Napier's name does not appear in the list of those being awarded degrees in the subsequent years so he must have left St Andrews to study in Europe before completing a degree. Of other facts we can also be certain. Napier did not acquire his knowledge of higher mathematics at St Andrews nor did he acquire his deep knowledge of classical literature there. Both these must have been acquired during his studies in Europe but no record exists to show where he studied, although the University of Paris is highly likely and it is also probable that he spent some time in Italy and the Netherlands.

By 1571 Napier had returned to Scotland for he was present at his father's second marriage which took place in that year. It was in 1571 that Napier himself began to make arrangements for his own marriage but it was at nearly two years before that took place. In 1572 most of the estates of the Napier family were made over to John Napier and a castle was planned for the estate at Gartness.

When the castle was completed in 1574, Napier and his wife took up residence there. Napier devoted himself to running his estates. This task he took very seriously and, being a great genius as an inventor, he applied his skills to these tasks. He approached agriculture in a scientific way and he experimented with:-

Napier's study of mathematics was only a hobby and in his mathematical works he writes that he often found it hard to find the time for the necessary calculations between working on theology. He is best known, however, for his invention of logarithms but his other mathematical contributions include a mnemonic for formulae used in solving spherical triangles, two formulae known as "Napier's analogies" used in solving spherical triangles and an invention called "Napier's bones" used for mechanically multiplying dividing and taking square roots and cube roots. Napier also found exponential expressions for trigonometric functions, and introduced the decimal notation for fractions. Unlike the logarithms used today, Napier's logarithms are not really to any base although in our present terminology it is not unreasonable (but perhaps a little misleading) to say that they are to base $1/e$. Certainly they involve a constant 10^7 which arose from the construction in a way that we will now explain. Napier did not think of logarithms in an algebraic way, in fact algebra was not well enough developed in Napier's time to make this a realistic approach. Rather he thought by dynamical analogy.

Babbage was not deterred, and by then was on to his next brainstorm, which he called the *Analytic Engine.* This device, large as a house and powered by 6 steam engines, would be more general purpose in nature because it would be programmable, thanks to the punched card technology of Jacquard. But it was Babbage who made an important intellectual leap regarding the punched cards.

In the Jacquard loom, the presence or absence of each hole in the card physically allows a coloured thread to pass or stops that thread (you can see this clearly in the earlier photo). Babbage saw that the pattern of holes could be used to represent an abstract idea such as a problem statement or the raw data required for that problem's solution. Babbage saw that there was no requirement that the problem matter itself physically pass thru the holes.

Furthermore, Babbage realized that punched paper could be employed as a storage mechanism, holding computed numbers for future reference. Because of the connection to the Jacquard loom, Babbage called the two main parts of his Analytic Engine the "Store" and the "Mill", as both terms are used in the weaving industry. The Store was where numbers were held and the Mill was where they were "woven" into new results. In a modern computer these same parts are called the *memory unit* and the *central processing unit* (CPU).

The Analytic Engine also had a key function that distinguishes computers from calculators: the conditional statement. A conditional statement allows a programme to achieve different results each time it is run. Based on the conditional statement, the path of the programme (that is, what statements are executed next) can be determined based upon a condition or situation that is detected at the very moment the programme is running.

You have probably observed that a modern stoplight at an intersection between a busy street and a less busy street will leave the green light on the busy street until a car approaches on the less busy street. This type of street light is controlled by a computer programme that can sense the approach of cars on the less busy street. That moment when the light changes from green to red is not fixed in the programme but rather varies with each traffic situation.

The conditional statement in the stoplight programme would be something like, "if a car approaches on the less busy street and the more busy street has already enjoyed the green light for at least a minute then move the green light to the less busy street". The conditional statement also allows a programme to react to the results of its own calculations. An example would be the programme that the I.R.S uses to detect tax fraud. This programme first computes a person's tax liability and then decides whether to alert the police based upon how that person's tax payments compare to his obligations.

Babbage befriended *Ada Byron*, the daughter of the famous poet Lord Byron. Though she was only 19, she was fascinated by Babbage's ideas and through letters and meetings with Babbage she learned enough about the design of the Analytic Engine to begin fashioning programmes for the still unbuilt machine. While Babbage refused to publish his knowledge for another 30 years, Ada wrote a series of "Notes" wherein she detailed sequences of instructions she had prepared for the Analytic Engine.

The Analytic Engine remained unbuilt (the British government refused to get involved with this one) but Ada earned her spot in history as the first computer programmer. Ada invented the subroutine and was the first to recognize the importance of looping.

Babbage himself went on to invent the modern postal system, cowcatchers on trains, and the ophthalmoscope, which is still used today to treat the eye. The next breakthrough occurred in America. The U.S. Constitution states that a census should be taken of all U.S. citizens every 10 years in order to determine the representation of the states in Congress. While the very first census of 1790 had only required 9 months, by 1880 the U.S. population had grown so much that the count for the 1880 census took 7.5 years. Automation was clearly needed for the next census. The census bureau offered a prize for an inventor to help with the 1890 census and this prize was won by Herman Hollerith, who proposed and then successfully adopted Jacquard's punched cards for the purpose of computation.

IBM continued to develop mechanical calculators for sale to businesses to help with financial accounting and inventory accounting. One characteristic of both financial accounting and inventory accounting is that although you need to subtract, you don't need negative numbers and you really don't have to multiply since multiplication can be accomplished via repeated addition.

But the U.S. military desired a mechanical calculator more optimized for scientific computation. By World War II the U.S. had battleships that could lob shells weighing as much as a small car over distances up to 25 miles. Physicists could write the equations that described how atmospheric drag, wind, gravity, muzzle velocity, etc. would determine the trajectory of the shell. But solving such equations was extremely laborious. This was the work performed by the human computers. Their results would be published in ballistic "firing tables" published in gunnery manuals.

During World War II the U.S. military scoured the country looking for math majors to hire for the job of computing these tables. But not enough humans could be found to keep up with the need for new tables. Sometimes artillery pieces had to be delivered to the battlefield without the necessary firing tables and this meant they were close to useless because they couldn't be aimed properly. Faced with this situation, the U.S. military was willing to invest in even hair-brained schemes to automate this type of computation. One early success was the Harvard *Mark I* computer, which was built as a partnership between Harvard and IBM in 1944. This was the first programmable digital computer made in the U.S. But it was not a purely electronic computer. The machine weighed 5 tons, incorporated 500 miles of wire, was 8 feet tall and 51 feet long, and had a 50 ft rotating shaft running its length, turned by a 5 horsepower electric motor. The Mark I ran non-stop for 15 years, sounding like a roomful of ladies knitting.

COMPUTER TECHNOLOGY

But things changed fast. By the 1990's a university student would typically own his own computer and have exclusive use of it in his dorm room.

This transformation was a result of the invention of the *microprocessor*. A microprocessor (uP) is a computer that is fabricated on an integrated circuit (IC). Computers had been around for 20 years before the first microprocessor was developed at *Intel* in 1971.

The micro in the name microprocessor refers to the physical size. Intel didn't invent the electronic computer. But they were the first to succeed in cramming an entire computer on a single *chip* (IC). Intel was started in 1968 and initially produced only semiconductor memory.

In 1969 they were approached by Busicom, a Japanese manufacturer of high performance calculators. Busicom wanted Intel to produce custom calculator chips: one chip dedicated to the keyboard, another chip dedicated to the display, another for the printer, etc.

But integrated circuits were expensive to design and this approach would have required Busicom to bear the full expense of developing new chips since these chips would only be of use to them.

But a new Intel employee convinced Busicom to instead accept a general purpose computer chip which, like all computers, could be reprogrammed for many different tasks. Intel argued that since the chip could be reprogrammed for alternative purposes, the cost of developing it could be spread out over more users and hence would be less expensive to each user. The general purpose computer is adapted to each new purpose by writing a *programme* which is a sequence of instructions stored in memory.

EVOLUTION OF COMPUTER

- The first counting device was the abacus, originally from Asia. It worked on a place-value notion meaning that the place of a bead or rock on the apparatus determined how much it was worth.
- 1600s: John Napier discovers logarithms. Robert Bissaker invents the slide rule which will remain in popular use until 19??.
- 1642: Blaise Pascal, a French mathematician and philosopher, invents the first mechanical digital calculator using gears, called the Pascaline. Although this machine could perform addition and subtraction on whole numbers, it was too expensive and only Pascal himself could repare it.
- 1804: Joseph Marie Jacquard used punch cards to automate a weaving loom.
- 1812: Charles P. Babbage, the "father of the computer", discovered that many long calculations involved many similar, repeated operations. Therefore, he designed

a machine, the difference engine which would be steam-powered, fully automatic and commanded by a fixed instruction programme. In 1833, Babbage quit working on this machine to concentrate on the analytical engine.

- 1840s: Augusta Ada. "The first programmer" suggested that a binary system shouled be used for staorage rather than a decimal system.
- 1850s: George Boole developed Boolean logic which would later be used in the design of computer circuitry.
- 1890: Dr. Herman Hollerith introduced the first electromechanical, punched-card data-processing machine which was used to compile information for the 1890 U.S. census. Hollerith's tabulator became so successful that he started his own business to market it. His company would eventually become International Business Machines (IBM).
- 1906: American physicist Lee De Forest invents the vacuum tube.
- 1939: Dr. John V. Atanasoff and his assistant Clifford Berry build the first electronic digital computer. Their machine, the Atanasoff-Berry-Computer (ABC) provided the foundation for the advances in electronic digital computers.
- 1941, Konrad Zuse (recently deceased in January of 1996), from Germany, introduced the first programmable computer designed to solve complex engineering equations. This machine, called the Z3, was also the first to work on the binary system instead of the decimal system.
- 1943: British mathematician Alan Turing developed hypothetical devices, the Turing machine which would be designed to perform logical operation and could read and write. It would presage programmable computers. He also used vacuum technology to build British Colossus, a machine used to counteract the German code-scrambling device, Enigma.

- 1944: Howard Aiken, in collaboration with engineers from IBM, constructed a large automatic digital sequence-controlled computer called the Harvard Mark I. This computer could handle all four arithmetic operations, and had special built-in programmes for logarithms and trigonometric functions.
- 1945: Dr. John von Neumann presented a paper outlining the stored-programme concept.
- 1947: The giant ENIAC (Electrical Numerical Integrator and Calculator) machine was developed by John W. Mauchly and J. Presper Eckert, Jr. at the University of Pennsylvania. It used 18, 000 vacuums, punch card input, weighed thirty tons and occupied a thirty-by-fifty-foot space. It wasn't programmable but was productive from 1946 to 1955 and was used to compute artillery-firing tables. That same year, William Shockley, John Bardeen and Walter Brattain of Bell Labs invented the transistor. It would rid computers of vacuum tubes and radios.
- 1949: Maurice V. Wilkes built the EDSAC (Electronic Delay Storage Automatic Computer), the first stored-programme computer. EDVAC (Electronic Discrete Variable Automatic Computer), the second stored-programme computer was built by Mauchly, Eckert, and von Neumann. An Wang developed magnetic-core memory which Jay Forrester would reorganize to be more efficient.
- 1950: Turing built the ACE, considered by some to be the first programmable digital computer.

GENERATION OF COMPUTERS

The history of computer development is often referred to in reference to the different generations of computing devices A generation refers to the state of improvement in the development of a product.

This term is also used in the different advancements of computer technology. With each new generation, the circuitry has gotten smaller and more advanced than the previous generation before it. As a result of the miniaturization, speed, power, and memory of computers has proportionally increased. New discoveries are constantly being developed that affect the way we live, work and play.

Each generation of computer is characterized by major technological development that fundamentally changed the way computers operate, resulting in increasingly smaller, cheaper, more powerful and more efficient and reliable devices. Read about each generation and the developments that led to the current devices that we use today.

FIRST GENERATION - 1940-1956: VACUUM TUBES

The first computers used vacuum tubes for circuitry and magnetic drums for memory, and were often enormous, taking up entire rooms. A magnetic drum, also referred to as drum, is a metal cylinder coated with magnetic iron-oxide material on which data and programmes can be stored. Magnetic drums were once used as a primary storage device but have since been implemented as auxiliary storage devices.

The tracks on a magnetic drum are assigned to channels located around the circumference of the drum, forming adjacent circular bands that wind around the drum. Single drum can have up to 200 tracks. As the drum rotates at a speed of up to 3,000 rpm, the device's read/write heads deposit magnetized spots on the drum during the write operation and sense these spots during a read operation. This action is similar to that of a magnetic tape or disk drive.

They were very expensive to operate and in addition to using a great deal of electricity, generated a lot of heat, which was often the cause of malfunctions. First generation computers relied on machine language to perform operations, and they could only solve one problem at a time. Machine languages are the only languages understood by computers.

While easily understood by computers, machine languages are almost impossible for humans to use because they consist entirely of numbers. Programmers, therefore, use either a high-level programming language or an assembly language. An assembly language contains the same instructions as a machine language, but the instructions and variables have names instead of being just numbers.

Programmes written in high-level languages retranslated into assembly language or machine language by a compiler. Assembly language programmes retranslated into machine language by a programme called an assembler.

Every CPU has its own unique machine language. Programmes must be rewritten or recompiled, therefore, to run on different types of computers. Input was based on punched cards and paper tape, and output was displayed on printouts. The UNIVAC and ENIAC computers are examples of first-generation computing devices. The UNIVAC was the first commercial computer delivered to a business client. Acronym for Electronic Numerical Integrator And Computer, the world's first operational electronic digital computer, developed by Army Ordnance to compute World War II ballistic firing tables.

The ENIAC, weighing 30 tons, using 200 kilowatts of electric power and consisting of 18,000 vacuum tubes,1,500 relays, and hundreds of thousands of resistors, capacitors, and inductors, was completed in 1945. In addition to ballistics, the ENIAC's field of application included weather prediction, atomic-energy calculations, cosmic-ray studies, thermal ignition, random-number studies, wind-tunnel design, and other scientific uses. The ENIAC soon became obsolete as themed arose for faster computing speeds.

SECOND GENERATION - 1956-1963: TRANSISTORS

Transistors replaced vacuum tubes and ushered in the second generation of computers. Transistor is a device composed of semiconductor material that amplifies a signal or opens or closes a circuit. Invented in 1947at Bell Labs, transistors have become the key ingredient of all digital circuits, including computers. Today's microprocessors contain tens of millions of microscopic transistors. Prior to the invention of transistors, digital circuits were composed of vacuum tubes, which had many disadvantages. They were much larger, required more energy, dissipated more heat, and were more prone to failures. It's safe to say that without the invention of transistors, computing, as we know it today would not be possible.

The transistor was invented in 1947 but did not see widespread use in computers until the late 50s. The transistor was far superior to the vacuum tube, allowing computers to become smaller, faster, cheaper, more energy-efficient and more reliable than their first-generation predecessors. Though the transistor still generated a great deal of heat that subjected the computer to damage, it was a vast improve-ment over the vacuum tube. Second-generation computers still relied on punched cards for input and printouts for output.

Second-generation computers moved from cryptic binary machine language to symbolic, or assembly, languages, which allowed programmers to specify instructions inwards. High-level programming languages were also being developed at this time, such as early versions of COBOL and FORTRAN. These were also the first computers that stored their instructions in their memory, which moved from a magnetic drum to magnetic core technology. The first computers of this generation were developed for the atomic energy industry.

THIRD GENERATION - 1964-1971: INTEGRATED CIRCUITS

The development of the integrated circuit was the hallmark of the third generation of computers. Transistors were miniaturized and placed on siliconchips, called semiconductors, which drastically increased the speed and efficiency of computers.

A nonmetallic chemical element in the carbon family of elements. Silicon - atomic symbol "Si" - is the second most abundant element in the earth's crust, surpassed only by oxygen. Silicon does not occur uncombined in nature. Sand and almost all rocks contain silicon combined with oxygen, forming silica. When silicon combines with other elements, such as iron, aluminum or potassium, a silicate is formed. Compounds of silicon also occur in the atmosphere, natural waters, and many plants and in the bodies of some animals. Silicon is the basic material used to make computer chips, transistors, silicon diodes and other electronic circuits and switching devices because its atomic structure makes the element an ideal semiconductor. Silicon is commonly doped, or mixed, with other elements, such as boron, phosphorous and arsenic, to alter its conductive properties.

A chip is a small piece of semi conducting material (usually silicon) on which an integrated circuit is embedded. A typical chip is less than ¼-square inches and can contain millions of electronic components(transistors). Computers consist of many chips placed on electronic boards called printed circuit boards. There are different types of chips. For example, CPU chips (also called microprocessors) contain an entire processing unit, whereas memory chips contain blank memory. Semiconductor is a material that is neither a good conductor of electricity (like copper) nor a good insulator (like rubber). The most common semiconductor materials are silicon and germanium. These materials are then doped to create an excess or lack of electrons.

Computer chips, both for CPU and memory, are composed of semiconductor materials. Semiconductors make it possible to miniaturize electronic components, such as transistors. Not only does miniaturization mean that the components take up less space, it also means that they are faster and require less energy. Instead of punched cards and printouts, users interacted with third generation computers through keyboards and monitors and interfaced with an operating system, which allowed the device to run many different applications at one time with a central programme that monitored the memory. Computers for the first time became accessible to a mass audience because they were smaller and cheaper than their predecessors.

FOURTH GENERATION - 1971-PRESENT: MICROPROCESSORS

The microprocessor brought the fourth generation of computers, as thousands of integrated circuits were built onto a single silicon chip. A silicon chip that contains a CPU. In the world of personal computers, the terms microprocessor and CPU are used interchangeably. At the heart of all personal computers and most workstations sits a microprocessor. Microprocessors also control the logic of almost all digital devices, from clock radios to fuel-injection systems for automobiles.

Three basic characteristics differentiate microprocessors:

- *Instruction Set*: The set of instructions that the microprocessor can execute.
- *Bandwidth*: The number of bits processed in a single instruction.
- *Clock Speed*: Given in megahertz (MHz), the clock speed determines how many instructions per second the processor can execute.

In both cases, the higher the value, the more powerful the CPU. For example, a 32-bit microprocessor that runs at 50MHz is more powerful than a 16-bitmicroprocessor that runs at 25MHz. What in the first generation filled an entire room could now fit in the palm of the hand. The Intel 4004chip, developed in 1971, located all the components of the computer - from the central processing unit and memory to input/output controls - on a single chip.

Abbreviation of central processing unit, and pronounced as separate letters. The CPU is the brains of the computer. Sometimes referred to simply as the processor or central processor, the CPU is where most calculations take place. In terms of computing power, the CPU is the most important element of a computer system.

On large machines, CPUs require one or more printed circuit boards. On personal computers and small workstations, the CPU is housed in a single chip called a microprocessor.

Two typical components of a CPU are:

- The arithmetic logic unit (ALU), which performs arithmetic and logical operations.
- The control unit, which extracts instructions from memory and decodes and executes them, calling on the ALU when necessary.

In 1981 IBM introduced its first computer for the home user, and in 1984 Apple introduced the Macintosh. Microprocessors also moved out of the realm of desktop computers and into many areas of life as more and more everyday products began to use microprocessors.

As these small computers became more powerful, they could be linked together to form networks, which eventually led to the development of the Internet. Fourth generation computers also saw the development of GUIs, the mouse and handheld devices

FIFTH GENERATION - ARTIFICIAL INTELLIGENCE

Fifth generation computing devices, based on artificial intelligence, are still in development, though there are some applications, such as voice recognition, that are being used today. Artificial Intelligence is the branch of computer science concerned with making computers behave like humans. John McCarthy at the Massachusetts Institute of Technology.

Artificial intelligence includes coined the term in 1956:

- *Games Playing*: Programming computers to play games such as chess and checkers
- *Expert Systems*: Programming computers to make decisions in real-life situations (for example, some expert systems help doctors diagnose diseases based on symptoms)
- *Natural Language*: Programming computers to understand natural human languages
- Neural Networks: Systems that simulate intelligence by attempting to reproduce the types of physical connections that occur in animal brains
- *Robotics*: Programming computers to see and hear and react to other sensory stimuli

Currently, no computers exhibit full artificial intelligence (that is, are able to simulate human behaviour). The greatest advances have occurred in the field of games playing. The best computer chess programmes are now capable of beating humans. In May,1997, an IBM super-computer called Deep Blue defeated world chess champion Gary Kasparov in a chess match. In the area of robotics, computers are now widely used in assembly plants, but they are capable only of very limited tasks. Robots have great difficulty identifying objects based on appearance or feel, and they still move and handle objects clumsily.

Natural-language processing offers the greatest potential rewards because it would allow people to interact with computers without needing any specialized knowledge. You could simply walk up to a computer and talk to it. Unfortunately, programming computers to understand natural languages has proved to be more difficult than originally thought. Some rudimentary translation systems that translate from one human language to another are in existence, but they are not nearly as good as human translators.

There are also voice recognition systems that can convert spoken sounds into written words, but they do not understand what they are writing; they simply take dictation. Even these systems are quite limited — you must speak slowly and distinctly.

In the early 1980s, expert systems were believed tore present the future of artificial intelligence and of computers in general. To date, however, they have not lived up to expectations. Many expert systems help human experts in such fields as medicine and engineering, but they are very expensive to produce and are helpful only in special situations.

Today, the hottest area of artificial intelligence is a neural network, which is proving successful in a number of disciplines such as voice recognition and natural language processing. There are several programming languages that are known as AI languages because they are used almost exclusively for AI applications. The two most common are LISP and Prolog.

VOICE RECOGNITION

The field of computer science that deals with designing computer systems that can recognize spoken words. Note that voice recognition implies only that the computer can take dictation, not that it understands what is being said.

Comprehending human languages falls under a different field of computer science called natural language processing. A number of voice recognition systems are available on the market.

The most powerful can recognize thousands of words. However, they generally require an extended training session during which the computer system becomes accustomed to a particular voice and accent. Such systems are said to be speaker dependent.

Many systems also require that the speaker speak slowly and distinctly and separate each word with a short pause. These systems are called discrete speech systems. Recently, great strides have been made in continuous speech systems – voice recognition systems that allow you to speak naturally. There are now several continuous-speech systems available for personal computers.

Because of their limitations and high cost, voice recognition systems have traditionally been used only in a few specialized situations. For example, such systems are useful in instances when the user is unable to use a keyboard to enter data because his or her hands are occupied or disabled.

Instead of typing commands, the user can simply speak into a headset. Increasingly, however, as the cost decreases and performance improves, speech recognition systems are entering the mainstream and are being used as an alternative to keyboards.

The use of parallel processing and superconductors is helping to make artificial intelligence a reality. Parallel processing is the simultaneous use of more than one CPU to execute a programme. Ideally, parallel processing makes a programme run faster because there are more engines (CPUs) running it. In practice, it is often difficult to divide a programme in such a way that separate CPUs can execute different portions without interfering with each other.

Most computers have just one CPU, but some models have several. There are even computers with thousands of CPUs. With single-CPU computers, it is possible to perform parallel processing by connecting the computers in a network.

However, this type of parallel processing requires very sophisticated software called distributed processing software. Note that parallel processing differs from multitasking, in which a single CPU executes several programmes at once. Parallel processing is also called parallel computing. Quantum computation and molecular and nanotechnology will radically change the face of computers in years to come.

First proposed in the 1970s, quantum computing relies on quantum physics by taking advantage of certain quantum physics properties of atoms or nuclei that allow them to work together as quantum bits, or qubits, to be the computer's processor and memory. By interacting with each other while being isolated from the external environment, qubits can perform certain calculations exponentially faster than conventional computers. Qubits do not rely on the traditional binary nature of computing.While traditional computers encode information into bits using binary numbers, either a 0or 1, and can only do calculations on one set of numbers at once, quantum computers encode information as a series of quantum-mechanical states such as spin directions of electrons or polarization orientations of a photon that might represent a 1 or a 0, might represent a combination of the two or might represent a number expressing that the state of the quite is somewhere between 1 and 0, or a superposition of many different numbers at once.

A quantum computer can do an arbitrary reversible classical computation on all the numbers simultaneously, which a binary system cannot do, and also has some ability to produce interference between various different numbers. By doing a computation on many different numbers at once, then interfering the results to get a single answer, a quantum computer has the potential to be much more powerful than a classical computer of the same size. In using only a single processing unit, a quantum computer can naturally perform myriad operations in parallel. Quantum computing is not well suited for tasks such as word processing and email, but it is ideal for tasks such as cryptography and modeling and indexing very large databases. Nanotechnology is a field of science whose goal is to control individual atoms and molecules to create computer chips and other devices that are thousands of times smaller than current technologies permit.

Current manufacturing processes use lithography to imprint circuits on semiconductor materials. While lithography has improved dramatically over the last two decades – to the point where some manufacturing plants can produce circuits smaller than one micron (1,000 nanometers) – it still deals with aggregates of millions of atoms.

It is widely believed that lithography is quickly approaching its physical limits. To continue reducing the size of semiconductors, new technologies that juggle individual atoms will be necessary. Although research in this field dates back to Richard P. Feynman's classic talk in 1959, the termnanotechnology was first coined by K. Eric Drexler in1986 in the book Engines of Creation.

In the popular press, the term Nan technology is sometimes used to refer to any sub-micron process, including lithography. Because of this, many scientists are beginning to use the term molecular nanotechnology when talking about true nano technology at the molecular level. The goal of fifth-generation computing is to develop devices that respond to natural language input and are capable of learning and self-organization. Here natural language means a human language. For example, English, French, and Chinese are natural languages. Computer languages, such as FORTRAN and C, are not. Probably the single most challenging problem in computer science is to develop computers that can understand natural languages. So far, the complete solution to this problem has proved elusive, although a great deal of progress has been made. Fourth-generation languages are the programming languages closest to natural languages.

TYPES OF COMPUTERS

A computer is a machine that can be programmed to manipulate symbols. Its principal characteristics are:

- It responds to a specific set of instructions in a well-defined manner.

- It can execute a prerecorded list of instructions (a programme).
- It can quickly store and retrieve large amounts of data.

Therefore computers can perform complex and repetitive procedures quickly, precisely and reliably. Modern computers are electronic and digital. The actual machinery (wires, transistors, and circuits) is called hardware; the instructions and data are called software.

All general-purpose computers require the following hardware components:

- *Central processing unit (CPU)*: The heart of the computer, this is the component that actually executes instructions organized in programmes ("software") which tell the computer what to do.
- *Memory (fast, expensive, short-term memory)*: Enables a computer to store, at least temporarily, data, programmes, and intermediate results.
- *Mass storage device (slower, cheaper, long-term memory)*: Allows a computer to permanently retain large amounts of data and programmes between jobs. Common mass storage devices include disk drives and tape drives.
- *Input device*: Usually a keyboard and mouse, the input device is the conduit through which data and instructions enter a computer.
- *Output device*: A display screen, printer, or other device that lets you see what the computer has accomplished.

In addition to these components, many others make it possible for the basic components to work together efficiently. For example, every computer requires a bus that transmits data from one part of the computer to another.

COMPUTER SIZES AND POWER

Computers can be generally classified by size and power as follows, though there is considerable overlap:

- *Personal computer*: A small, single-user computer based on a microprocessor.

- *Workstation*: A powerful, single-user computer. A workstation is like a personal computer, but it has a more powerful microprocessor and, in general, a higher-quality monitor.
- *Minicomputer*: A multi-user computer capable of supporting up to hundreds of users simultaneously.
- *Mainframe*: A powerful multi-user computer capable of supporting many hundreds or thousands of users simultaneously.
- *Supercomputer*: An extremely fast computer that can perform hundreds of millions of instructions per second.

SUPERCOMPUTER AND MAINFRAME

Supercomputer is a broad term for one of the fastest computers currently available. Supercomputers are very expensive and are employed for specialized applications that require immense amounts of mathematical calculations. For example, weather forecasting requires a supercomputer. Other uses of supercomputers scientific simulations, (animated) graphics, fluid dynamic calculations, nuclear energy research, electronic design, and analysis of geological data (e.g. in petrochemical prospecting).

Mainframe was a term originally referring to the cabinet containing the central processor unit or "main frame" of a room-filling Stone Age batch machine. After the emergence of smaller "minicomputer" designs in the early 1970s, the traditional big iron machines were described as "mainframe computers" and eventually just as mainframes. Nowadays a Mainframe is a very large and expensive computer capable of supporting hundreds, or even thousands, of users simultaneously.

The chief difference between a supercomputer and a mainframe is that a supercomputer channels all its power into executing a few programmes as fast as possible, whereas a mainframe uses its power to execute many programmes concurrently. In some ways, mainframes are more powerful than supercomputers because they support more simultaneous programmes. But supercomputers can execute a single programme faster than a mainframe. The distinction between small mainframes and minicomputers is vague, depending really on how the manufacturer wants to market its machines.

MINICOMPUTER

It is a midsize computer. In the past decade, the distinction between large minicomputers and small mainframes has blurred, however, as has the distinction between small minicomputers and workstations. But in general, a minicomputer is a multiprocessing system capable of supporting from up to 200 users simultaneously.

WORKSTATION

It is a type of computer used for engineering applications (CAD/CAM), desktop publishing, software development, and other types of applications that require a moderate amount of computing power and relatively high quality graphics capabilities. Workstations generally come with a large, high-resolution graphics screen, at large amount of RAM, built-in network support, and a graphical user interface.

Most workstations also have a mass storage device such as a disk drive, but a special type of workstation, called a diskless workstation, comes without a disk drive. The most common operating systems for workstations are UNIX and Windows NT. Like personal computers, most workstations are single-user computers. However, workstations are typically linked together to form a local-area network, although they can also be used as stand-alone systems.

PERSONAL COMPUTER

It can be defined as a small, relatively inexpensive computer designed for an individual user. In price, personal computers range anywhere from a few hundred pounds to over five thousand pounds.

All are based on the microprocessor technology that enables manufacturers to put an entire CPU on one chip. Businesses use personal computers for word processing, accounting, desktop publishing, and for running spreadsheet and database management applications. At home, the most popular use for personal computers is for playing games and recently for surfing the Internet.

Personal computers first appeared in the late 1970s. One of the first and most popular personal computers was the Apple II, introduced in 1977 by Apple Computer. During the late 1970s and early 1980s, new models and competing operating systems seemed to appear daily. Then, in 1981, IBM entered the fray with its first personal computer, known as the IBM PC.

The IBM PC quickly became the personal computer of choice, and most other personal computer manufacturers fell by the wayside. P.C. is short for personal computer or IBM PC. One of the few companies to survive IBM's onslaught was Apple Computer, which remains a major player in the personal computer marketplace.

Other companies adjusted to IBM's dominance by building IBM clones, computers that were internally almost the same as the IBM PC, but that cost less. Because IBM clones used the same microprocessors as IBM PCs, they were capable of running the same software.

Over the years, IBM has lost much of its influence in directing the evolution of PCs. Therefore after the release of the first PC by IBM the term PC increasingly came to mean IBM or IBM-compatible personal computers, to the exclusion of other types of personal computers, such as Macintoshes. In recent years, the term PC has become more and more difficult to pin down.

In general, though, it applies to any personal computer based on an Intel microprocessor, or on an Intel-compatible microprocessor. For nearly every other component, including the operating system, there are several options, all of which fall under the rubric of PC Today, the world of personal computers is basically divided between Apple Macintoshes and PCs.

The principal characteristics of personal computers are that they are single-user systems and are based on microprocessors. However, although personal computers are designed as single-user systems, it is common to link them together to form a network. In terms of power, there is great variety. At the high end, the distinction between personal computers and workstations has faded. High-end models of the Macintosh and PC offer the same computing power and graphics capability as low-end workstations by Sun Microsystems, Hewlett-Packard, and DEC.

PERSONAL COMPUTER TYPES

Actual personal computers can be generally classified by size and chassis / case. The chassis or case is the metal frame that serves as the structural support for electronic components. Every computer system requires at least one chassis to house the circuit boards and wiring. The chassis also contains slots for expansion boards.

If you want to insert more boards than there are slots, you will need an expansion chassis, which provides additional slots. There are two basic flavours of chassis designs–desktop models and tower models–but there are many variations on these two basic types. Then come the portable computers that are computers small enough to carry. Portable computers include notebook and subnotebook computers, hand-held computers, palmtops, and PDAs.

Tower Model

The term refers to a computer in which the power supply, motherboard, and mass storage devices are stacked on top of each other in a cabinet. This is in contrast to desktop models, in which these components are housed in a more compact box. The main advantage of tower models is that there are fewer space constraints, which makes installation of additional storage devices easier.

Desktop Model

A computer designed to fit comfortably on top of a desk, typically with the monitor sitting on top of the computer. Desktop model computers are broad and low, whereas tower model computers are narrow and tall. Because of their shape, desktop model computers are generally limited to three internal mass storage devices. Desktop models designed to be very small are sometimes referred to as slim line models.

Notebook Computer

An extremely lightweight personal computer. Notebook computers typically weigh less than 6 pounds and are small enough to fit easily in a briefcase. Aside from size, the principal difference between a notebook computer and a personal computer is the display screen. Notebook computers use a variety of techniques, known as flat-panel technologies, to produce a lightweight and non-bulky display screen. The quality of notebook display screens varies considerably.

In terms of computing power, modern notebook computers are nearly equivalent to personal computers. They have the same CPUs, memory capacity, and disk drives. However, all this power in a small package is expensive. Notebook computers cost about twice as much as equivalent regular-sized computers. Notebook computers come with battery packs that enable you to run them without plugging them in. However, the batteries need to be recharged every few hours.

Laptop Computer

A small, portable computer — small enough that it can sit on your lap. Nowadays, laptop computers are more frequently called notebook computers.

Sub notebook Computer

A portable computer that is slightly lighter and smaller than a full-sized notebook computer. Typically, sub notebook computers have a smaller keyboard and screen, but are otherwise equivalent to notebook computers.

Hand-held Computer

A portable computer that is small enough to be held in one's hand. Although extremely convenient to carry, handheld computers have not replaced notebook computers because of their small keyboards and screens. The most popular hand-held computers are those that are specifically designed to provide PIM (personal information manager) functions, such as a calendar and address book. Some manufacturers are trying to solve the small keyboard problem by replacing the keyboard with an electronic pen. However, these pen-based devices rely on handwriting recognition technologies, which are still in their infancy. Hand-held computers are also called PDAs, palmtops and pocket computers.

Palmtop

A small computer that literally fits in your palm. Compared to full-size computers, palmtops are severely limited, but they are practical for certain functions such as phone books and calendars. Palmtops that use a pen rather than a keyboard for input are often called hand-held computers or PDAs. Because of their small size, most palmtop computers do not include disk drives. However, many contain PCMCIA slots in which you can insert disk drives, modems, memory, and other devices. Palmtops are also called PDAs, hand-held computers and pocket computers.

PDA

Short for personal digital assistant, a handheld device that combines computing, telephone/fax, and networking features. A typical PDA can function as a cellular phone, fax sender, and personal organizer. Unlike portable computers, most PDAs are pen-based, using a stylus rather than a keyboard for input. This means that they also incorporate handwriting recognition features.

Some PDAs can also react to voice input by using voice recognition technologies. The field of PDA was pioneered by Apple Computer, which introduced the Newton MessagePad in 1993. Shortly thereafter, several other manufacturers offered similar products. To date, PDAs have had only modest success in the marketplace, due to their high price tags and limited applications. However, many experts believe that PDAs will eventually become common gadgets.

Chapter 2

Components of Computer

COMPUTER HARDWARE

Computer hardware is the physical part of the computer including the digital circuits inside the computer as opposed to the software that carry out the computing instructions. The hardware of a computer is unlikely to change frequently unless due to the crash or for upgrading them. The devices that is capable of storing, executing system instructions and controlling other logical outputs.

Hardware comprises all of the physical part of the computer such as Monitor, CPU, motherboard, ram, CD-Rom, printer, scanner, hard disk, flash drive (AKA pen drive), processor, pci buses, floppy disk, power supply, VGA card, sound card, network interface card, peripherals, joystick, mouse, keyboard, foot pedal, computer fan, camera, headset and others.

On the other hard software is a logical part of a computer and is used to carry out the instructions, storing, executing and developing other software programmes. A typical PC consists of a case or chassis in the desktop or tower case and these components.

PC OR PERSONAL COMPUTER

Is a system, consisting of many components. Some of those components, like Windows XP, and all your other programmes, are software. The stuff you can actually see and touch, and would likely break if you threw it out a fifth-story window, is hardware.

Not everybody has exactly the same hardware. But those of you who have a desktop system, like the example Figure, probably have most of the components shown in that same figure. Those of you with notebook computers probably have most of the same components. Only in your case the components are all integrated into a single book-sized portable unit.

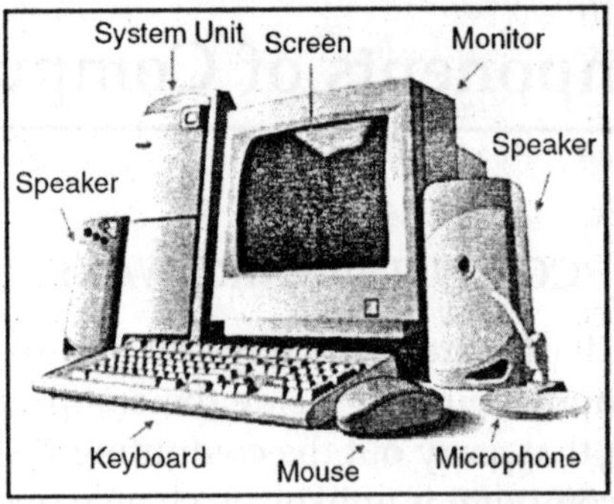

The *system unit* is the actual computer; everything else is called a *peripheral* device. Your computer's system unit probably has at least one floppy disk drive, and one CD or DVD drive, into which you can insert floppy disks and CDs. There's another disk drive, called the hard disk inside the system unit, as shown in Figure. You can't remove that disk, or even see it. But it's there. And everything that's currently "in your computer" is actually stored on that hard disk.

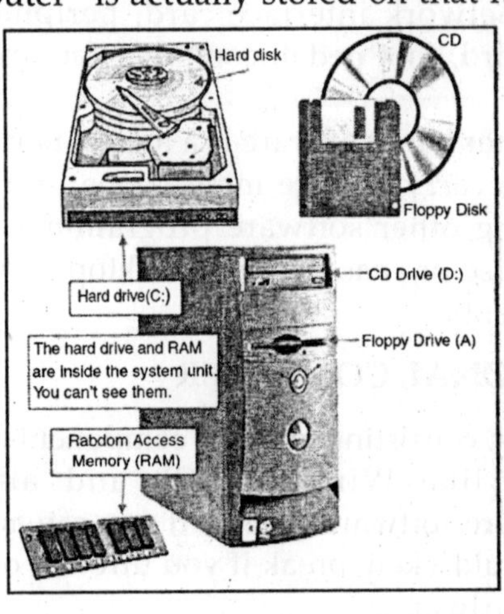

The floppy drive and CD drive are often referred to as *drives with removable media* or *removable drives* for short, because you can remove whatever disk is currently in the drive, and replace it with another. Your computer's hard disk can store as much information as tens of thousands of floppy disks, so don't worry about running out of space on your hard disk any time soon. As a rule, you want to store everything you create or download on your hard disk. Use the floppy disks and CDs to send copies of files through the mail, or to make backup copies of important items.

RANDOM ACCESS MEMORY (RAM)

There's too much "stuff" on your computer's hard disk to use it all at the same time. During the average session sitting at the computer, you'll probably use only a small amount of all that's available. The stuff you're working with at any given moment is stored in random access memory (often abbreviated RAM, and often called simply "memory"). The advantage using RAM to store whatever you're working on at the moment is that RAM is very fast. Much faster than any disk. For you, "fast" translates to less time waiting and more time being productive.

So if RAM is so fast, why not put everything in it? Why has a hard disk at all? The answer to that lies in the fact that RAM is volatile. As soon as the computer is shut off, whether intentionally or by an accidental power outage, every thing in RAM disappears, just as quickly as a light bulb goes out when the plug is pulled. So you don't want to rely on RAM to hold everything. A disk, on the other hand, holds its information whether the power is on or off.

HARD DISK

All of the information that's "in your computer", so to speak, is stored on your computer's *hard disk.* You never see that actual hard disk because it's sealed inside a special housing and needs to stay that way. Unlike RAM, which is volatile, the hard disk can hold information forever — with or without electricity. Most modern hard disks have tens of billions of *bytes* of storage space on them. Which, in English, means that you can create, save, and download files for months or years without using up all the storage space it provides? In the unlikely event that you do manage to fill up your hard disk, Windows will start showing a little message on the screen that reads "You are running low on disk space" well in advance of any problems. In fact, if that message appears, it won't until you're down to about 800 MB of free space. And 800 MB of empty space is equal to about 600 blank floppy disks.

MOUSE

Obviously you know how to use your mouse, since you must have used it to get here. But let's take a look at the facts and buzzwords anyway. Your mouse probably has at least two buttons on it. The button on the left is called the *primary mouse button*, the button on the right is called the *secondary mouse button* or just the *right mouse button*. I'll just refer to them as the left and right mouse buttons. Many mice have a small wheel between the two mouse buttons, as illustrated in Figure.

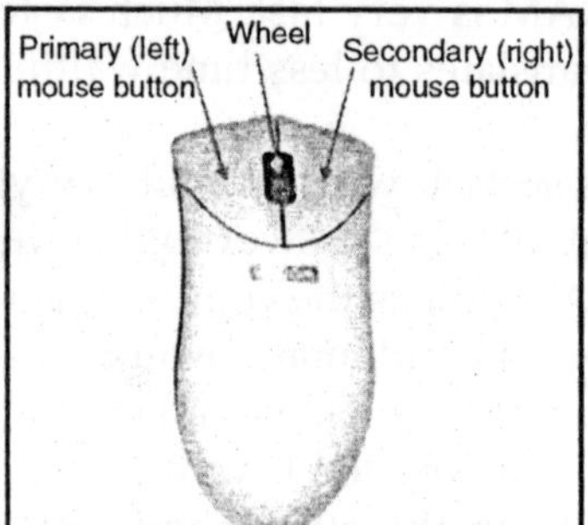

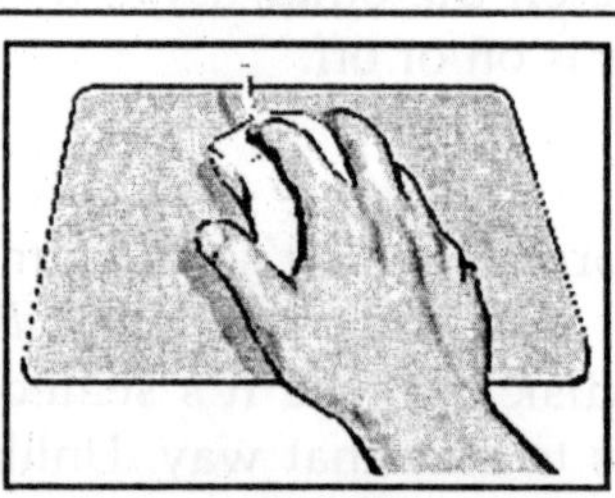

The idea is to rest your hand comfortably on the mouse, with your index finger touching (but not pressing on) the left mouse button. Then, as you move the mouse, the *mouse pointer* (the little arrow on the screen) moves in the same direction. When moving the mouse, try to keep the buttons aimed toward the monitor — don't "twist" the mouse as that just makes it all the harder to control the position of the mouse pointer.

If you find yourself reaching too far to get the mouse pointer where you want it to be on the screen, just pick up the mouse, move it to where it's comfortable to hold it, and place it back down on the mouse pad or desk.

The buzzwords that describe how you use the mouse are as follows:

- *Point*: To point to an item means to move the mouse pointer so that it's touching the item.
- *Click*: Point to the item, then tap (press and release) the left mouse button.
- *Double-click*: Point to the item, and tap the left mouse button twice in rapid succession - click-click as fast as you can.
- *Right-click*: Point to the item, then tap the mouse button on the right.
- *Drag*: Point to an item, then hold down the left mouse button as you move the mouse. To *drop* the item, release the left mouse button.
- *Right-drag*: Point to an item, then hold down the right mouse button as you move the mouse. To *drop* the item, release the right mouse button.

KEYBOARD

Like the mouse, the keyboard is a means of interacting with your computer. You really only need to use the keyboard when you're typing text. Most of the keys on the keyboard are laid out like the keys on a typewriter. But there are some special keys like Esc (Escape), Ctrl (Control), and Alt (Alternate).

There are also some keys across the top of the keyboard labeled F1, F2, F3, and so forth. Those are called the *function keys*, and the exact role they play depends on which programme you happen to be using at the moment. Most keyboards also have a *numeric keypad* with the keys laid out like the keys on a typical adding machine. If you're accustomed to using an adding machine, you might want to use the numeric keypad, rather than the numbers across the top of the keyboard, to type numbers. It doesn't really matter which keys you use. The numeric keypad is just there as a convenience to people who are accustomed to adding machines.

Most keyboards also contain a set of *navigation keys*. You can use the navigation keys to move around around through text on the screen. The navigation keys won't move the mouse pointer. Only the mouse moves the mouse pointer. On smaller keyboards where space is limited, such as on a notebook computer, the navigation keys and numeric keypad might be one in the same. There will be a Num Lock key on the keypad. When the Num Lock key is "on", the numeric keypad keys type numbers. When the Num Lock key is "off", the navigation keys come into play. The Num Lock key acts as a toggle. Which is to say, when you tap it, it switches to the opposite state. For example, if Num Lock is on, tapping that key turns it off. If Num Lock is off, tapping that key turns Num Lock on.

Combination Keystrokes (Shortcut keys)

Those mysterious Ctrl and Alt keys are often used in combination with other keys to perform some task. We often refer to these combination keystrokes as shortcut keys, because they provide an alternative to using the mouse to select menu options in programmes.

Shortcut keys are always expressed as:

key1 + key2

where the idea is to hold down key1, tap key2, then release key1. For example, to press Ctrl+Esc hold down the Ctrl key (usually with your pinkie), tap the Esc key, then release the Ctrl key. To press Alt+F you hold down the Alt key, tap the letter F, then release the Alt key.

COMPUTER SOFTWARE

Computer software is most commonly created by computer programmers using a programming language. The programmer writes commands in the programming language that are similar to what someone might use in everyday speech. These commands are called *source code*. Another computer programme called a *compiler* is then used on the source code, transforming the commands into a language that the computer can understand.

The result is an executable computer programme, which is another name for software. Various types of computer software are used to simplify the operations and applications of computer programmes. Computer software enables the computer system to perform in accordance with the given tasks. Computer software involves all types of software related applications. Electronic media content is also explained by the computer software.

CATEGORIES OF COMPUTER SOFTWARE

System Software

System Software represents programmes that allow the hardware to run properly. System software is the most commonly used variety of computer software. System software offers a protective shield to all software applications.

It also provides support to the physical components of computers. System software coordinates all external devices of computer system like printer, keyboard, displays etc. System software is a set of programmes that control the operations of a computer and devices attached with the computer. It creates links between user and computer as well as controls the execution of application programmes. System software are essential for a computer to do work, Without this software no link can be created between user and computer.

The examples of system software are:

- Operating systems.
- Utility programmes.
- Device Drivers.
- Language Processors.

Operating System

The operating system is system software that is stored on the storage device such as hard disk, CD-ROM, floppy disk (or in ROM). When a computer is switched on, the operating system is transferred from the storage device into main memory through ROM programme. The handheld devices have the entire operating system in the ROM. This type of operating system is difficult to update. An operating system controls and co-ordinates the overall operations of the computer system. It manages the computer hardware, controls the execution of application programmes and provides the set of services to the users. The operating system acts as an interface between user and the computer.

The users interact with the operating system indirectly through application programme. Operating system manages all the operations of the computer and performs basic tasks such as;

- Accepts input from input devices.
- Sends output to output devices.
- Manages the application programmes in memory.
- Manages the files on the storage devices.
- Manages & controls the I/O devices etc.

The operating system is responsible for managing hardware resources. An application programme cannot access input/output devices or execute programme instructions itself. The operating system performs these tasks through CPU on behalf of application programmes.

The operating system acts as a platform on which various application programmes are executed. The user requests the application programme to perform a particular task and the application programme refers the request of user to operating system. Figure below shows the actual position of an operating in a computer system.

Usually, operating system is divided into two parts:

- *Resident part*: This part of operating system is known as kernel. It contains the critical, functions. It is loaded into the main memory during the booting process of computer. It performs various functions residing in the main memory. The kernel will be discussed in the next topic.
- *Non-resident part*: This part of operating system is loaded into main memory when required.

The Examples of operating systems are:

- Disk Operating System (DOS) developed by Microsoft.
- Operating System 2 (QS/2) developed by IBM.
- XENIX or ZENIX developed by Microsoft.
- WTNOWS developed by Microsoft and also WINDOWS- NE Now-a- days, the most popular operating system is Windows operating system.

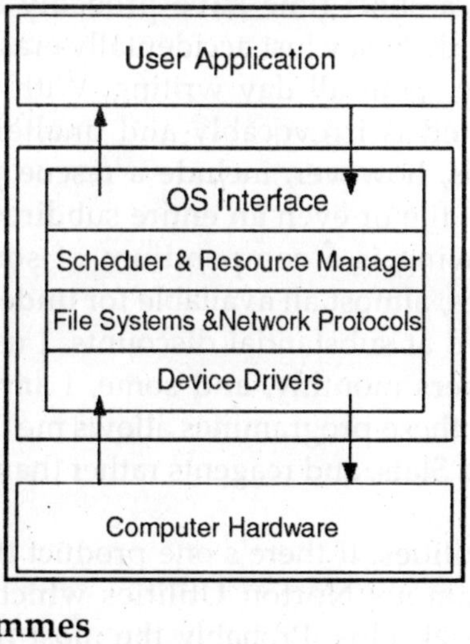

Utility Programmes

In recent year, the personal computer has become almost as common a fixture in the clinical laboratory as the microscope. PCs are used for every conceivable application and in every lab department. Computer are used for word processing, database management, stastical analysis, budgeting, and scheduling.

Over the last two years, use of utility programmes has gained much importance. The softwares are available at much cheaper cost, has made the user to have a dozen programmes that help his computer to run faster and efficient while protecting data from accidental loss or corruption.

IBM (and compatible) computers primarily utilize MS-DOS as an operating system, a combination of external disk-based programmes, such as chkdsk.exe and format.exe, and interal ROM-based programmes, such as copy, del, and dir. These DOS programmes are designed to manage da-to-day computer activities. Unfortunately, many vital features are either missing in DOs or so cumbersome to use that they are generally ignored.

Utility programmes concentrate on one or two specific functions or equip to user with a whole range of DOS substitutions. For example, those who have used a computer for more than a short time have probably experienced the sinking feeling that they just accidentally erased an important document they spent all day writing. With DOS, a file that has been deleted is irrevocably and unalterably gone. The Norton Utilities, however, include a rescue programme that will undelete a file or even an entire subdirectory.

The following is a compendium of some of the more popular utilities, almost all available for under 200 each. Most can be obtained at substantial discounts. I use some of them every day, others monthly, and some, I am grateful to say, rarely. Having these programmes allows me to keep my mind on T4/T8 ratios, Stats, and reagents rather than worrying about my computer.

Norton Utilities. If there's one product than nobody will be left with famous Norton Utilities which is a Symantec product. Fastback Plus. Probably the most neglected part of computer housekeeping is copying important files to disks or tape. Backing up is essential because even rescue utility programmes can't prevent a hard disk succumbing to some intractable disorder, heretofore unknown to even computer experts—and failing. For an inexpensive insurance policy, try Fastback Plus, from Fifth Generation Systems. The programme quickly and easily creates foolproof backups. It copies designated files to just about any format disk, including tape units and Bernoulli cartridges. As the backup proceeds, files are compressed, thus saving floppy disk space.

Magellan. Lotus Development Corporation's Magellan is a hard disk and file management tool for finding, viewing, and organizing all the information on your computer. It's similar to XTREE and QDOS—programmes that act as shells for DOS—but it does substantially more. Magellan will win you over within minutes because of its unique and easily accessed features.

Imagine searching through 80 megabytes of your hard disk and finding files by file name or by any word in a file name in a few seconds. Once Magellan has found the file for you, it doesn't merely give you the file name but also allows you to see the contents of the file, just as if you were working in it. This is accomplished through viewers specifically designed for programmes like WordStar, dBase, Lotus 1-2-3, Paradox, WordPerfect, and many more.

Language Processor

A hardware device designed or used to perform tasks, such as processing programme code to machine code. Language processors are found in languages such as Fortran and COBOL.

Application Software

Represents programmes that allow users to do something besides simply run the hardware. Some experts also include a third category, programming software, though others put those programmes into one of the other previously mentioned categories. A set of programmes used to solve particular problems of user through computer is called Application software. It is also known as application package. The ready packages are also available in market on CDs for various purposes. These are used by user who does not know the computer programming. The users solve their problems by using ready packages more easily and quickly.

Some of application packages are:

- Word processing software.
- Spreadsheet software.
- Database Management System software.
- Graphics software.
- Communication software.

Word Processing Software

This software is used to create and to edit documents such as letters, reports, essays etc. The word processing software provides several features for document editing and formatting. In. editing process, text is entered into the document, deleted, copied or moved to another location etc.

In formatting process, different formats can be applied on the text to make the document more attractive before to print on the printer. The most popular word processing software programmes are: Microsoft Word, Word Perfect etc.

Spreadsheet Software

Spreadsheet software is used to store and process data in an electronic sheet having columns and rows. The data is entered into the cells of the sheet. The intersection of a row and a column is known as cell. Each cell is a unique address. The numbers and formulas are entered into the cells and the computer can automatically perform the calculation on numerical data in cells.

The spreadsheet software is commonly used for business application such as for performing financial calculations and recording transactions. The most popular example of spreadsheet software is Microsoft Excel etc.

Database Management Software

Database management software is used to create and manage databases. A database is a collection of related information or records on any subject such as records of the books in a library, information about the students of a college etc. Database Management Software stores and manages records in databases. These records can be accessed very quickly when required. The Microsoft Access, Oracle etc. are most popular examples of Database Management Software.

Presentation Graphics Software

The presentation graphic software is used to create slides for making presentations. The presentation graphic software also has pre-drawn clip art images, which can be inserted into slides and can be modified. The PowerPoint is an example of presentation graphic software.

Communication Software

The Communication software is used to exchange information electronically. It is most commonly used software to send and receive information on the Internet. It also allows for sending and receiving faxes directly. The computer files can also be transferred from one PC to another through this software. The Internet Explorer is an example of this software.

TYPES OF COMPUTER SOFTWARE

Programming Software

This is one of the most commonly known and popularly used forms of computer software. These software come in forms of tools that assist a programmer in writing computer programmes. Computer programmes are sets of logical instructions that make a computer system perform certain tasks. The tools that help the programmers in instructing a computer system include text editors, compilers and interpreters.

System Software

It helps in running the computer hardware and the computer system. System software is a collection of operating systems; devise drivers, servers, windowing systems and utilities. System software helps an application programmer in abstracting away from hardware, memory and other internal complexities of a computer.

Application Software

It enables the end users to accomplish certain specific tasks. Business software, databases and educational software are some forms of application software. Different word processors, which are dedicated for specialized tasks to be performed by the user, are other examples of application software.

Inventory Management Software

This type of software helps an organization in tracking its goods and materials on the basis of quality as well as quantity. Warehouse inventory management functions encompass the internal warehouse movements and storage. Inventory software helps a company in organizing inventory and optimizing the flow of goods in the organization, thus leading to an improved customer service.

Utility Software

Also known as service routine, utility software helps in the management of computer hardware and application software. It performs a small range of tasks. Disk defragmenters, systems utilities and virus scanners are some of the typical examples of utility software.

Data Backup and Recovery Software

An ideal data backup and recovery software provides functionalities beyond simple copying of data files. This software often supports user needs of specifying what is to be backed up and when. Backup and recovery software preserve the original organization of files and allow an easy retrieval of the backed up data.

Computer Games Software

A form of entertainment software that has many genres.

Some of these genres include MMOs (Massive Multiplayer Online games), first-person shooters, action games, role-playing games, and adventure games.

Driver Software

Programmes that allow a computer to interact with additional hardware devices such as printers, scanners, and video cards.

Educational Software

Programmes and games that teach the user or provide drills to help memorize facts. Educational software is diverse, and can teach anything from computer-related activities like typing to higher education subjects like chemistry.

Media Players and Media Development Software

Software designed to play and/or edit digital media files such as music and videos.

Productivity Software

An older term that refers to any programmes that would allow the user to be more productive in a business sense. Word processors, database management utilities, and presentation software all fall into this category.

Operating Systems

Software that coordinates system resources and allows other programmes to run. A few examples are Windows Vista, Mac OS X, and Linux. This was an overview of the major types of software.

Computer software are widely popular today and hence we cannot imagine a world of computers without them. We would not have been able to use computers if not for the software.

What is fascinating about the world of computers is that it has its own languages, its ways of communication with our human world and human interaction with the computers is possible, thanks to computer software. I wonder, if the word 'soft' in 'software' implies 'soft-spoken ness', which is an important quality of a pleasant communication.

BLOCK DIAGRAM OF COMPUTER

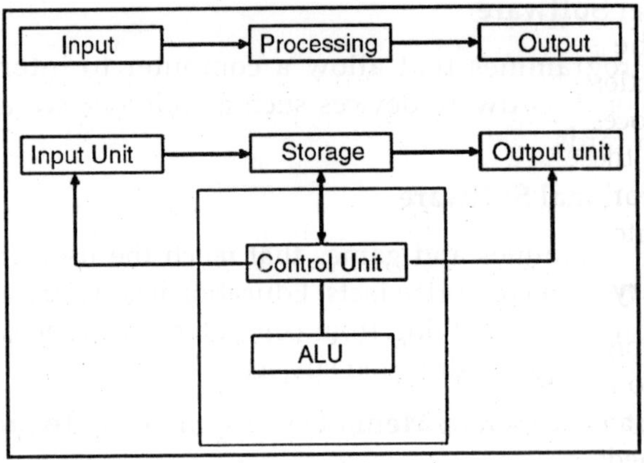

A computer can process data, pictures, sound and graphics. They can solve highly complicated problems quickly and accurately.

INPUT UNIT

Computers need to receive data and instruction in order to solve any problem. Therefore we need to input the data and instructions into the computers.

Data and instructions must be entered into the computer system for processing, and results obtained from computations must be displayed or recorded for the user. The input device serves the purpose of receiving data and instructions in a form that can be understood by the computer.

The input unit consists of one or more input devices. Keyboard is the one of the most commonly used input device. Other commonly used input devices are the mouse, floppy disk drive, magnetic tape, etc.

All the input devices perform the following functions:

- Accept the data and instructions from the outside world.
- Convert it to a form that the computer can understand.

- Supply the converted data to the computer system for further processing.

STORAGE UNIT

The storage unit of the computer holds data and instructions that are entered through the input unit, before they are processed. It preserves the intermediate and final results before these are sent to the output devices. It also saves the data for the later use. The various storage devices of a computer system are divided into two categories.

Primary Storage

Stores and provides very fast. This memory is generally used to hold the programme being currently executed in the computer, the data being received from the input unit, the intermediate and final results of the programme. The primary memory is temporary in nature.

The data is lost, when the computer is switched off. In order to store the data permanently, the data has to be transferred to the secondary memory. The cost of the primary storage is more compared to the secondary storage. Therefore most computers have limited primary storage capacity.

Secondary Storage

Secondary storage is used like an archive. It stores several programmes, documents, data bases etc. The programmes that you run on the computer are first transferred to the primary memory before it is actually run. Whenever the results are saved, again they get stored in the secondary memory. The secondary memory is slower and cheaper than the primary memory. Some of the commonly used secondary memory devices are Hard disk, CD, etc.,

MEMORY SIZE

All digital computers use the binary system, i.e. 0's and 1's. Each character or a number is represented by an 8 bit code.

The set of 8 bits is called a byte.

A character occupies 1 byte space.

A numeric occupies 2 byte space.

Byte is the space occupied in the memory.

The size of the primary storage is specified in KB (Kilobytes) or MB (Megabyte). One KB is equal to 1024 bytes and one MB is equal to 1000KB. The size of the primary storage in a typical PC usually starts at 16MB. PCs having 32 MB, 48MB, 128 MB, 256MB memory are quite common.

OUTPUT UNIT

The output unit of a computer provides the information and results of a computation to outside world. Printers, Visual Display Unit (VDU) are the commonly used output devices. Other commonly used output devices are floppy disk drive, hard disk drive, and magnetic tape drive. The processed data, stored in the memory of the computer is sent to the output unit, which then converts it into a form that can be understood by the user. The output is usually produced in one of the two ways – on the display device, or on paper

ARITHMETIC LOGICAL UNIT

All calculations are performed in the Arithmetic Logic Unit (ALU) of the computer. It also does comparison and takes decision. All calculations and comparisons, based on the instructions provided, are carried out within the ALU. It performs arithmetic functions like addition, subtraction, multiplication, and division and also logical operations like greater than, less than and equal to.

The ALU can perform basic operations such as addition, subtraction, multiplication, division, etc and does logic operations viz, >, <, =, 'etc. Whenever calculations are required, the control unit transfers the data from storage unit to ALU once the computations are done, the results are transferred to the storage unit by the control unit and then it is send to the output unit for displaying results.

CONTROL UNIT

It controls all other units in the computer. The control unit instructs the input unit, where to store the data after receiving it from the user. It controls the flow of data and instructions from the storage unit to ALU. It also controls the flow of results from the ALU to the storage unit. The control unit is generally referred as the central nervous system of the computer that control and synchronizes its working.

CENTRAL PROCESSING UNIT

The central processing unit, CPU, or processor, is the nerve centre of the computer system. It performs the central control functions. All the computational, logical, and operational decisions are made here. It contains the logic circuitry for performing the various computational activities. It controls the operation of all the functional units. It fetches machine instructions from memory, decodes these instructions and insures that the operations called for by the instructions are executed correctly.

In order to do all this, it communicates or interfaces with the input and output units and the memory. Digitally coded information travels among the CPU, memory, and Input/Output units on electrical connections called busses. Each I/O unit of the computer system is given an address and each information location in memory is given an address. To locate specific information in memory, a digital code - the address of the information - is sent on the address bus to memory by the CPU.

At the same time, other digital codes representing control signals are sent on the control bus to tell the memory what to do - either to read or to write information from the memory location designated by the address on the address bus. The CPU controls when and at what time each operation is to be accomplished.

It does this by following instructions stored in memory in a step-by-step sequence called the programme. Inside the computer, the information is not recognizable as written letters or numbers because it is all converted to electrical signals of digital codes so that it may be handled easily inside the computer system. The digital codes carrying the information inside the computer system must be coupled from one unit to another. The multiple wires which do this are called busses. The three principal busses in a computer system - the address bus, the control bus, and the data bus - are illustrated to the right.

Data and instructions (programmes) are stored in the computer's memory after which all the major calculations and computations are carried out within the CPU. The CPU is also responsible for controlling the operations of various units of the computer system.

Sometimes an additional special processor is used to provide more efficient system operations by relieving some of the control requirements of the CPU. When used as such, the I/O processor is referred to as a data channel, direct memory access channel, or peripheral processor. For more efficiency, some computer systems use a supplementary processor to control the interaction between the CPU and external devices.

Logical functions like AND, OR, and NOT form the basis of many different types of digital devices. They are called logic circuits because they make logic decisions electronically. The logic circuit is called such because electronically it performs the logical AND functions. Decisions such as "A" AND "B", "A" OR "B" and NOT "A" or NOT "B" being a particular value are the types used over and over again in computer systems hardware.

These circuits can be represented symbolically. Individual inputs and outputs in digital circuits are always in either of only two possible states: "1" or "0". The signal level can only have one of two states; therefore, it is called a binary circuit and it can only represent one bit of information which can either have a value of "1" or "0".

A "truth table," illustrated below, is used to demonstrate the combination of logical or binary input signals which yield a binary output for a specific gate type.

The output goes high when both inputs are high. The output drops when either input drops. Output "C" is a "1" only when "A" AND "B" are both a "1" at the same time. The OR gate is different from the AND gate in that it requires only one of the two input signals to be a one (or 2.4 volts) at any given instant of time in order for the output "C" to be a logical one. Only when both of the input signals "A" and "B" are zero ("0") will the output signal "C" be zero. The NOT gate simply performs an inversion on a signal. When the input signal is a one, the output is a zero and visa versa.

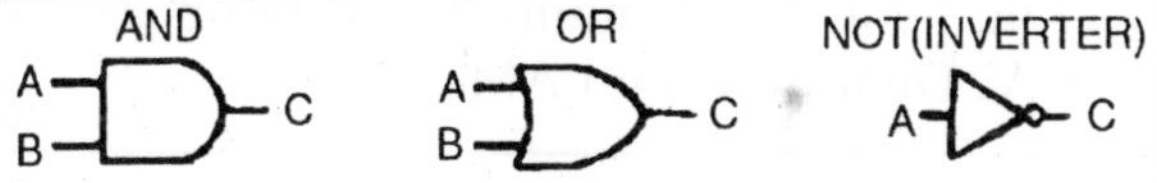

A	B	C
0	0	0
0	1	0
1	0	0
1	1	1

A	B	C
0	0	0
0	1	1
1	0	1
1	1	1

A	C
0	1
1	0

Integrated circuits contributed significantly to the advancement of the use of computers. Large numbers of logic circuits are contained on a single integrated circuit. The density of modern IC's is possible in part because of the similarity of the circuitry in them.

The computer is made up of thousands and sometimes millions of such circuits. These circuits handle the digital information in digital codes, detect the codes, and execute the operations called for in the codes. Because all of this is being done within the machine in digital code, the codes are called machine language or machine instructions.

0011 0111 0110 0011 1001 0101 1101 0011 0110 1111 1111 1010 1111 0011 1001 1011 1011 0001 1100 1010 1110 1001 1011 1010 1011 1101 0010 1001 1100 1101 1101 1000 1110 0101 1111 0100 1101 1001 0101 1111 1001 0100 1110 0110 1110 1100 0111 0010 1011 1010 0110 1111 1111 1111 1111 0100 1010 0111 1011 1111 0110 0011 1001 0101 1101 0011 1111 0101 0111 1111 0101 0011 1001 1011 1011 0001 1100 1110 1110 1001 1011 0010 1011 1101 0110 1111 1101 1101 1101 1000 1111 0101 0111 0100 1101 1001 0101 1110 1111 0100 1110 0101 0100 1001 1100 1101 1000 1110 0101 1111 0100 1111

The control unit and ALU of the computer are together known *as the Central Processing Unit (CPU).*

The CPU is like brain performs the following functions:

- It performs all calculations.
- It takes all decisions.
- It controls all units of the computer.

A PC may have CPU-IC such as Intel 8088, 80286, 80386, 80486, Celeron, Pentium, Pentium Pro, Pentium II, Pentium III, Pentium IV, Dual Core, and AMD etc.

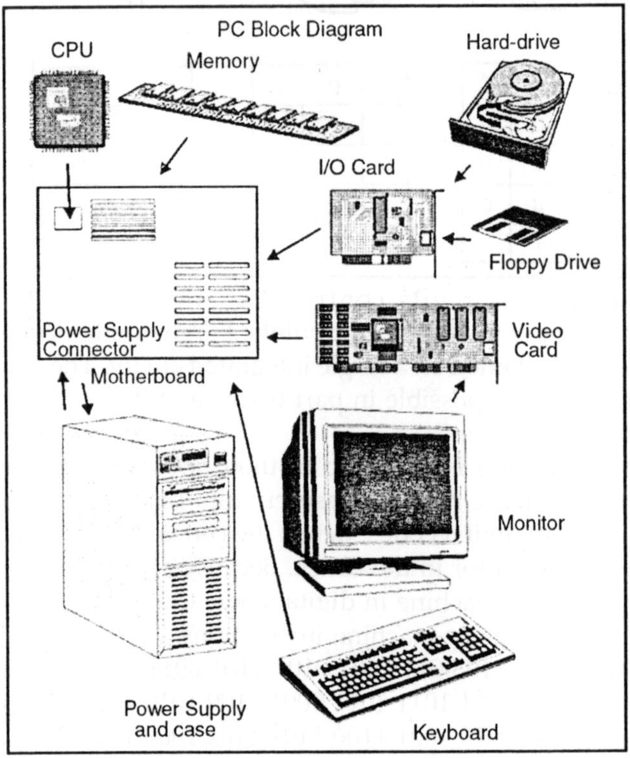

INPUT AND OUTPUT DEVICES

INPUT DEVICES

Component or peripheral (such as a barcode reader, graphic tablet, keyboard, magnetic-stripe reader, modem, mouse, scanner, stylus) that feeds data or instruction into a computer for display, processing, storage, or outputting or transmission.

Input devices convert the user's actions and analog data (sound, graphics, pictures) into digital electronic signals that can be 'handled' or 'read' by a computer. Digital data (such as from barcode readers, modems, scanners, etc.) does not require any conversion and is input direct into a computer. It is through input devices that a user exercises control over a computer, its operations, and outputs.

An input device is any device that provides input to a computer. There are dozens of possible input devices, but the two most common ones are a keyboard and mouse. Every key you press on the keyboard and every movement or click you make with the mouse sends a specific input signal to the computer. These commands allow you to open programmes, type messages, drag objects, and perform many other functions on your computer.

Since the job of a computer is primarily to process input, computers are pretty useless without input devices. Just imagine how much fun you would have using your computer without a keyboard or mouse. Not very much. Therefore, input devices are a vital part of every computer system.

While most computers come with a keyboard and mouse, other input devices may also be used to send information to the computer. Some examples include joysticks, MIDI keyboards, microphones, scanners, digital cameras, web cams, card readers, UPC scanners, and scientific measuring equipment. All these devices send information to the computer and therefore are categorized as input devices.

To be of any use at all a computer has to be able to take input, yet this basic premise can easily escape the modern computer user. With the quality and range of input devices now available, it seems hard to believe that computer input had once to be literally hardwired.

New circuits had to be constructed to solve individual problems by arranging cables and jack sockets on vast circuit boards. Clearly at that time word processing was simply beyond imagining, but years of developments have made this seem absurd, and word processing has become a staple of the computer's work.

Word processing, of course, relies on perhaps the most basic computer input device: the keyboard. Plainly modelled on the typewriter, in Western countries most modern computer keyboards are based on the QWERTY layout, or closely-related variants such as the French AZERTY layout.

There are additional keys not normally found on typewriters such as function keys, a numeric keypad and so on, and even in countries where different alphabets or writing systems are in use, the physical layout of the keys is often quite similar. The original 1981 IBM PC's keyboard was severely criticized by typists for its non-standard placement of the return and left shift keys.

In 1984, IBM corrected this on its AT keyboard, but shortened the backspace key, making it harder to reach. Then, in 1987, it introduced the enhanced keyboard, which relocated all the function keys, the Ctrl keys, and the Esc key to the positions we commonly see them today.

In recent years, so-called "Internet keyboards" have also become popular, including extra buttons for specific applications or functions (typically a browser or email client). Laptops might also have vendor specific keys included in the keyboard.

TYPES OF INPUT DEVICES

Read Only Memory (ROM)

Memory is like the banks of switches we have been thinking about that simply contain 1/0 binary patterns. Read Only Memory (abbreviated ROM) is a special kind of memory that cannot be changed. The most basic instructions for the CPU are built in to the ROM at the factory. To the end user, there really is very little to worry about regarding ROM. The amount of ROM in your computer doesn't really matter to you. All your programmes and information will go into another kind of memory that we will learn about soon.

Keyboard

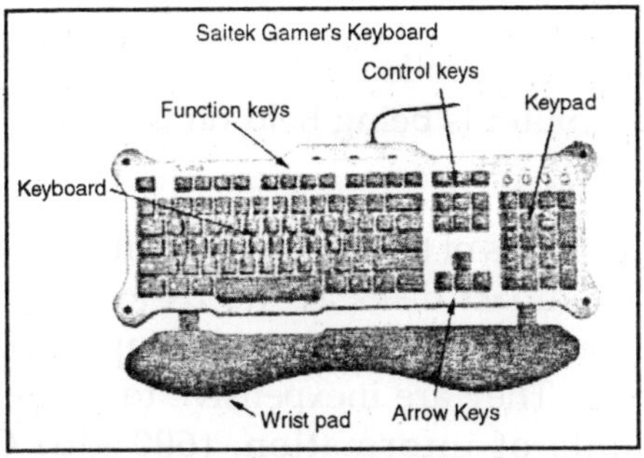

The keyboard is probably the easiest kind of input device to understand. When the user presses a key, a code is sent to the cpu, which translates the code into some sort of storage format (usually ASCII.) There is generally no way for the cpu to send information back to the keyboard, so it is an input only device. Usually, you buy a keyboard as part of a computer system, but there may be a reason you want a specialized model. Certain keyboards are designed to be more ergonomically safe to prevent Carpal-Tunnel Syndrome.

Mouse

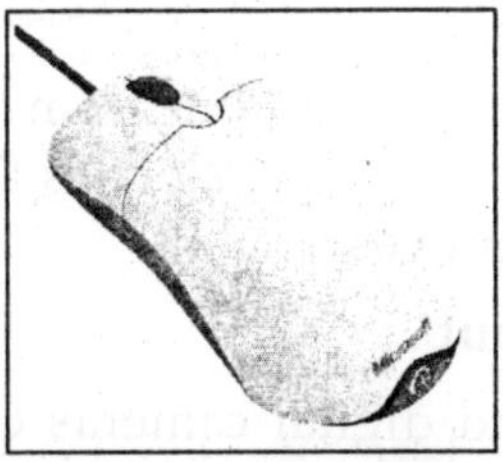

Many modern computers rely heavily on the mouse. This is a small object, usually with a roller ball on the bottom that can be dragged along the desktop. Mice usually have one or more buttons on them that can be activated with the hand controlling the mouse. As the mouse is moved on the desk, a pointer moves on the screen.

This mouse pointer is analogous to the user's hand. Many find this a more natural way of controlling the computer than typing on a keyboard. There are a number of "mouse substitutes" available, but they all basically work in the same way. Laptop computers often have a small ball embedded in the keyboard that can be rolled so the mouse can be activated even when the computer is being held on the user's lap.

CD-ROM

The same kinds of technology that enable us to store music digitally on compact disks allows us to store other kinds of information on the same medium. Compact Disks essentially store numbers. They are inexpensive to create, and can hold large amounts of information. (600 Mb) CD-ROMs are frequently used to sell software which has become too large to fit on floppy disks. Unfortunately, a CD - ROM cannot be written to with typical home technology. The ROM part of CD-ROM refers to this characteristic. A CD - ROM is an input device because it can send information to the CPU, but the CPU cannot send information to it. CD Drives are measured in comparison to the speed of music CDs. An audio CD always runs at a constant speed. A 2X CD drive is twice the speed of an audio CD player. 6X and 8x drives are available at this writing. Even these drives are not as fast as typical hard drives. Erasable CD drives are becoming popular, because they hold as much information as a regular CD, but the user can store things to them as well as reading from them. Such devices will probably be much more prevalent as their price comes down and reliability improves.

Audio/Video Input

Web cams and digital cameras can also be considered input devices. They provide visual data to the computer in the form of images and video. Some web cams can even be used as pointing devices by tracking the location of a person's hands or face. Microphones and digital musical instruments, such as midi keyboards, are audio input devices that provide the computer with audio data. Even an electric guitar, when hooked up to a computer, can be an input device.

Microphone

A microphone is a great input device to add to your

computer, simply because it gives you greater capabilities when calling someone online, or trying to use a video conference. By purchasing a microphone, anyone you wish will be able to hear you. You may also record things to your computer with the microphone, giving you multiple functions with one input device.

Webcam

Webcams help to round out the video conferencing experience. Webcams rarely actually come with desktop computers (but may be built into some laptops). Purchasing a webcam can be a great investment, however, for anyone who is looking to have a video conference, or to simply see someone as you talk with them. Webcams are available at low prices, as well as high prices, depending on the quality you expect.

Scanner

Scanners are often though about in the office, but are rarely thought about as an input device for a computer. When you have a scanner, you can scan newspaper clippings, articles, and pictures. This gives you the ability to save everything onto your computer. There are multiple types of scanners available; some even come on the printer you already have.

Other Input-Only Devices

There are other devices available for input, but they tend to be specialty devices. Some examples are:

- Touch - sensitive screens for mall kiosks.
- Adaptive keyboards for individuals with physical disabilities
- Infrared mice for a mouse without cords
- Special presentation devices that allow a speaker to send input to the computer while delivering a presentation away from the keyboard.

OUTPUT DEVICES

Any device that outputs information from a computer is called, not surprisingly, an output device. Since most information from a computer is output in either a visual or auditory format, the most common output devices are the monitor and speakers. These two devices provide instant feedback to the user's input, such as displaying characters as they are typed or playing a song selected from a playlist. While monitors and speakers are the most common output devices, there are many others. Some examples include headphones, printers, projectors, lighting control systems, audio recording devices, and robotic machines. A computer without an output device connected to it is pretty useless, since the output is what we interact with. Anyone who has ever had a monitor or printer stop working knows just how true this is.

TYPES OF OUTPUT DEVICES

Printer

Printers take information from the CPU and transfer it to paper. There are a number of different printer technologies available.

Dot Matrix

Dot Matrix printers are inexpensive and reliable, but they are loud and slow. They do not have nearly the print quality of some of the other types of printers.

Ink Jet

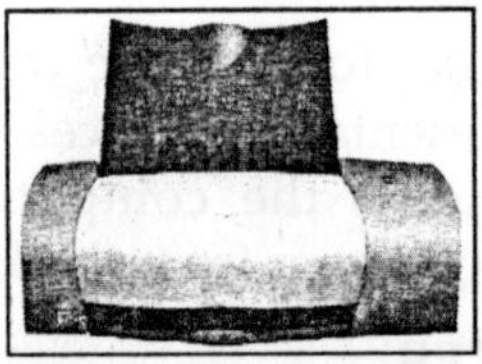

Ink Jet printers squirt small streams of ink onto the paper. They tend to be slightly more expensive than dot matrix printers, but the quiet operation and improved print quality make them very popular with buyers of home computers. Some ink jet printers can make colour prints. These can be very entertaining, but the ink becomes expensive.

Laser Printers

Laser Printers use a combination of laser and copying technology to make very clear copies. Laser printers tend to make clearer copies than the other types of printers, and operate much more quickly, but they can be quite expensive to purchase and maintain.

Many people try to save money on a printer purchase and are disappointed. If the main reason you will use your computer is to type letters, remember that the people you write to will not see your monitor. What they will see is only what comes out of your printer. If printed documents are an important part of what you will use a computer for, consider a higher quality printer. Ink Jets are probably most appropriate for home use, and laser printers are more popular in an office setting. A dot matrix machine is fine for test printing or use on a kid's computer, but you will be disappointed with the results if you try to use it for business correspondence. Before buying an ink jet, find out how much the ink cartridges cost, and how long they tend to last. With a laser printer, be sure to check on the cost of toner cartridges.

Monitors

The monitor is the part of the system that you look at most of the time. Monitors resemble televisions. Most computer monitors use the same technology as televisions, but with much higher resolution. Often the monitor will come packaged with a computer system, but you may wish to upgrade.

Desktop Monitor Liquid Crystal Display

Size

The size of a monitor can make a big impact. You might get a headache squinting at a screen that is too small. The size of a monitor is measured in diagonal inches. a 15 inch monitor is 15 inches diagonally from corner to corner of the screen.

Dot Pitch and DPI

Monitors are also measured by their precision. There are two main measures, Dot Pitch, and DPI. Dot pitch is a measure of the size of each tiny dot the monitor can display. The smaller each dot is, the nicer the picture will look, but the more expensive the monitor will be. When discussing Dot Pitch, smaller is better!! DPI stands for Dots Per Inch. As you can guess, the smaller the dot pitch rating for a monitor is, the more of those tiny dots you could squeeze into a square inch. If you are considering DPI, Larger is better. Computer sales people are not above taking advantage of this confusion.

Video Controller Card

Dealing with graphics takes a lot of work. Modern computers usually have a separate computer built in just to help with controlling the monitor. This little computer has its own cpu and memory! The power and speed of this little computer, as well as its memory capacity, have a huge effect on how graphics are drawn to your screen. This little computer is referred to as a graphics controller card. The most common cards now are called SVGA. Of course it gets way more complicated than this, but all you have to know is that there are fancier cards that do more and cost more, but you may not need the fanciest one out there for your first computer.

Projectors

A hardware device that enables an image, such as a computer screen, to be projected onto a flat surface. These devices are commonly used in meetings and presentations as they allow for a large image to be shown so everyone in a room can see. A general diagram of projector as an example image of what a projector may look like is shown below. As can be seen in this image the projector is a small device often a little bigger than a toaster and typically weighs a few pounds.

Speakers

A hardware device connected to a computer's sound card that outputs sounds generated by the card. Below is a graphic image example of the general speakers with subwoofer; speakers like the ones shown below are an example of what most computer speakers resemble.

Plotters

A plotter can be used to produce very large drawings on paper sizes up to A0 (16 times as big as A4). A plotter draws onto the paper using very fine pens. There are two types of plotter. They differ in the way that the pen can be moved about on the piece of paper to draw lines :

Flatbed Plotter

The paper is fixed and the pen moves left and right and up and down across the paper to draw lines.

Drum Plotter

The pen moves up and down on the paper and the paper is moved left and right by rotating a drum on which the paper is placed.

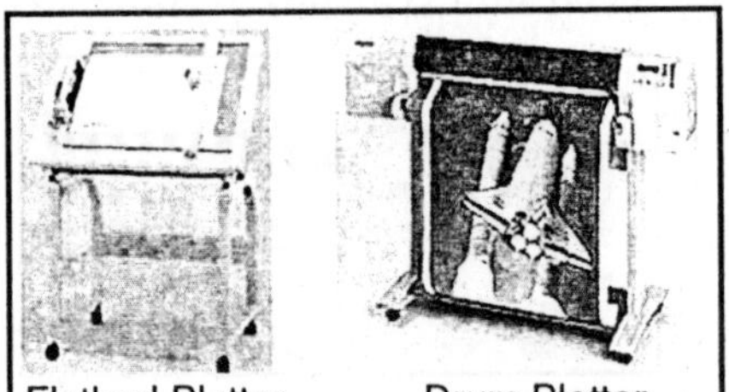

Flatbed Plotter Drum Plotter

Plotters can automatically change their pens and so can produce colour output. The lines drawn by a plotter are continuous and very accurate. Plotters are very slow but produce high quality output. They are usually used for Computer Aided Design (CAD) and Computer Aided Manufacturing (CAM) applications such as printing out plans for houses or car parts. The quality of the output produced by ink jet printers is now very good and large format (big) ink-jet printers are steadily replacing plotters for most tasks.

COMMON INPUT OUTPUT DEVICES

RAM

RAM is perhaps the most important of the input/output devices. When we talk about computer memory, we are mainly talking about RAM. In this class, when we think about the banks of light switches that can be manipulated, we are thinking of RAM memory. The term Random Access is pretty unfortunate. There is nothing random about how memory is accessed. The programme running will determine what is in memory. (of course, the programme itself is in memory too!)

RAM can be read from by the CPU. This means that the CPU can 'look' at any address in RAM and get the contents of that address. It can also be written to by the CPU, meaning that the CPU can change the value of memory cells on the fly.

One VERY important aspect of RAM memory is that it requires power. RAM can only hold values while power is going through it. If the power is interrupted, the RAM will lose ALL the values in it. This is why it is so important to save your work frequently when working on a computer. RAM memory is volatile. When the room you are working on is hit by a tsunami and the power goes out of your computer, you lose everything that was in RAM. This could be bad. The answer is to make copies of RAM, and place these copies on other kinds of media. That's what disk drives are for.

The amount of RAM in your computer is obviously a pretty important factor. The more memory you have, the more 'room' there is in your computer for information and programmes. Modern programmes have gotten HUGE, and the kinds of information you can work with have gotten much larger. Some early home computers had 4 or 16 K of RAM. The original IBM PC had 640 K of RAM.

In its day, this was thought of as an extravagant amount of memory that would never be fully used. Modern computers with less than 16 Megabytes (16,000 K) are considered a bit lame. (pun completely intended.) Older computers can be quite happy with much less RAM, but they will not be able to run the newer programmes. If you are buying or upgrading a computer, you should seriously consider as much RAM as you can afford. There is probably no more cost-effective upgrade than RAM. If you find that you need more memory, It is relatively cheap and easy to do a memory upgrade. Note that not all types of RAM are interchangeable. Look in the book that came with your computer for specifically which type of RAM you need when you are ready to upgrade.

Disk Drives

Disk drives are special devices that allow us to make copies of parts of RAM and store them magnetically. If RAM memory is electronic, think of disk drives as a special kind of magnetic memory. When you save something to a disk, the electronic impulses in RAM are copied and stored to the disk as a series of magnetic impulses.

All a disk drive does is translate electronic impulses and magnetic impulses back and forth. Disk drives are handy because magnetic impulses are more permanent than electronic ones.

The disk drive does not require electricity to keep values in memory, so if you store something to a disk, the information will be there when the tidal wave knocks the power out to your computer. (Assuming, of course, that the disk stayed dry and clean) Disks are sometimes thought of as secondary storage for this reason. There are a number of different kinds of disks. We will discuss a couple of main types:

Floppy Drives

A floppy drive is a machine that is designed to read floppy disks. Floppy disks are the removable devices that you stick in slots in the front of the machine. I know, they look square, not disk-shaped, and they don't look floppy at all, but they are indeed floppy disks. Floppy disks come in hard plastic cases to make them a little more sturdy and easier to handle, but inside the plastic case, there is an actual disk.

It is made of a plastic-like substance called mylar which really is floppy. Floppy disks come in two main sizes; 5 1/4 inch, and 3 1/2 inch. The 5 1/4 disks are becoming obsolete, but you still see them from time to time. The 3 1/2 inch disks, although physically smaller, can usually hold more information!

There are different flavours of floppy disks. In a modern computer, the only kind of floppy you need to purchase is High Density 1.44 MB. As you can guess, they hold 1.44 MegaBytes of information, which is a pretty good amount. (You could hold several hundred pages of text or about a dozen full colour pictures on a 1.44 MB disk) This type of disk may carry some other markings as well, such as DSHD or HD. The HD is the important part. That tells you it can handle 1.44

MB. If you have an older computer, you may find that it needs a different type or size of disks. Check your documentation to be sure.

Hard Drives

A hard drive is a special disk that is usually mounted permanently inside your computer's cabinet. You rarely see the hard drive, and almost never take it out. Hard drives are made of different material than floppies, and they are physically hard (although if you touched the actual hard surface, you would destroy it!) They spin much more quickly than floppies, and require much more precision.

They are sealed inside a special case, and that is sealed inside the computer case. A hard drive has a much larger capacity than a floppy, and is much faster at saving and retrieving information. Modern computers frequently have hard drives with 500 MB or more of capacity. As this capacity grows, people are beginning to measure it in terms of gigabytes. Software programmes are always becoming larger and taking more room on hard drives. It never takes long to completely fill up the capacity of a drive. If you can afford a large drive when you buy the computer, you won't be sorry, but you can usually add another drive or upgrade later.

Fancier Kinds of Drives

There are a number of other types of drives you may encounter when buying or upgrading a computer. You may encounter such things as Bernoulli tape drives, WORM (write once, read many) drives, optical floppies, and removable hard drives. All these things are really cool, but you may want to stick with the basics until you are a little more comfortable with the technology. Any computer system ought to have at least one 3.5 inch floppy drive, as large a hard drive as possible, and a CD-ROM drive.

Drive Controller Cards

Most computers come with a small card installed that helps control all your disk drives. It is called the Drive

Controller Card. There are two major kinds, IDE and SCSI. The only time you will ever care about this is when you buy a hard drive. Just know that the terms IDE and SCSI are terms that describe the drive controller card.

NETWORK CARD

In a home computer, you will generally not have a network card, but these devices are very common for computers in office settings. A network card is a special card which allows your computer to talk to other computers that are physically attached via cables.

Depending on how the network is set up, you can send messages from computer to computer, run programmes that are stored on different computers, and share devices like hard drives and printers. In many offices, the network also gives you access to the Internet. Network connections are generally faster than modem connections.

Modem

Modems were once thought of as somewhat extravagant, but with the advent of the Internet, they are becoming a necessity for home computers. They allow you to connect your computer to the Internet or other computer systems through a telephone connection. The term Modem stands for Modulator / Demodulator. It is a device that converts back and forth from the digital signals that computers understand to analog signals (sounds) that can be transferred over telephone lines.

Modems can be internal or external. The external ones have their own little case and power supply, and are generally a little more expensive than the internal ones, which are little cards that fit inside the computer. Modems are rated by their transmission speed, which is measured in BAUD (Bits of Audio Data / Second).

If you want to do any Internet connections, you need a baud rate of 1440 BAUD (also sometimes called 14400 BPS or 14.4 KBPS) You can also purchase faster modems, but they are of course more expensive. In the near future, something will happen in this arena. It is likely that we will be switching to a completely new kind of communication technology for home computers, but nobody knows exactly what that will be just yet. Some modems also include faxing and voice mail capabilities. These features can be very convenient for people with home offices.

Sound Card

Sound cards are another peripheral device that was once thought to be extravagant, but is now pretty much standard equipment on any new machine. A sound card is a device which enables the computer to handle sounds (duh!). It can handle sounds in two major ways. It can create sound effects entirely through programming, or it can record sounds through a standard microphone. Sound cards are attached to speakers which recreate the sound.

Obviously, sound cards are a big boost to computer game players, but they are frequently being used for more serious pursuits as well. People can attach voice annotations to documents they have written, musicians can test and modify a composition with a computer, and people with visual disabilities can have screens of text read to them.

The basic sound card is referred to as an 8-bit sound card, because it processes 8 bits of information at a time. You can now find 16-bit, and even 32-bit sound cards if you are willing to pay for them. As always, it depends on what you want your computer to do for you.

INPUT/OUTPUT INTERFACE

Input and output in IF/Prolog take place using device drivers which are managed on the basis of a driver model. A device driver is responsible for operations for a particular stream type, e.g. files, character strings or pipes. Prolog can manage different streams with the same set of generic built-in predicates.

Prolog provides the following built-in devices:

- File is the device for operating system files
- Null is the "bit bucket" device
- Pipe is the device for operating system pipes

- Standard is the device for the standard streams of the Prolog system
- String is the device for input/output using character strings
- Socket is the device for interprocess communication The I/O-related COM interfaces which are defined by header files in the oskit/io directory.

Most of these interfaces are fairly generic and can be used in a wide variety of situations. Some of these interfaces, such as the bufio interface, are extensions to other more primitive interfaces, and allow objects to export the same functionality in different forms, permitting clients to select the service that most directly meets their needs thereby reducing interface crossing overhead and increasing overall performance.

MACHINE LANGUAGE

DEFINITION

A language that need not be modified, translated, or interpreted before the processor for which it was designed can use it. The arithmetic and control unit circuits of the processor for which the language is designed can directly sense the operation codes and addresses used in instructions written in machine language.

It is also called as the Instructions written in an assembly language or a high-level language must be translated into machine language before a processor can execute them. Sometimes referred to as machine code or object code, machine language is a collection of binary digits or bits that the computer reads and interprets. Machine language is the only language a computer is capable of understanding. Computer designers rather than computer users usually use machine languages.

A system of codes directly understandable by a computer's CPU is termed this CPU's native or machine language. Although *machine code* may seem similar to *assembly language* they are in fact two different types of languages. *Assembly code* consists of both binary numbers and simple words whereas *machine code* is composed only of the two binary digits 0 and 1. Every CPU has its own machine language, although there is considerable overlap between some. If CPU *A* understands the full language of CPU *B* it is said that *A* is compatible with *B*. CPU *B* may not be compatible with CPU *A*, as *A* may know a few codes that *B* does not.

The "words" of a machine language are called *instructions*; each of these gives a basic command to the CPU. A programme is just a long list of instructions that are *executed* by a CPU. Older processors executed instructions one after the other, but newer super scalar processors are capable of executing several instructions at once. Programme flow may be influenced by special *jump* instructions that transfer execution to an instruction other than the following one. Conditional jumps are taken (execution continues at another address) or not (execution continues at the next instruction) depending on some condition.

Instructions are simply a pattern of bits—different patterns correspond to different commands to the machine. The more readable rendition of a machine language is called assembly language. Some languages give all their instructions the same number of bits, while the instruction length differs in others.

How the patterns are organised depends largely on the specific language. Common to most is the division of an instruction into *fields*, of which one or more specify the exact operation (for example "add"). Other fields may give the type of the operands, their location, or their value directly (operands contained in an instruction are called *immediate*).

ASSEMBLY LANGUAGE

DEFINITION

Assembly language is nothing more than a symbolic representation of machine code, which also allows symbolic designation of memory locations. Thus, an instruction to add the contents of a memory location to an internal CPU register called the accumulator might be add a number instead of a string of binary digits (bits). No matter how close assembly language is to machine code, the computer still cannot understand it. The assembly-language programme must be translated into machine code by a separate programme called an assembler.

The assembler programme recognizes the character strings that make up the symbolic names of the various machine operations, and substitutes the required machine code for each instruction. At the same time, it also calculates the required address in memory for each symbolic name of a memory location, and substitutes those addresses for the names.

The final result is a machine-language programme that can run on its own at any time; the assembler and the assembly-language programme are no longer needed. To help distinguish between the "before" and "after" versions of the programme, the original assembly-language programme is also known as the source code, while the final machine-language programme is designated the object code.

If an assembly-language programme needs to be changed or corrected, it is necessary to make the changes to the source code and then re-assemble it to create a new object programme.

OVERVIEW

Although the numbers of the above programme make perfect sense to a computer, they are about as clear as mud to a human. Who would have guessed that they put a dollar sign on the screen? Clearly, entering numbers by hand is a lousy way to write a programme.

It doesn't have to be this way, though. A long time ago, someone came up with the idea that computer programmes could be written using words instead of numbers. A special programme called an *assembler* would then take the programmer's words and convert them to numbers that the computer could understand.

This new method, called writing a programme in *assembly language,* saved programmers thousands of hours, since they no longer had to look up hard-to-remember numbers in the backs of programming books, but could use simple words instead.

The programme above, written in assembly language, looks like this:

```
MOV AX, 47104
MOV DS, AX
MOV [3998], 36
INT 32
```

When an assembler reads this sample programme, it converts each line of code into one CPU-level instruction. This programme uses two types of instructions, MOV and INT. On Intel processors, the MOV instruction moves data around, while the INT instruction transfers processor control to the device drivers or operating system.

The programme still isn't quite clear, but it is much easier to understand than it was before. The first instruction, MOV AX, 47104, tells the computer to copy the number 47104 into the location AX. The next instruction, MOV DS, AX, tells the computer to copy the number in AX into the location DS. The next instruction, MOV [3998], 36 tells the computer to put the number 36 into memory location 3998. Finally, INT 32 exits the programme by returning to the operating system.

Before we go on, I would like to explain just how this programme works. Inside the CPU are a number of locations, called registers, which can store a number. Some registers, such as AX, are general purpose, and don't do anything special. Other registers, such as DS, control the way the CPU works. DS just happens to be a *segment register*, and is used to pick which area of memory the CPU can write to. In our programme, we put the number 47104 into DS, which tells the CPU to access the memory on the video card.

The next thing our programme does is to put the number 36 into location 3998 of the video card's memory. Since 36 is the code for the dollar sign, and 3998 is the memory location of the bottom right hand corner of the screen, a dollar sign shows up on the screen a few microseconds later. Finally, our programme tells the CPU to perform what is called an *interrupt*. An interrupt is used to stop one programme and execute another in its place. In our case, we want interrupt 32, which ends our programme and goes back to MS-DOS, or whatever other programme was used to start our programme.

RUNNING THE PROGRAMME

Let's go ahead and run this programme. First, be sure to print these instructions out, since you will need to refer to them as we go on. Next, click on your start menu, and run the programme called MS-DOS Prompt. A black screen with white text should appear.

We are now in MS-DOS, the way computers used to be 20 years ago. MS-DOS was before the days of the mouse, so you must type commands on the keyboard to make the computer do things.

The cursor should move down a line, and you should see the Debug prompt, which is a simple dash. We are now in a programme called *Debug*. Debug is a powerful utility that lets you directly access the registers and memory of your computer for various purposes. In our case, we want to enter our programme into memory and run it, so we'll use Debug's a command, for *assemble.*

Go ahead and type a100 now. The cursor will move down another line, and you will see something like 1073:0100. This is the memory location we are going to enter assembly language instructions at. The first number is the segment, and the second number is the memory location within the segment. Your Debug programme will probably pick a different segment for your programme than mine did, so don't worry if it's different.

Another thing to note is that Debug only understands hexadecimal numbers, which are a sort of computer shorthand. Hexadecimal numbers sometimes contain letters as well as well as digits.

Let's go ahead and enter your programme now. Type each of the instructions below into Debug exactly as they appear, and press enter after each one. When you finish entering the last instruction, press enter twice to tell Debug that we are done entering instructions.

```
mov ax,B800
mov ds,ax
mov byte[0F9E],24
int 20
```

As you can see, I've converted all the numbers into hexadecimal, and have made a few other changes so Debug can understand what's going on. If you make a mistake while entering the above programme, press enter twice, type a100, and start entering instructions again at the beginning of the programme. Once you have entered the programme, you can go ahead and run it. Simply type g for *go* and press enter when you are ready to start the programme. You should see a dollar sign in the lower right hand corner of your screen and the words Programme terminated normally. These words are put out by Debug to let you know that the programme ended normally.

HIGH LEVEL LANGUAGES

OVERVIEW

Very early in the development of computers attempts were made to make programming easier by reducing the amount of knowledge of the internal workings of the computer that was needed to write programmes. If programmes could be presented in a language that was more familiar to the person solving the problem, then fewer mistakes would be made. High-level programming languages allow the specification of a problem solution in terms closer to those used by human beings. These languages were designed to make programming far easier, less error-prone and to remove the programmer from having to know the details of the internal structure of a particular computer. These high-level languages were much closer to human language. One of the first of these languages was Fortran II which was introduced in about 1958. In Fortran II our programme above would be written as:

$$C = A + B$$

which is obviously much more readable, quicker to write and less error-prone. As with assembly languages the computer does not understand these high-level languages directly and hence they have to be processed by passing them through a programme called a compiler which translates them into internal machine language before they can be executed.

Another advantage accrues from the use of high-level languages if some international body standardizes the languages. Then each manufacturer produces a compiler to compile programmes that conform to the standard into their own internal machine language. Then it should be easy to take a programme, which conforms to the standard, and implement it on many different computers merely by re-compiling it on the appropriate computer.

This great advantage of portability of programmes has been achieved for several high-level languages and it is now possible to move programmes from one computer to another without too much difficulty. Unfortunately many compiler writers add new features of their own which means that if a programmer uses these features then their programme becomes non-portable. It is well worth becoming familiar with the standard and writing programmes which obey it, so that your programmes are more likely to be portable. As with assembly language human time is saved at the expense of the compilation time required to translate the programme to internal machine language. The compilation time used in the computer is trivial compared with the human time saved, typically seconds as compared with weeks. Many high level languages have appeared since Fortran II (and many have also disappeared!), among the most widely used have been:

COBOL	Business applications
FORTRAN	Engineering & Scientific Applications
PASCAL	General use and as a teaching tool
C & C++	General Purpose - currently most popular
PROLOG	Artificial Intelligence
JAVA	General Purpose - gaining popularity rapidly

All these languages are available on a large variety of computers. High-level languages are those programming languages, which are customised and pretty convenient to use. These languages can be operated with several platforms. Some of the high-level languages have relevance even when not associated central processing unit.

CHARACTERISTICS OF HIGH-LEVEL LANGUAGES

In terms of technology, high-level languages are not better than the low-level versions. Rather the computing techniques used in high-level languages are simpler than those applied in low-level programming languages. The term high-level indicates greater degree of abstraction from the so-called computer languages. Unlike low-level programming languages, the high-level languages never come with opcodes. Among the other common features of high-level languages, object-oriented features, string handling schedules and modes for input or outputs of files are worth mentioning.

FUNCTIONS OF HIGH-LEVEL LANGUAGES

The main function of a high-level language is to simplify the use of programming systems to the users. The high-level languages break up the complicated chains of commands into simpler parts. For an efficient computer programming, the codes must be developed in low-level languages. However to make the best possible use of those codes, high-level languages are required. Over the passage of time, the architectures of computers are becoming more complicated than before. Today's microprocessors require cutting-edge techniques to run the computer systems efficiently. Here comes the role of high-level languages. These programming languages are capable of designing cods that perfectly suit the requirements of modern computing.

DIFFERENT STAGES OF OPERATION

High-level languages operate through different models of programming. Interpreted and compiled are the two programming languages used in the intermediate steps. Intermediate representa-tions and machine code generation are some other steps involved in the operation of high-level languages.

Chapter 3

System Programming

DEFINITION

System programming is the activity of programming system software. The primary distinguishing characteristic of systems programming when compared to application programming is that application programming aims to produce software which provides services to the user (e.g. word processor), whereas systems programming aims to produce software which provides services to the computer hardware. It also requires a greater degree of hardware awareness.

The architects of the earliest computer systems gave little thought to software. (The very word was still a decade in the future.) Building the machine itself was the serious intellectual challenge; converting mathematical formulas into programme statements looked like a routine clerical task. The awful truth came out soon enough. Maurice V.Wilkes, who wrote what may have been the first working computer programme, had his personal epiphany in 1949, when "the realization came over me with full force that a good part of the remainder of my life was going to be spent in finding errors in my own programmes." Half a century later, we're still debugging.

The very first programmes were written in pure binary notation: Both data and instructions had to be encoded in long, featureless strings of 1s and 0s. Moreover, it was up to the programmer to keep track of where everything was stored in the machine's memory. Before you could call a subroutine, you had to calculate its address. The technology that lifted these burdens from the programmer was assembly language, in which raw binary codes were replaced by symbols such as load, store, add, sub. The symbols were translated into binary by a programme called an assembler, which also calculated addresses. This was the first of many instances in which the computer was recruited to help with its own programming. Assembly language was a crucial early advance, but still the programmer had to keep in mind all the minutiae in the instruction set of a specific computer.

Evaluating a short mathematical expression such as x2+y2 might require dozens of assembly-language instructions. Higher-level languages freed the programmer to think in terms of variables and equations rather than registers and addresses. In Fortran, for example, x2+y2 would be written simply as X** 2+Y**2. Expressions of this kind are translated into binary form by a programme called a compiler. With Fortran and the languages that followed, programmers finally had the tools they needed to get into really serious trouble.

By the 1960s large software projects were notorious for being late, overbudget and buggy; soon came the appalling news that the cost of software was overtaking that of hardware. Frederick P. Brooks, Jr., who managed the OS/360 software programme at IBM, called large- system programming a "tar pit" and remarked,"Everyone seems to have been surprised by the stickiness of the problem."

One response to this crisis was structured programming, a reform movement whose manifesto was Edsger W. Dijkstra's brief letter to the editor titled "Go to statement considered harmful." Structured programmes were to be built out of subunits that have a single entrance point and a single exit (eschewing the goto command,which allows jumps into or out of the middle of a routine).

Three such constructs were recommended: sequencing (do A, then B, then C), alternation (either do A or do B) and iteration (repeat A until some condition is satisfied). Corrado Böhm and Giuseppe Jacopini proved that these three idioms are sufficient to express essentially all programmes. Structured programming came packaged with a number of related principles and imperatives. Top-down design and stepwise refinement urged the programmer to set forth the broad outlines of a procedure first and only later fill in the details. Modularity called for self-contained units with simple interfaces between them. Encapsulation, or data hiding,required that the internal workings of a module be kept private, so that later changes to the module would not affect other areas of the programme. All of these ideas have proved their worth and remain a part of software practice today. But they did not rescue programmers from the tar pit.

SYSTEM PROGRAMMING LANGUAGE

System programming languages are higher level and they are strongly typed languages. The term "higher level" means that many details are handled automatically so that programmers can write less code to get the same job done. System programming languages are well suited to building components where the complexity is in the data structures and algorithms.

System programming support following features:

- Register allocation is handled by the compiler so that programmers need not write code to move information between registers and memory.
- Programmers can use simple keywords such as while and if for control structures; the compiler generates all the detailed instructions to implement the control structures.
- Procedure calling sequences are generated automatically: programmers need not worry about moving arguments to and from the call stack.

EMBEDDED SYSTEM PROGRAMMING

Embedded System Programming was first used in Apollo guidance computer to guide Apollo. Technological advancement brought the price of embedded system (ICs) lower making it possible to use them for commercial purpose. Today embedded systems are widely used in various devices performing specific functions with drastic improvement in processing power. Embedded system programming has been derived from the word embedded system. An embedded system is nothing but a special purpose system in which the computer is fully encapsulated by the device it controls. Embedded software designs have advanced enough to produce widely used devices performing specific function devices such as ATM, PDA, mobile phones etc.

This widely used technological term in the field of Information Technology, is the combination of computer hardware and software which is either fixed in facility or programmable. In short it is purposely designed for a meticulous kind of application device. Systems that hosts this embedded systems are various industrial machines, automobiles, medical equipment, cameras, household appliances, and airplanes, vending machines, toys, cellular phone and PDA.

Seeing its importance and worth embedded systems programming has gained lot popularity and people are looking for companies providing this service. If you are looking for a company providing embedded systems programming then your search is over as Softage is there for you.

Softage is Russia's leading IT service provider providing best and advanced embedded systems programming. Embedded systems programming is specially dedicated to unequivocal tasks so that design engineers can optimize it by reducing the magnitude and cost of the product. In fact nowadays, embedded systems are frequently mass-produced. This has resulted in the cost savings that may be multiplied by millions of items. Apart from the other devices embedded systems also range from portable devices such as MP3 players, to large stationary installations like traffic lights or factory controllers.

According to the experts embedded systems are easily programmable and are provided with a programming interface. Embedded system programming is a tough and professional work which is efficiently handled by Softage. Backed by years of experience Softage hosts some of the best and professional programmers those are experts in embedded system software programming. Embedded systems programming is basically done in various languages such as J2e, C/C++, x86 assembler, ADSP assembler, and SQL accessing appropriate language for specific devices. All these languages are supported and provided by Softage and that too easily affordable. Thus, what you are waiting for if you are looking for embedded systems programming then Softage is there for you.

WINDOWS SYSTEM PROGRAMMING

In old days, the operating system programme executes the program's instructions in sequence one instruction after another as they arranged by the programmer. When the programme calls a function or interacts with the Operating System (OS) by calling one of the OS's service functions, the function's instructions executed in similar way and the execution continue sequentially until the end of the last instruction of the main programme.

In this traditional way of programming the programme only need one main function to start the execution. Nowadays, in event driven programming environment such as Windows, the interaction between the programme and the OS is a message-based interaction. In this interaction the programme start in a wait mode until the user create an event like for example, press a key or click a mouse button.

The OS generates appropriate message and inserts it in application's message queue. The programme, when it ready, should dispatch the messages (read a message from the queue and send it back to the OS) one message after another for time scheduling purpose. After that, the OS then send the message again to the programme and the programme respond by taking appropriate actions. In this kind of interaction, a simple programme need at least two functions, the main function that start the message loop (WinMain ()) and the other called by the OS (Windows Function())and respond to the passed message.

UNIX SYSTEMS PROGRAMMING

The Unix systems programming API has been standardised by a large number of POSIX standards documents from the IEEE. For the majority of programmers the most important of these is POSIX 1003.1 which covers process primitives and environments, directories and files, I/O primitives and device specific functions. Later standards cover other issues, such as Shells and Utilities (POSIX 1003.2) and Administration (POSIX 1387.2).

One of the unusual characteristics of POSIX 1003.1 is its use of the C language throughout. Whereas IEEE standards would normally be expected to be language independent, the history of Unix is so bound up with C that this was the only feasible route. The document claims that it will be the basis for definitions that are independent of particular programming languages. In fact, new language dependent versions have arisen, such as Ada (POSIX 1003.5) and Fortran.

Irrespective of the formal standards mechanisms, designers of libraries for other languages have used POSIX 1003.1 as the specification for their own libraries. For example, tcl [Ousterhout] and Perl [Wall] have well-developed Unix bindings that copy the syntax, and rely on the semantics, of POSIX 1003.1.

Java [Arnold] is the latest flavour in programming languages for all sorts of excellent reasons, despite some serious shortcomings. It is a full O/O language (although not as pure as SmallTalk or Eiffel); it is based on C/C++, but avoids the worst of both languages (not completely, though); by use of a virtual machine it is cross-platform (although some vendors have variant versions); it has a rich set set of libraries that deal with, for example, graphics and networking. These are combining to produce the "Web programming" environment where applications or applets are written once to run on any platform. Java extends the open authoring environment of HTML to an open programming environment.

How do Unix and Java co-exist? Very well in general terms. A Java application can do exactly the same things in a Unix environment that it can do in a Mac or Windows environment. With care, applications can even be written that transparently handle such issues as forward- versus back-slashes for directory separators. Java currently lacks the depth of hooks into the POSIX API that tcl and Perl have. The standard must continue to have this lack or it will lose its universal applicability. However, *extensions* by *non-standard* libraries can supply this depth, as long as they are done in an appropriate manner. This paper reports on a project to make the POSIX API available to Java applications or applets using a non-standard library. It encapulates POSIX calls within Java methods for a new set of classes in the posix package.

This project must be contrasted in aims and methods to the Microsoft policy with J++: their attempt is to make J++ the best environment for doing Windows programming in Java J++, and this implicitly rejects the notion of a cross-platform environment. It may even turn out to be difficult for the programmer using J++ to be certain of how general their code is. The statements from Microsoft do not seem to dispel any uncertainty.

This project, on the other hand, makes it explicit about the introduction of non-standard features, by placing all the new classes in a package that is non-standard. No application using the posix package will ever pass the "Java Pure" tests. On the other hand, this package will develop by an open process method: the source code will be freely available to all, and can be freely modified. If interest is high enough, it can be divorced from individual control and given to a suitable co-ordinating authority.

LINKERS

DEFINITION

In computer science, a linker is a programme that takes one or more objects generated by a compiler and assembles them into a single executable programme. In IBM mainframe environments such as OS/360 this programme is known as a "linkage editor". On Unix variants the term loader is often used as a synonym for linker. Because this usage blurs the distinction between the compile-time process and the run-time process, this article will use "linking" for the former and "loading" for the latter. However, in some operating systems the same programme handles both the jobs of linking and loading a programme; see "dynamic linking".

Computer programmes are typically comprised of several parts or modules; these parts, if not all contained within a single object file, refer to each other by means of symbols.

Typically, an object file can contain three kinds of symbols:

- Defined symbols, which allow it to be called by other modules.
- Undefined symbols, which call the other modules where these symbols are defined.
- Local symbols, used internally within the object file to facilitate relocation.

When a programme comprises multiple object files, the linker combines these files into a unified executable programme, resolving the symbols as it goes along. Linkers can take objects from a collection called a "library". Some linkers do not include the whole library in the output; they only include its symbols that are referenced from other object files or libraries. Libraries exist for diverse purposes, and one or more system libraries are usually linked in by default. The linker also takes care of arranging the objects in a program's address space.

This may involve "relocating" code that assumes a specific base address to another base. Since a compiler seldom knows where an object will reside, it often assumes a fixed base location (for example, zero). Relocating machine code may involve re-targeting of absolute jumps, loads and stores. The executable output by the linker may need another relocation pass when it is finally loaded into memory (just before execution). This pass is usually omitted on hardware offering virtual memory — every programme is put into its own address space, so there is no conflict even if all programmes load at the same base address. This pass may also be omitted if the executable is a position independent executable.

CONCEPT

The basic job of any linker is simple: it binds more abstract names to more concrete names, which permits programmers to write code using the more abstract names. That is, it takes a name written by a programmer such as get line and binds it to "the location 612 bytes from the beginning of the executable code in module iosys." Or it may take a more abstract numeric address such as "the location 450 bytes beyond the beginning of the static data for this module" and bind it to a numeric address. A linkers is used in the development of computer programming in systems.

The earliest computers were programmed entirely in machine language. Programmers would write out the symbolic programmes on sheets of paper, hand assemble them into machine code and then toggle the machine code into the computer, or perhaps punch it on paper tape or cards. If the programmer used symbolic addresses at all, the symbols were bound to addresses as the programmer did his or her hand translation.

If it turned out that an instruction had to be added or deleted, the entire programme had to be hand-inspected and any addresses affected by the added or deleted instruction adjusted. The problem was that the names were bound to addresses too early. Assemblers solved that problem by letting programmers write programmes in terms of symbolic names, with the assembler binding the names to machine addresses. If the programme changed, the programmer had to reassemble it, but the work of assigning the addresses is pushed off from the programmer to the computer. Libraries of code compound the address assignment problem. Since the basic operations that computers can perform are so simple, useful programmes are composed of subprograms that perform higher level and more complex operations.

Computer installations keep a library of pre-written and debugged subprograms that programmers can draw upon to use in new programmes they write, rather than requiring programmers to write all their own subprograms. The programmer then loads the subprograms in with the main programme to form a complete working programme. Programmers were using libraries of subprograms even before they used assemblers. By 1947, John Mauchly, who led the

ENIAC project, wrote about loading programmes along with subprograms selected from a catalog of programmes stored on tapes, and of the need to relocate the subprograms' code to reflect the addresses at which they were loaded. Perhaps surprisingly, these two basic linker functions, relocation and library search, appear to predate even assemblers, as Mauchly expected both the programme and subprograms to be written in machine language.

The relocating loader allowed the authors and users of the subprograms to write each subprogram as though it would start at location zero, and to defer the actual address binding until the subprograms were linked with a particular main programme. With the advent of operating systems, relocating loaders separate from linkers and libraries became necessary. Before operating systems, each programme had the machine's entire memory at its disposal, so the programme could be assembled and linked for fixed memory addresses, knowing that all addresses in the computer would be available. But with operating systems, the programme had to share the computer's memory with the operating system and perhaps even with other programmes, This means that the actual addresses at which the programme would be running weren't known until the operating system loaded the programme into memory, deferring final address binding past link time to load time.

Linkers and loaders now divided up the work, with linkers doing part of the address binding, assigning relative addresses within each programme, and the loader doing a final relocation step to assign actual addresses. As systems became more complex, they called upon linkers to do more and more complex name management and address binding.

Fortran programmes used multiple subprograms and common blocks, areas of data shared by multiple subprograms, and it was up to the linker to lay out storage and assign the addresses both for the subprograms and the common blocks. Linkers increasingly had to deal with object code libraries. Including both application libraries written in Fortran and other languages, and compiler support libraries called implicitly from compiled code to handle I/O and other high-level operations. Programmes quickly became larger than available memory, so linkers provided overlays, a technique that let programmers arrange for different parts of a programme to share the same memory, with each overlay loaded on demand when another part of the programme called into it.

Overlays were widely used on mainframes from the advent of disks around 1960 until the spread of virtual memory in the mid-1970s, then reappeared on microcomputers in the early 1980s in exactly the same form, and faded as virtual memory appeared on PCs in the 1990s.

They're still used in memory limited embedded environments, and may yet reappear in other places where precise programmer or compiler control of memory usage improves performance. With the advent of hardware relocation and virtual memory, linkers and loaders actually got less complex, since each programme could again have an entire address space.

Programmes could be linked to be loaded at fixed addresses, with hardware rather than software relocation taking care of any load-time relocation. But computers with hardware relocation invariably run more than one programme, frequently multiple copies of the same programme. When a computer runs multiple instances of one programme, some parts of the programme are the same among all running instance (the executable code, in particular), while other parts are unique to each instance.

If the parts that don't change can be separated out from the parts that do change, the operating system can use a single copy of the unchanging part, saving considerable storage. Compilers and assemblers were modified to create object code in multiple sections, with one section for read only code and another section for writable data, the linker had to be able to combine all of sections of each type so that the linked programme would have all the code in one place and all of the data in another. This didn't delay address binding any more than it already was, since addresses were still assigned at link time, but more work was deferred to the linker to assign addresses for all the sections.

LINKER ACTION

Programme Loading

Copy a programme from secondary storage (which since about 1968 invariably means a disk) into main memory so it's ready to run. In some cases loading just involves copying the data from disk to memory, in others it involves allocating storage, setting protection bits, or arranging for virtual memory to map virtual addresses to disk pages.

Relocation

Compilers and assemblers generally create each file of object code with the programme addresses starting at zero, but few computers let you load your programme at location zero. If a programme is created from multiple subprograms, all the subprograms have to be loaded at non-overlapping addresses. Relocation is the process of assigning load addresses to the various parts of the programme, adjusting the code and data in the programme to reflect the assigned addresses.

In many systems, relocation happens more than once. It's quite common for a linker to create a programme from multiple subprograms, and create one linked output programme that starts at zero, with the various subprograms relocated to locations within the big programme. Then when the programme is loaded, the system picks the actual load address and the linked programme is relocated as a whole to the load address.

Symbol Resolution

When a programme is built from multiple subprograms, the references from one subprogram to another are made using symbols; a main programme might use a square root routine

called sqrt, and the math library defines sqrt. A linker resolves the symbol by noting the location assigned to sqrt in the library, and patching the caller's object code to so the call instruction refers to that location. Although there's considerable overlap between linking and loading, it's reasonable to define a programme that does programme loading as a loader, and one that does symbol resolution as a linker. Either can do relocation, and there have been all-in-one linking loaders that do all three functions. The line between relocation and symbol resolution can be fuzzy. Since linkers already can resolve references to symbols, one way to handle code relocation is to assign a symbol to the base address of each part of the programme, and treat relocatable addresses as references to the base address symbols.

TWO-PASS LINKING PROCESS

Now we turn to the general structure of linkers. Linking, like compiling or assembling, is fundamentally a two pass process. A linker takes as its input a set of input object files, libraries, and perhaps command files, and produces as its result an output object file, and perhaps ancillary information such as a load map or a file containing debugger symbols.

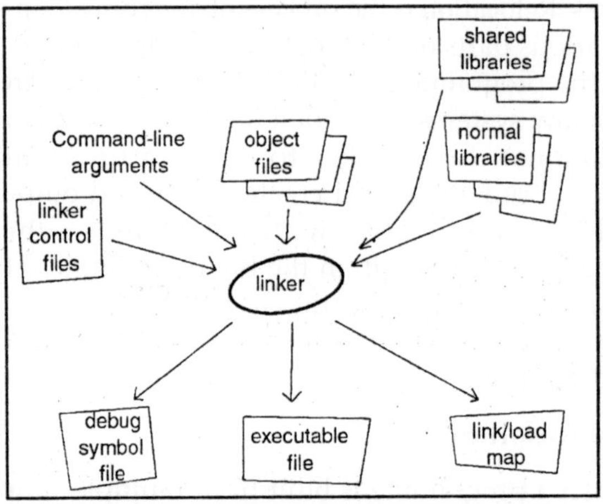

Each input file contains a set of *segments*, contiguous chunks of code or data to be placed in the output file. Each input file also contains at least one *symbol table*. Some symbols are exported, defined within the file for use in other files, generally the names of routines within the file that can be called from elsewhere. Other symbols are imported, used in the file but not defined, generally the names of routines called from but not present in the file.

When a linker runs, it first has to scan the input files to find the sizes of the segments and to collect the definitions and references of all of the symbols It creates a segment table listing all of the segments defined in the input files, and a symbol table with all of the symbols imported or exported.

Using the data from the first pass, the linker assigns numeric locations to symbols, determines the sizes and location of the segments in the output address space, and figures out where everything goes in the output file. The second pass uses the information collected in the first pass to control the actual linking process. It reads and relocates the object code, substituting numeric addresses for symbol references, and adjusting memory addresses in code and data to reflect relocated segment addresses, and writes the relocated code to the output file. It then writes the output file, generally with header information, the relocated segments, and symbol table information. If the programme uses dynamic linking, the symbol table contains the info the runtime linker will need to resolve dynamic symbols.

In many cases, the linker itself will generate small amounts of code or data in the output file, such as "glue code" used to call routines in overlays or dynamically linked libraries, or an array of pointers to initialization routines that need to be called at programme startup time. Whether or not the programme uses dynamic linking, the file may also contain a symbol table for relinking or debugging that isn't used by the programme itself, but may be used by other programmes that deal with the output file.

Some object formats are relinkable, that is, the output file from one linker run can be used as the input to a subsequent linker run. This requires that the output file contain a symbol table like one in an input file, as well as all of the other auxiliary information present in an input file. Nearly all object formats have provision for debugging symbols, so that when the programme is run under the control of a debugger, the debugger can use those symbols to let the programmer control the programme in terms of the line numbers and names used in the source programme.

Depending on the details of the object format, the debugging symbols may be intermixed in a single symbol table with symbols needed by the linker, or there may be one table for the linker and a separate, somewhat redundant table for the debugger.

A few linkers appear to work in one pass. They do that by buffering some or all of the contents of the input file in memory or disk during the linking process, then reading the buffered material later. Since this is an implementation trick that doesn't fundamentally affect the two-pass nature of linking, we don't address it further here.

RELOCATION AND CODE MODIFICATION

The heart of a linker or loader's actions is relocation and code modification. When a compiler or assembler generates and object file, it generates the code using the unrelocated addresses of code and data defined within the file, and usually zeros for code and data defined elsewhere. As part of the linking process, the linker modifies the object code to reflect the actual addresses assigned. For example, consider this snippet of x86 code that moves the contents of variable a to variable b using the eax register.

```
mov a,%eax
mov %eax,b
```

If a is defined in the same file at location 1234 hex and b is imported from somewhere else, the generated object code will be: A1 34 12 00 00 mov a,%eax A3 00 00 00 00 mov %eax,b Each instruction contains a one-byte operation code followed by a fourbyte address.

The first instruction has a reference to 1234 (byte reversed, since the x86 uses a right to left byte order) and the second a reference to zero since the location of b is unknown. Now assume that the linker links this code so that the section in which a is located is relocated by hex 10000 bytes, and b turns out to be at hex 9A12.

The linker modifies the code to be:

A1 34 12 01 00 mov a,%eax

A3 12 9A 00 00 mov %eax,b

That is, it adds 10000 to the address in the first instruction so now it refers to a's relocated address which is 11234, and it patches in the address for b. These adjustments affect instructions, but any pointers in the data part of an object file have to be adjusted as well. On older computers with small address spaces and direct addressing, the modification process is fairly simple, since there are only only one or two address formats that a linker has to handle. Modern computers, including all RISCs, require considerably more complex code modification.

No single instruction contains enough bits to hold a direct address, so the compiler and linker have to use complicated addressing tricks to handle data at arbitrary addresses. In some cases, it's possible to concoct an address using two or three instructions, each of which contains part of the address, and use bit manipulation to combine the parts into a full address. In this case, the linker has to be prepared to modify each of the instructions appropriately, inserting some of the bits of the address into each instruction.

In other cases, all of the addresses used by a routine or group of routines are placed in an array used as an "address pool", initialization code sets one of the machine registers to point to that array, and code loads pointers out of the address pool as needed using that register as a base register. The linker may have to create the array from all of the addresses used in a programme, then modify instructions that so that they refer to the appropriate address pool entry.

LINKER COMMAND LANGUAGES

Every linker has some sort of command language to control the linking process. At the very least the linker needs the list of object files and libraries to link. Generally there is a long list of possible options: whether to keep debugging symbols, whether to use shared or unshared libraries, which of several possible output formats to use. Most linkers permit some way to specify the address at which the linked code is to be bound, which comes in handy when using a linker to link a system kernel or other programme that doesn't run under control of an operating system. In linkers that support multiple code and data segments, a linker command language can specify the order in which segments are to be linked, special treatment for certain kinds of segments, and other application-specific options.

- *Command line:* Most systems have a command line or the equivalent, via which one can pass a mixture of file names and switches. This is the usual approach for Unix and Windows linkers. On systems with limited length command lines, there's usually a way to direct the linker to read commands from a file and treat them as though they were on the command line.

Intermixed with Object Files

Some linkers, such as IBM mainframe linkers, accept alternating object files and linker commands in a single input file. This dates from the era of card decks, when one would pile up object decks and hand-punched command cards in a card reader.

Embedded in Object Files

Some object formats, notably Microsoft's, permit linker commands to be embedded inside object files. This permits a compiler to pass any options needed to link an object file in the file itself. For example, the C compiler passes commands to search the standard C library.

Separate Configuration Language

A few linkers have a full fledged configuration language to control linking. The GNU linker, which can handle an enormous range of object file formats, machine architectures, and address space conventions, has a complex control language that lets a programmer specify the order in which segments should be linked, rules for combining similar segments, segment addresses, and a wide range of other options. Other linkers have less complex languages to handle specific features such as programmer-defined overlays.

LOADER

It is the Loader's function to fix absolute addresses for the relocated values in a relocatable module, thereby converting a relocatable module into an "executable" output file. The Loader is usually called automatically by the Linker but it may also be called separately by the user. As indicated below, several different Loaders are (optionally) available for use with Introl-C and, if the user has elected to obtain such optional Loaders, a variety of executable output file formats can be generated, depending on the Loader being used.

Each resident Introl-C compiler package, and each Introl-C cross-compiler package, nominally includes a single, specific type of Introl Loader which is considered as being the "standard" Loader for that compiler's particular host system configuration. For resident Introl-C Compiler packages, the 'standard' Loader that is furnished is an "operating system dependent" type of Loader which generates an output file that is executable on that particular Compiler's host system.

For cross-compiler versions of Introl-C, the "standard" Loader furnished is typically a "hex" type Loader that generates a file of output load records, which can be either Motorola S-Records, intel Hex, Tektronix Hex, or Tektronix Extended Hex at user option. Besides the "standard" Loader that accompanies any given Compiler type, it is also possible for the user to optionally obtain and use other compatible "cross-Loaders" which generate output formats unrelated to the Compiler's host operating system. For example, "hex-type" Loaders are optionally available for

use with resident versions of Introl-C; "operating system dependent" type Loaders are optionally available for use with cross-compiler versions; etc. There are, therefore, several different species of Loaders, (as well as several different types of related Standard Libraries) that may potentially be used under Introl-C. The "standard" Loader supplied with your Introl-C package, as well as any other Loaders that may have been optionally ordered, are described in detail in the Loader Appendix of this Linker Reference Manual. This Loader section describes the general features that are common to all Loader types. Normally the input to the Loader is expected to be a relocatable file which has no unresolved external references; if unresolved references do exist in its input, loading will normally not be successful.

A Loader option is provided, however, to force a file to be loaded even if it contains unresolved references. Usually a relocatable file has to be linked before it can be used as input to the Loader. It is also possible, of course, to assemble a file which makes no external references and then use the relocatable output file produced by the Assembler directly as input to the Loader (ie without having actually linked it)

FUNCTIONS OF LOADER

- Allocate space in memory for the programme (allocation).
- Resolve symbolic references between object programmes (linking).
- Adjust all address dependent locations, such as address constraints, to correspond to the allocated space (relocation).
- Physically place the machine instruction and data into memory(loading) for execution.
- *Loader*: System programme that performs the loading function.
- *Linker* (or linkage editor): System programme that performs the linking operations (i.e. linking and relocation).

KINDS OF LOADER

Absolute Loader

Performs Loading Only:

- Object programme contains:
  H card (or record)
  T cards (or record)
  E card (or record)

- Check the starting address and memory size required (i.e. specified in H record), load Text records into memory sequentially, and then jump to the starting address specified by End record.

Absolute Loader Algorithm

begin
read Header record
verify programme name and length
read first Text record
while record type '" 'E' do
begin
{if object code is in character form, convert into internal representation}
move object code to specified location in memory
read next object programme record
end
jump to address specified in End record
end

Relocatable Loader

Perform allocation, relocation, and loading:

- *Modification record*: Used to describe the starting address and length of code to be modified.
- *SIC computer*: Most instructions use direct addressing. Too many modification records are needed.
- *Another approach*: Use relocation bit to indicate that the word should be modified or not.

Linkage Editor

Performing linking only:

- Produce a linked version of the programme (called load module, executable image, or image programme).
- Solve external reference and library search, and perform relocation of all sections relative to the start of the linked programme.
- Although all linking has been performed, information concerning external reference is retained in the linked programme for further re-linking if necessary.

Linkage editor commands:
Example: New version of library routine
Include Planner (PROGLIB)
Delete Project
Include Project (NEWLY)
Replace Planner (PROGLIB)
Example: Combine subroutines into a package
Include Readr(FINLIB)
Include Writer(FIN LIB)
Include Block(FINLIB)
Save Finio(SUBLIB)

→The linked module name Finio could be indexed in the directory of SUBLIB under the same name as the original subroutines.

- Linkage editor performs linking operation before the programme is loaded for execution. Linking loader perform linking operation at load time.
- Dynamic linking (or dynamic binding, load on call) perform linking operation until execution.
  - When a subroutine call is encountered and the subroutine is not resident in memory, load the subroutine into memory, perform linking, and finally jump to the subroutine.
  - Advantages: Load the routines when they are needed, the memory space will be saved.

Linking Loader

Perform allocation, linking, relocation, and loading:

- *Modification record*: Used to describe the starting address and length of code to be modified.
- *SIC computer*: Most instructions use direct addressing. Too many modification records are needed.
- *Another approach*: Use relocation bit to indicate that the word should be modified or not.

LOADER COMMAND LINE

The "standard" Loader supplied with your Introl-C package is normally automatically called by the Linker when the Linker pass finishes. However, linker command line options exist (see Linker Section of this manual) that mav be used to alternatively force the Linker to automatically call other optional Loaders. Situations also arise when it is desirable to explicitly call the Loader alone, without first executing the Linker. When such situations arise, the Loader may be independently called by the user with a loader command line of the general form:

```
<c>ld <file> {<option>}
```

where <c>ld represents the Introl filename of the specific Loader being called, <file> is the name of the (linked) relocatable module which is to be loaded, and (<option>) represents zero or more Loader option specifiers.

Each of the potentially usable Introl Loaders is uniquely identified by a 3-letter Loader filename, the last two letters of which are always "ld". The <c> designator indicated in the "<c>ld" loader call on the command line therefore represents the first letter in the three-letter Loader name.

For example, to call the Introl hex type of Loader, which has the filename "hld", the "<c>ld" entry on the command line would actually become "hld". For further specifics on the names of the loaders which can be legally accessed. The relocatable file that is input to the Loader is expected to have a filenarne extension; if none is specified, the default filename extension ".RL" is assumed.

Normally the name of the executable output file will be identical to the name of the input file, but with a filename extension typically added by the Loader. The filename extensions each Loader appends are discussed in the Loader Appendices to this manual.

LOADER OPTIONS

Each type of Loader available for use with the Introl-C has its own, generally unique set of options. When the Loader is being called separately, Loader options are specified directly on the loader command line when the Loader is being automatically called by the Linker, Loader options are specified on the link command line, together with the Linker options. If Loader options are specified on the link command line, any such options (ie those that do not apply to the Linker) will be automatically sent on to the Loader. For the most part Linker and Loader option specifiers tend to be distinct, so that there is little ambiguity when Loader options are specified on the link command line.

LIBRARY FILES

A library file is a file which contains one or more linkable object modules of the type produced by the Introl Assembler. When a file is compiled and assembled, the result is exactly one linkable module which is placed into a file. This file is actually a library which happens to contain only a single module. When the user links a programme, one or more of these "libraries" are specified on the link command line. Usually the "libraries" are those produced as a result of a compilation and contain only a single module, however, they may also contain several modules. The Library Manager, "libman", is a programme which allows the user to place several modules into a single library file. When the user has a large set of modules which are commonly used in programmes, it is usually convenient to place them all in one library and then simply specify the library once on the link command line. The Linker will extract only those modules it requires in order to satisfy the external references of the programme.

The Linker is designed to automatically search the "Standard Library", libc.R, if it still has external references to satisfy after it has exhausted all the alternatives provided by the modules specified an the link command line. For many C programmes, the Standard Library is usually where most of the external references are satisfied. Many users find it useful to add to, or modify routines in, the Standard Library. The Library Manager is the utility programme which allows the user to create new libraries and also to maintain existing ones.

MODES OF OPERATION

The Library Manager has three modes of operation: Direct Mode, Interactive Mode, and Command File Mode. The most convenient to use for simple additions and deletions to the library is the Direct Mode. For more extensive modifications the user may instead wish to use Interactive mode. The third mode is the Command File mode which causes the Library Manager to read its commands from a file rather than getting them from the user terminal.

Direct Mode: In Direct Mode the user is permitted to specify a single command on the library manager command line. When the Library Manager is called, it executes this single command function and then immediately exits from the Library Manager.

When modifying libraries, however, a single command function is often all that is necessary to accomplish the change desired by the user. When Direct Mode is being used, the desired command is specified right on the command line, following the <lib> library specification. Any Library Manager command may be used in the Direct Mode. Interactive Mode: if no command is specified on the Library Manager call line, the Library Manager will enter its Interactive Mode of operation.

In Interactive Mode the Library Manager will print a colon (".") as a promet and will accept a succession of commands directly from the user terminal.

Interactive Mode is useful when the user must make extensive changes to a library, or when the user wishes to step through the library checking and/or changing modules in an "interactive" manner. Once selected, the Interactive Mode will remain in effect until the user enters a "quit" or "omit" command.

Command File Mode: One of the commands which the user can specify as an Interactive code or a Direct Mode command entry is the "Comfile" command. This command instructs the Library Manager to read subsequent instructions from a command file.

When a "Comfile command is entered, the Library Manager will read from the file specified until it reads a "quit" or "omit" command or, alternatively, until it reaches the end of the file. when exiting the Command File Mode, the Library

Manager will return to whatever mode it was in before the Command File Mode was entered. If the Command File Mode was entered as the result of a Direct Mode command, then the Library Manager will terminate when Command File Mode is exited. If entered from the Interactive Mode, it will return to the Interactive Mode.

ASSEMBLER

DEFINITION

An assembler is a programme that converts simple commands into machine code. The simple commands, written in an assembly language, are used in groups to perform more complicated tasks.

FUNCTION

The function of the assembler is to translate programmes written in the assembler language into object modules. The code will then be in a suitable form for processing by the Linkage Editor. The assembler language is a symbolic representation of machine language.

The correspondence between the two can be best understood by examining the listings produced by an assembler. The assembler, like the linkage editor, is supplied as part of VSE, CMS, and MVS, and executes under control of the appropriate control programme. It accepts, as input, a source programme written in the Assembler Language.

This consists of three types of instructions:

- C Machine instructions.
- C Assembler instructions.
- C Macro instructions.

As expected with an IBM language, code can also be copied in from a source statement library (VSE) or a pds (MVS) or MACLIB (CMS).

SEGMENTS AND OFFSETS IN ASSEMBLER

The original designers of the 8088, decided that nobody will every need to use more that one megabyte of memory. So they built the machine so it couldn't access above that. The problem is to access a whole megabyte 20 bits are needed (one bit being either a one or a zero).

Registers only have 16 bits, and they didn't want to use two because that would be 32 bits and that was too much for anyone. They decided to do the addressing with two registers but not 32 bits. Is this confusing? Blame the designers of the 8088.

```
OFFSET = SEGMENT * 16
SEGMENT = OFFSET / 16 (the lower 4 bits are lost)
SEGMENT * 16 |0010010000010000—| range (0 to
65535) * 16
+OFFSET |—0100100000100010| range (0 to 65535)
=20 bit address |00101000100100100010| range 0
to 1048575 (1 MEG)
 ====== DS ======
 ====== SI ======
```

(note DS and SI overlap). This is how DS:SI is used to make a 20 bit address. The segment is in DS and the offset is in SI.

Segment registers are: CS, DS, ES, SS. On the 386+ there are also FS & GS. *Offset registers are*: BX, DI, SI, BP, SP, IP. In 386+ protected mode, ANY general register (not a segment register) can be used as an Offset register. (Except IP, which you can't access.)

REGISTERS

- *AX*: This is split into half - into AL and AH (for low and high). They store the high part and the low part of the number in ax.
- *BX (BH/BL)*: Same as AX
- *CX (CH/CL)*: Same as AX (used for loops)
- *DX (DH/DL)*: Same as AX (used for multiplication/ division)
- *DI and SI*: Are index registers and can be used as offset registers.
- *SP*: Stack Pointer. Does just that. Points to the current position in the stack. *Don't* alter unless you REALLY know what you are doing.

INTERPRETER

DEFINITION

- An interpreter runs programme code by converting it to machine code on the fly. You save some time in the front by avoiding the compiling and linking steps, but interpreters generally run slower because they have to convert the same code (in a loop, say) again and again. An example of a common interpreter is the one that executes, bat files.
- An *interpreter* is also a programme that translates a high-level language into a low-level one, but it does it at the moment the programme is run. You write the programme using a text editor or something similar, and then instruct the interpreter to run the programme. It takes the programme, one line at a time, and translates each line before running it: It translates the first line and runs it, then translates the second line and runs it etc. The interpreter has no "memory" for the translated lines, so if it comes across lines of the programme within a loop, it must translate them afresh every time that particular line runs.

  Consider this simple Basic programme:
- 10 FOR COUNT = 1 TO 1000
- 20 PRINT COUNT * COUNT
- 30 NEXT COUNT
- Line 20 of the programme displays the square of the value stored in COUNT and this line has to be carried out 1000 times. The interpreter must also translate that line 1000 times, which is clearly an inefficient process. However, interpreted languages do have their uses, as we will see in a later section.
- Examples of interpreted languages are Basic, JavaScript and LISP
- The Interpreter pattern discusses: defining a domain language (i.e. problem characterization) as a simple

language grammar, representing domain rules as language sentences, and interpreting these sentences to solve the problem. The pattern uses a class to represent each grammar rule. And since grammars are usually hierarchical in structure, an inheritance hierarchy of rule classes maps nicely.

- An abstract base class specifies the method interpret(). Each concrete subclass implements interpret() by accepting (as an argument) the current state of the language stream, and adding its contribution to the problem solving process.

STRUCTURE

- Interpreter suggests modeling the domain with a recursive grammar. Each rule in the grammar is either a "composite" (a rule that references other rules) or a terminal (a leaf node in a tree structure). Interpreter relies on the recursive traversal of the Composite pattern to interpret the "sentences" it is asked to process.

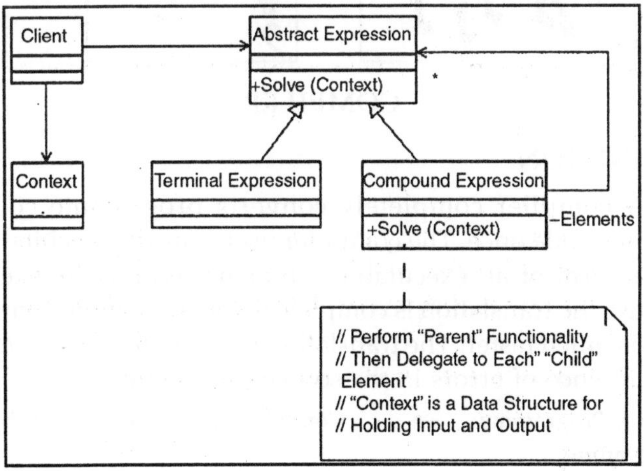

Example

- The Interpreter pattern defines a grammatical representation for a language and an interpreter to interpret the grammar. Musicians are examples of Interpreters. The pitch of a sound and its duration can be represented in musical notation on a staff. This notation provides the language of music. Musicians playing the music from the score are able to reproduce the original pitch and duration of each sound represented.

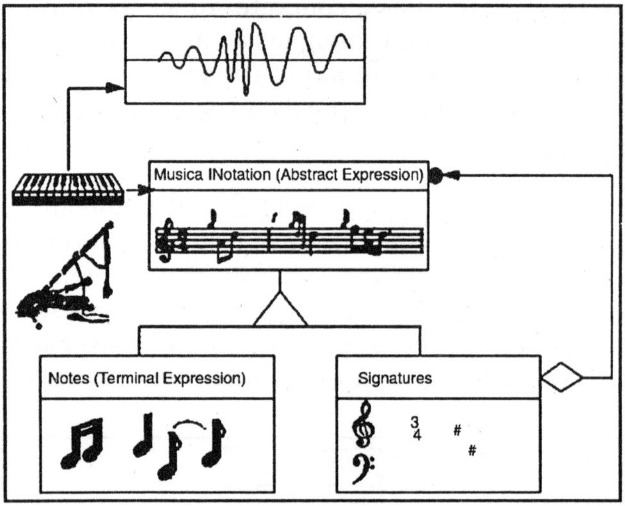

COMPILER

DEFINITION

A compiler completely converts programme code to machine code once. The computer user runs the machine code in the form of an executable command, ending in .exe say. Because the translation is complete before execution, compiled code is much faster. The translation process should also report the presence of errors in the source programme.

Source Programme → Compiler → Target Programme

↓

Error Messages

There are two parts of compilation. The analysis part breaks up the source programme into constant piece and creates an intermediate representation of the source programme. The synthesis part constructs the desired target programme from the intermediate representation. *Compilers* were the first sort of translator programme to be written. The idea is simple: You write the programme, then hand it to the compiler which translates it. Then run the result.

The compiler takes the file that you have written and produces another file from it. In the case of Pascal programmes, for instance, you might write a programme called my Prog.pas and the Pascal compiler would translate it into the file myProg.exe which you could then run. If you tried to examine the contents of myProg.exe using, say, a text editor, then it would just appear as gobbledy-gook.

The compiler has another task apart from translating your programme. It also checks it to make sure that it is grammatically correct. Only when it is sure that there are no grammatical errors does it do the translation. Any errors that the compiler detects are called compile-time errors or syntax errors. If it finds so much as one syntax error, it stops compiling and reports the error to you. Here is an example of the C++ compiler reporting a whole list of errors:

COMPILER PHASES

The compiler has a number of phases plus symbol table manager and an error handler:

Input Source Programme
↓
Lexical Analyzer
↓
Syntax Analyzer
↓
Symbol Table Manager — Semantic Analyzer — Error Handler
↓
Intermediate Code Generator
↓

Code Optimizer
↓
Code Generator
↓
Out Target Programme

The cousins of the compiler are:

- Preprocessor.
- Assembler.
- Loader and Link-editor.

Front End vs Back End of a Compilers. The phases of a compiler are collected into front end and back end. The front end includes all analysis phases end the intermediate code generator. The back end includes the code optimization phase and final code generation phase. The front end analyzes the source programme and produces intermediate code while the back end synthesizes the target programme from the intermediate code.

A naive approach (front force) to that front end might run the phases serially:

- Lexical analyzer takes the source programme as an input and produces a long string of tokens.
- Syntax Analyzer takes an out of lexical analyzer and produces a large tree.
- Semantic analyzer takes the output of syntax analyzer and produces another tree.
- Similarly, intermediate code generator takes a tree as an input produced by semantic analyzer and produces intermediate code.

Minus Points

- Requires enormous amount of space to store tokens and trees.
- Very slow since each phase would have to input and output to and from temporary disk

Remedy

- use syntax directed translation to inter leaves the actions of phases.

- Compiler construction tools.

Parser Generators

The specification of input based on regular expression. The organization is based on finite automation.

Scanner Generator

The specification of input based on regular expression. The organization is based on finite automation.

Syntax-Directed Translation

It walks the parse tee and as a result generate intermediate code.

Automatic Code Generators

Translates intermediate rampage into machine language.

Data-Flow Engines

It does code optimization using data-flow analysis.

WORKING OF COMPILER

Compiling a programme takes several stages of processing, which outlined as shown. The principles which are explained below also apply to interpreters, with the exception that the interpreters translate each programme one line at a time before running it, and then moving on to the next line.

Tokenising

This part of the process is also sometimes called *Lexical Analysis*. It involves turning the programme from a series of characters into a series of *tokens* that represent the building blocks of a programme. The tokens are keywords of the language i.e. important words such as *if, print* or *repeat*), variable names and mathematical operators (+, *, brackets etc.).

The tokeniser takes each of the characters in turn, and as soon as it recognises a legitimate token, it reports it to the next stage of the process. Each token has a label and a type, so a variable "count" in a programme would have the label corresponding to its name ("count") and the type "variable name". The tokeniser is also responsible for ignoring comments in the programme - these are words and phrases inserted purely for the benefit of any human reading the programme, and they have no function.

Syntax Analysis

Syntax means "grammar" and the syntax analyser in a compiler checks that the right tokens appear in the right order to make grammatically correct instructions. For instance, in C++, the instruction xyz++; is syntactically correct, but the instruction +;xyz+is not - the order of the tokens is wrong.

Semantic Analysis

The word "semantics" refers to *meaning*, and the semantic analyser checks the meaning of the programme. This refers to aspects such as whether the variables have been declared, e.g. xyz++; may be syntactically correct, but if the variable xyz has not been declared, then it is semantically incorrect!

The semantic analyser checks not only variable declarations and scope, but whether the programme has entered or left loops, or subroutines, whether classes are accessed correctly etc.

ADVANTAGES

Choosing the right C compiler for your embedded-system projects may be a bigger challenge than you expect. The embedded-system-industry trend is moving from using assembly to using the higher level languages. Assembly language gives you more control over your code size and execution speeds. However, embedded C is easy to understand and portable from platform to platform.

Another benefit is that developing code in C generally improves your product time to market. These features are advantageous if you expect your firmware to have longevity or if your staff changes periodically. A variety of embedded-C compilers is available in the market today. Embedded-C compilers are available as shareware from controller- or processor-IC vendors; or from high-end, reputable software companies whose selling prices often reflect the sophistication of the software. Some compiler-software companies have great advertisements and competitive prices but inferior products. So, how do you choose your compiler software for now and for the future?

There are many issues to consider when choosing your compiler. The most important are ANSI compliance, size and speed optimizations, portability, and supporting tools.

Adherence to the ANSI standard for the C language is critical for about 80 to 85% of code. This feature facilitates portability from part to part, as well as from software platform to software platform. ANSI-compliant software also integrates easy-to-understand code into your library. This type of code—if it is well-written—will have a shelf life like a good red wine. Even if portability is not an issue, it is important to understand how the compiler differs from ANSI and whether those differences will impact your development.

If the compiler of interest is ANSI-compliant, you should then examine the software's machine-code-generation capability. You might ask whether the compiler output code is optimized for small code (because memory is precious in controllers or processors) or whether the application executes in a timely or time-accurate manner. These features are somewhat mutually exclusive, but the compiler software should be able to optimize one or the other.

Portability between platforms is critical in larger companies that have a diverse range of products. However, it can also be convenient in smaller companies that may want the flexibility to quickly change controllers during development. Portability allows you to change quickly from one controller to another during application development. It also makes your code libraries more valuable over time.

If you want to easily complete your programming projects, the compiler cannot stand on its own. Every compiler needs an integrated suite of other tools. This tool suite should have, at a minimum, an integrated development environment that comes complete with a simulator and a hardware-debugging interface. Sometimes, you can mix and match these tools from other vendors, but use the vendor for your compiler as a first source. It can be difficult and frustrating to mix and then match tools from various vendors.

Some other characteristics that make up a good compiler are the availability of code libraries and library support. This concept does not fit into organizations with the NIH (not-invented-here) philosophy. An NIH organization deserves everything it gets (or doesn't get). Libraries with code that implements useful functions help expedite your projects to completion. Many times, these libraries have gone through evaluations and debugging to ensure their value.

Some of the final details in your compiler evaluation have to do with customer service. You need to ask whether your compiler company supports your questions and helps with its software bugs. You will find this information in the company's application-notes library, discussion forums, and software-release history. Although frequent releases can be a sign of responsiveness, they can also be an indication of serious stability concerns. The ideal compiler vendor has more support than you'll ever need.

In the past, most firmware designers would write embedded-firmware programmes in assembly language. The embedded-C compiler transforms your source code into machine code. The C compiler you use determines the size as well as the execution time of your code. Many ways exist for determining these factors, so running your own test programmes is also important. Don't depend on the results from a compiler-software company that runs its own tests. Many times, these companies can consciously or unconsciously skew the results.

Chapter 4

Operating System

PROCESS

The 1960's definition of an operating system is "the software that controls the hardware". However, today, due to microcode we need a better definition. We see an operating system as the programmes that make the hardware useable. In brief, an operating system is the set of programmes that controls a computer. Some examples of operating systems are UNIX, Mach, MS-DOS, MS-Windows, Windows/NT, Chicago, OS/2, MacOS, VMS, MVS, and VM.

Controlling the computer involves software at several levels. We will differentiate kernel services, library services, and application-level services, all of which are part of the operating system. Processes run Applications, which are linked together with libraries that perform standard services. The kernel supports the processes by providing a path to the peripheral devices. The kernel responds to service calls from the processes and interrupts from the devices.

The core of the operating system is the kernel, a control programme that functions in privileged state (an execution context that allows all hardware instructions to be executed), reacting to interrupts from external devices and to service requests and traps from processes. Generally, the kernel is a permanent resident of the computer. It creates and terminates processes and responds to their request for service.

Operating Systems are resource managers. The main resource is computer hardware in the form of processors, storage, input/output devices, communication devices, and data. Some of the operating system functions are: implementing the user interface, sharing hardware among users, allowing users to share data among themselves, preventing users from interfering with one another, scheduling resources among users, facilitating input/output, recovering from errors, accounting for resource usage, facilitating parallel operations, organizing data for secure and rapid access, and handling network communications.

OBJECTIVES

Modern Operating systems generally have following three major goals. Operating systems generally accomplish these goals by running processes in low privilege and providing service calls that invoke the operating system kernel in high-privilege state.

HIDING DETAILS OF HARDWARE

An abstraction is software that hides lower level details and provides a set of higher-level functions. An operating system transforms the physical world of devices, instructions, memory, and time into virtual world that is the result of abstractions built by the operating system. There are several reasons for abstraction.

First, the code needed to control peripheral devices is not standardized. Operating systems provide subroutines called device drivers that perform operations on behalf of programmes for example, input/output operations.

Second, the operating system introduces new functions as it abstracts the hardware. For instance, operating system introduces the file abstraction so that programmes do not have to deal with disks.

Third, the operating system transforms the computer hardware into multiple virtual computers, each belonging to a different programme. Each programme that is running is called a process. Each process views the hardware through the lens of abstraction.

Fourth, the operating system can enforce security through abstraction.

MANAGE RESOURCES

An operating system controls how processes (the active agents) may access resources (passive entities).

PLEASANT AND EFFECTIVE USER INTERFACE

The user interacts with the operating systems through the user interface and usually interested in the "look and feel" of the operating system.

The most important components of the user interface are the command interpreter, the file system, on-line help, and application integration. The recent trend has been toward increasingly integrated graphical user interfaces that encompass the activities of multiple processes on networks of computers.

One can view Operating Systems from two points of views: Resource manager and Extended machines. Form Resource manager point of view Operating Systems manage the different parts of the system efficiently and from extended machines point of view Operating Systems provide a virtual machine to users that is more convenient to use.

The structurally Operating Systems can be design as a monolithic system, a hierarchy of layers, a virtual machine system, an exokernel, or using the client-server model. The basic concepts of Operating Systems are processes, memory management, I/O management, the file systems, and security.

CONCEPTS

The CPU (Central Processing Unit) is the heart of any computer, but the operating system is the brain. Unfortunately, understanding exactly how these things really work can be difficult, because it's fairly hard to "play" with the operating system that you are actually using.

You can do quite a bit with sophisticated debuggers, but eventually you run into confusion and difficulty. And, as you try more complex tasks, you run the risk of interfering with the real machine's operating system.

Finally, modern CPU's are very complex, and that complexity can make it more difficult to understand basic concepts. Therefore thought it would be interesting to emulate CPU's and other hardware in software. By doing that, we can present simple ideas and build on that understanding. We'll start very simply, and build from there, eventually demonstrating more advanced concepts like virtual memory, disk filesystems, and even multitasking.

FUNDAMENTAL CONCEPT

*Fundamental concept of computer operating system*starts with the structure of the OS. Conceptually, an operating system can be broken down into the kernel, shell and system utilities. The kernel is the core of the operating system, and in some cases, the distinction between the kernel and the shell is clear; in others, the distinction is only conceptual.

A process is a programme in execution. New processes are spawned when needed and terminated to free memory and other resources. Files are a method of organizing the information on disk.

Files are usually organized in an inverted tree-like structure. A system call is a programme that requests something from the *operating system*. The roles of an operating system vary with the hardware and user programmes it was designed to work with.

The earliest operating systems were designed to help applications interact with hardware. This has grown to the point that the operating system now defines the machine. The operating system provides an interface to the underlying hardware, the application programmes, and the user.

The *operating system* manages:

- Hardware
- CPU
- Memory
- Device Drivers
- I / O
- Applications

There are four basic types of operating systems:

- Real time operating system
- Single user, single task operating system

- Single user, multi task operating system
- Multi user operating system

HISTORY

History of operating system was started with the first generation computers. They operated on a purely mechanical basis. There was no concept of an operating system. The user fed data and the programme into the computer using punched cards. The programmes were debugged using front panel switches and lights. The second-generation computers were batch systems where the jobs and instructions were put together so that they could be processed without interruptions.

The third generation computers used the concepts of multiprogramming and time-sharing. Spooling batch systems were the first and simplest of multiprogramming systems. The major advantage was that the output from the jobs was available as soon as the job was completed. The fourth generation saw the advent of modern operating systems for PCs, workstations and servers and also includes networking and distributed operating systems.

The early *operating systems* were diverse, with each vendor producing their own operating systems specific to their hardware. This continued until the 1960s when IBM developed the S/360 series of machines, where all machines ran the same operating system, OS/360. CP/M (Control Programme for Microcomputers) was the first generic operating system for microcomputers. Before CP/M, every brand of computer had its own unique operating system.

Because of this, programmes could not be shared between computers and software had to be rewritten for every type of computer. The nearest to the operating system was the "job control language" (JCL) required to submit a programme for execution on the mainframe.

CP/M was a complete software development environment that enabled to write software that was machine-independent, and move CP/M itself to other computers. OS/2 was the first operating system to provide intrinsic multitasking based on hardware support. It was text-mode only and allowed only one programme to be on the screen at a time, even though other programmes could be running in the background.

CONCEPTS OF REAL-TIME OPERATING SYSTEMS

FUNDAMENTALS

To most people, embedded systems are not recognizable as computers. Instead, they are hidden inside everyday objects that surround us and help us in our lives. Embedded systems typically do not interface with the outside world through familiar personal computer interface devices such as a mouse, keyboard and graphic user interface. Instead, they interface with the outside world through unusual interfaces such as sensors, actuators and specialized communication links.

Real-time and embedded systems operate in constrained environments in which computer memory and processing power are limited. They often need to provide their services within strict time deadlines to their users and to the surrounding world. It is these memory, speed and timing constraints that dictate the use of real-time operating systems in embedded software.

BASIC KERNEL SERVICES

In the discussion below, we will focus on the "kernel" – the part of an operating system that provides the most basic services to application software running on a processor.

The "kernel" of a real-time operating system ("RTOS") provides an "abstraction layer" that hides from application software the hardware details of the processor (or set of processors) upon which the application software will run..

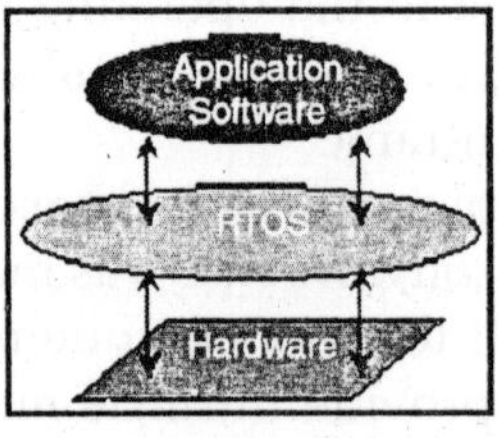

Fig. An RTOS Kernel Provides an Abstraction Layer

In providing this "abstraction layer" the RTOS kernel supplies five main categories of basic services to application software.

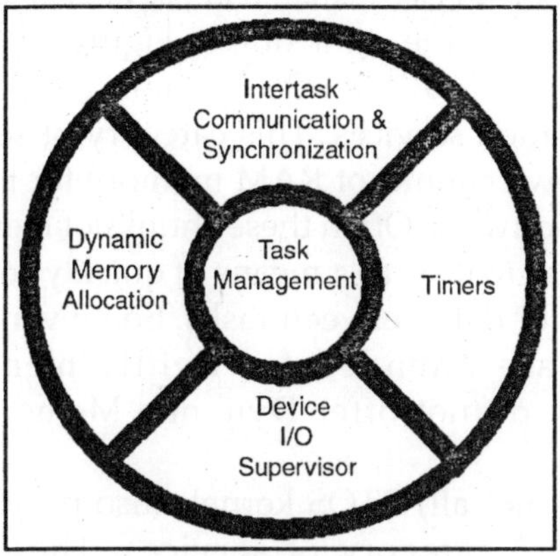

Fig. Basic Services Provided by a Real-Time Operating System Kernel

The most basic category of kernel services, at the very centre of Figure, is Task Management. This set of services allows application software developers to design their software as a number of separate "chunks" of software — each handling a distinct topic, a distinct goal, and perhaps its own real-time deadline. Each separate "chunk" of software is called a "task."

Services in this category include the ability to launch tasks and assign priorities to them. The main RTOS service in this category is the scheduling of tasks as the embedded system is in operation. The Task Scheduler controls the execution of application software tasks, and can make them run in a very timely and responsive fashion.

The second category of kernel services, shown at the top of Figure, is Intertask Communication and Synchronization. These services make it possible for tasks to pass information from one to another, without danger of that information ever being damaged. They also make it possible for tasks to coordinate, so that they can productively cooperate with one another. Without the help of these RTOS services, tasks might well communicate corrupted information or otherwise interfere with each other. Since many embedded systems have stringent timing requirements, most RTOS kernels also provide some basic Timer services, such as task delays and time-outs. These are shown on the right side of Figure.

Many (but not all) RTOS kernels provide Dynamic Memory Allocation services. This category of services allows tasks to "borrow" chunks of RAM memory for temporary use in application software. Often these chunks of memory are then passed from task to task, as a means of quickly communicating large amounts of data between tasks. Some very small RTOS kernels that are intended for tightly memory-limited environments, do not offer Dynamic Memory Allocation services.

Many (but not all) RTOS kernels also provide a "Device I/O Supervisor" category of services. These services, if available, provide a uniform framework for organizing and accessing the many hardware device drivers that are typical of an embedded system.

In addition to kernel services, many RTOSs offer a number of optional add-on operating system components for such high-level services as file system organization, network communication, network management, database management, user-interface graphics, etc. Although many of these add-on components are much larger and much more complex than the RTOS kernel, they rely on the presence of the RTOS kernel and take advantage of its basic services.

Each of these add-on components is included in an embedded system only if its services are needed for implementing the embedded application, in order to keep programme memory consumption to a minimum. In this paper, we will focus on the basic RTOS kernel services for task management, intertask communication and synchronization, and dynamic memory allocation.

GENERAL PURPOSE OPERATING SYSTEMS

Many non-real-time operating systems also provide similar kernel services. The key difference between general-computing operating systems and real-time operating systems is the need for " deterministic " timing behaviour in the real-time operating systems. Formally, "deterministic" timing means that operating system services consume only known and expected amounts of time.

In theory, these service times could be expressed as mathematical formulas. These formulas must be strictly algebraic and not include any random timing components. Random elements in service times could cause random delays in application software and could then make the application randomly miss real-time deadlines – a scenario clearly unacceptable for a real-time embedded system.

General-computing non-real-time operating systems are often quite non-deterministic. Their services can inject random delays into application software and thus cause slow responsiveness of an application at unexpected times. If you ask the developer of a non-real-time operating system for the algebraic formula describing the timing behaviour of one of its services (such as sending a message from task to task), you will invariably not get an algebraic formula.

Instead the developer of the non-real-time operating system (such as Windows, Unix or Linux) will just give you a puzzled look. Deterministic timing behaviour was simply not a design goal for these general-computing operating systems. On the other hand, real-time operating systems often go a step beyond basic determinism.

For most kernel services, these operating systems offer constant load-independent timing: In other words, the algebraic formula is as simple as: *T(message_send) = constant* , irrespective of the length of the message to be sent, or other factors such as the numbers of tasks and queues and messages being managed by the RTOS.

TASK SCHEDULING

Most RTOSs do their scheduling of tasks using a scheme called "priority-based preemptive scheduling." Each task in a software application must be assigned a priority, with higher priority values representing the need for quicker responsiveness. Very quick responsiveness is made possible by the "preemptive" nature of the task scheduling. "Preemptive" means that the scheduler is allowed to stop any task at any point in its execution, if it determines that another task needs to run immediately.

The basic rule that governs priority-based preemptive scheduling is that at every moment in time, "The Highest Priority Task that is Ready to Run, will be the Task that Must be Running." In other words, if both a low-priority task and a higher-priority task are ready to run, the scheduler will allow the higher-priority task to run first. The low-priority task will only get to run after the higher-priority task has finished with its current work.

What if a low-priority task has already begun to run, and then a higher-priority task becomes ready? This might occur because of an external world trigger such as a switch closing. A priority-based preemptive scheduler will behave as follows: It will allow the low-priority task to complete the current assembly-language instruction that it is executing.

But it won't allow it to complete an entire line of high-level language code; nor will it allow it to continue running until the next clock tick. It will then immediately stop the execution of the low-priority task, and allow the higher-priority task to run.

After the higher-priority task has finished its current work, the low-priority task will be allowed to continue running. This is shown in Figure, where the higher-priority task is called "Mid-Priority Task." Of course, while the mid-priority task is running, an even higher-priority task might become ready. This is represented in Figure by "Trigger_2" causing the "High-Priority Task" to become ready.

In that case, the running task ("Mid-Priority Task") would be preempted to allow the high-priority task to run. When the high-priority task has finished its current work, the mid-priority task would be allowed to continue. And after both the high-priority task and the mid-priority task complete their work, the low-priority task would be allowed to continue running. This situation might be called "nested preemption."

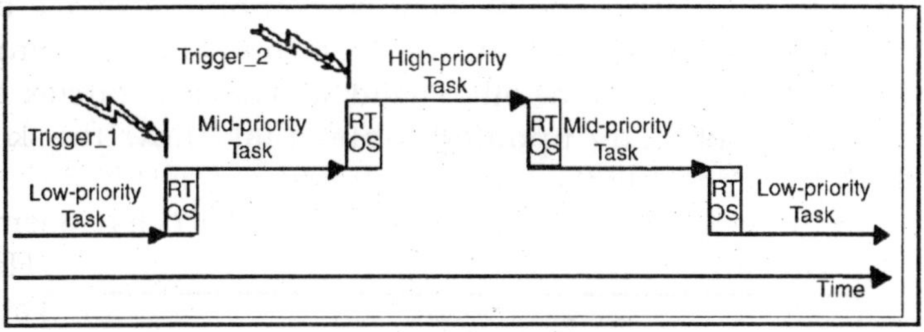

Fig. Timeline for Priority-based Preemptive Scheduling.

Each time the priority-based preemptive scheduler is alerted by an external world trigger (such as a switch closing) or a software trigger (such as a message arrival), it must go through the following 5 steps:

- Determine whether the currently running task should continue to run. If not.
- Determine which task should run next.
- Save the environment of the task that was stopped (so it can continue later).
- Set up the running environment of the task that will run next.
- Allow this task to run.

These 5 steps together are called "task switching."

FIXED-TIME TASK SWITCHING

The time it takes to do task switching is of interest when evaluating an operating system. A simple general-computing (non-preemptive) operating system might do task switching only at timer tick times, which might for example be ten milliseconds apart. Then if the need for a task switch arises anywhere within a 10-millisecond timeframe, the actual task switch would occur only at the end of the current 10-millisecond period. Such a delay would be unacceptable in most real-time embedded systems.

In more sophisticated preemptive task schedulers, the scheduler may need to search through arrays of tasks to determine which task should be made to run next. If there are more tasks to search through, the search will take longer. Such searches are often done by general-computing operating systems, thus making them non-deterministic. Real-time operating systems, on the other hand, avoid such searches by using incrementally updated tables that allow the task scheduler to identify the task that should run next in a rapid fixed-time fashion. These two types of timing behaviour for task switching.

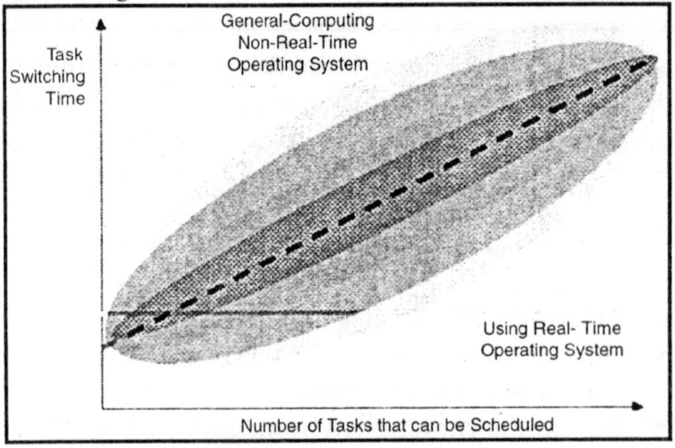

Fig. Task Switching Timing

In this figure, we see that for a general-computing (non-real-time) operating system, the task switching time generally rises as a software system includes more tasks that can be scheduled. However, the actual time for a task switch is not the time shown by the dashed black line. Instead, in any given task switch instance, it might be well above or well below the time shown by the dashed black line. The shaded regions surrounding the dashed black line simply show the likelihood of the actual task switch time being that far above or below the dashed black line.

On the other hand, the horizontal solid green line shows the task switching time characteristic of a real-time operating system. It is constant, independent of any load factor such as the number of tasks in a software system. Please note that in some instances, such as the leftmost area of the graph, the task switching time might in special cases be quicker for a general-computing non-real-time operating system, than for a real-time operating system. This does not detract from the appropriateness of a real-time operating system for real-time embedded applications. For, in fact, the term "real-time" does not mean "as fast as possible" but rather "real-time" demands consistent, repeatable, known timing performance.

Although a non-real-time operating system might do some faster task switching for small numbers of tasks, it might equally well introduce a long time delay the next time it does the same task switch. The strength of a real-time operating system is in its known, repeatable timing performance, which is also typically faster than that of a non-deterministic task scheduler in situations of large numbers of tasks in a software system.

Most often, the real-time operating system will exhibit task-switching times much faster than its non-real-time competitor when the number of tasks grows above 5 or 10.

COMMUNICATION AND SYNCHRONIZATION

Most operating systems, including RTOSs, offer a variety of mechanisms for communication and synchronization between tasks. These mechanisms are necessary in a preemptive environment of many tasks, because without them the tasks might well communicate corrupted information or otherwise interfere with each other.

For instance, a task might be preempted when it is in the middle of updating a table of data. If a second task that preempts it reads from that table, it will read a combination of some areas of newly-updated data plus some areas of data that have not yet been updated. [New Yorkers would call this a "mish-mash."]

These updated and old data areas together may be incorrect in combination, or may not even make sense. An example is a data table containing temperature measurements that begins with the contents "10 C." A task begins updating this table with the new value "99 F", writing into the table character-by-character. If that task is preempted in the middle of the update, a second task that preempts it could possibly read a value like "90°C" or "99°C." or "99°F", depending on precisely when the preemption took place. The partially updated values are clearly incorrect, and are caused by delicate timing coincidences that are very hard to debug or reproduce consistently.

An RTOS's mechanisms for communication and synchronization between tasks are provided to avoid these kinds of errors. Most RTOSs provide several mechanisms, with each mechanism optimized for reliably passing a different kind of information from task to task.

Probably the most popular kind of communication between tasks in embedded systems is the passing of data from one task to another. Most RTOSs offer a message passing mechanism for doing this, as seen in Figure. Each message can contain an array or buffer of data.

Fig. Intertask Message Communication

If messages can be sent more quickly than they can be handled, the RTOS will provide message queues for holding the messages until they can be processed. This is shown in Figure.

Another kind of communication between tasks in embedded systems is the passing of what might be called "synchronization information" from one task to another. "Synchronization information" is like a command, where some commands could be positive, and some negative. For example, a negative command to a task would be something like "Please don't print right now, because my task is using the printer." Or more generally, "I want to lock the . . . for my own use only." A positive command would be something like "I've detected a cardiac emergency, and I want you to help me handle it." Or more generally, "Please join me in handling . . ." Most RTOSs offer a semaphore or mutex mechanism for handling negative synchronization (sometimes called "mutual exclusion"). These mechanisms allow tasks to lock certain embedded system resources for their use only, and subsequently to unlock the resource when they're done.

For positive synchronization, different RTOSs offer different mechanisms. Some RTOSs offer event-flags, while others offer signals. And yet others rely on message passing for positive synchronization as well as data passing duties.

DETERMINING HIGH-SPEED MESSAGE

Intertask message communication is another area where different operating systems show different timing characteristics. Most operating systems actually copy messages twice as they transfer them from task to task via a message queue. The first copying is from the message-sender task to an operating system-owned "secret" area of RAM memory (implementing the "message queue"); and the second copying is from the operating system's "secret" RAM area to the message-receiver task. Clearly this is non-deterministic in its timing, as these copying activities take longer as message length increases.

Fig. Message Transfer via Message Queue

An approach that avoids this non-determinism and also accelerates performance, is to have the operating system copy a pointer to the message and deliver that pointer to the message-receiver task without moving the message contents at all. In order to avoid access collisions, the operating system then needs to go back to the message-sender task and obliterate its copy of the pointer to the message. For large messages, this eliminates the need for lengthy copying and eliminates non-determinism.

DYNAMIC MEMORY ALLOCATION

Determinism of service times is also an issue in the area of dynamic allocation of RAM memory. Many general-computing non-real-time operating systems offer memory allocation services from what is termed a "Heap." The famous "malloc" and "free" services known to C-language programmers work from a heap. Tasks can temporarily borrow some memory from the operating system's heap by calling "malloc", and specifying the size of memory buffer needed. When this task (or another task) is finished with this memory buffer it can return the buffer to the operating system by calling "free." The operating system will then return the buffer to the heap, where its memory might be used again, perhaps as part of a larger buffer. Or perhaps it may in the future be broken into several smaller buffers.

Heaps suffer from a phenomenon called "External Memory Fragmentation" that may cause the heap services to degrade. This fragmentation is caused by the fact that when a buffer is returned to the heap, it may in the future be broken into smaller buffers when "malloc" requests for smaller buffer sizes occur. After a heap undergoes many cycles of "malloc"s and "free"s, small slivers of memory may appear between memory buffers that are being used by tasks. These slivers are so small that they are useless to tasks. But they are trapped between buffers that are being used by tasks, so they can't be coagulated ("glued") together into bigger, useful buffer sizes. Over time, a heap will have more and more of these slivers.

This will eventually result in situations where tasks will ask for memory buffers ("malloc") of a certain size, and they will be refused by the operating system — even though the operating system has enough available memory in its heap. The problem: That memory is scattered in small slivers distributed in various separate parts of the heap. In operating system terminology, the slivers are called "fragments", and this problem is called "external memory fragmentation."

This fragmentation problem can be solved by so-called "garbage collection" (defragmentation) software. Unfortunately, "garbage collection" algorithms are often wildly non-deterministic – injecting randomly-appearing random-duration delays into heap services. These are often seen in the memory allocation services of general-computing non-real-time operating systems. This puts the embedded system developer who wants to use a general-computing non-real-time operating system into a quandry: Should the embedded system be allowed to suffer occasional randomly-appearing random-duration delays if / when "garbage collection" kicks in?... Or, alternatively, should the embedded system be allowed to fragment its memory until application software "malloc" requests to the heap are refused even though a sufficient total amount of free memory is still available? Neither alternative is acceptable for embedded systems that need to provide service continually for long periods of time.

Real-time operating systems, on the other hand, solve this quandry by altogether avoiding both memory fragmentation and "garbage collection", and their consequences. RTOSs offer non-fragmenting memory allocation techniques instead of heaps. They do this by limiting the variety of memory chunk sizes they make available to application software. While this approach is less flexible than the approach taken by memory heaps, they do avoid external memory fragmentation and avoid the need for defragmentation. For example, the "Pools" memory allocation mechanism allows application software to allocate chunks of memory of perhaps 4 or 8 different buffer sizes per pool. Pools totally avoid external memory fragmentation, by not permitting a buffer that is returned to the pool to be broken into smaller buffers in the future. Instead, when a buffer is returned the pool, it is put onto a "free buffer list" of buffers of its own size that are available for future re-use at their original buffer size.

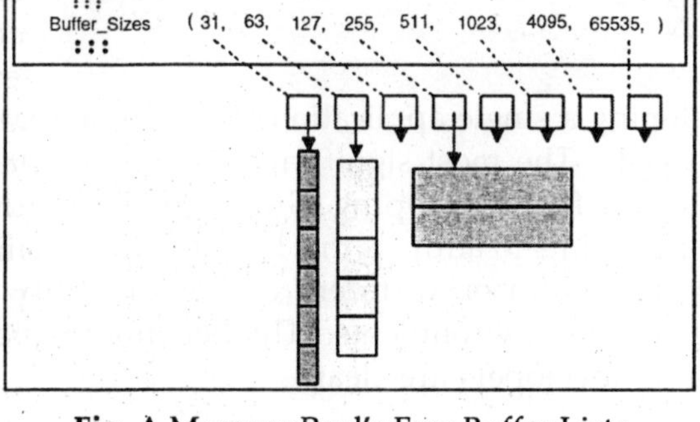

Fig. A Memory Pool's Free Buffer Lists

Memory is allocated and de-allocated from a pool with deterministic, often constant, timing.

USES

Real-time and embedded systems are used in many applications such as airborne computers, medical instruments and communication systems. Embedded systems are characterized by limited processor memory, limited processing power, and unusual interfaces to the outside world. Real-time requirements impose stringent time deadlines for delivering the results of embedded processing. RTOS kernels hide from application software the low-level details of system hardware, and at the same time provide several categories of services to application software. These include: task management with priority-based preemptive scheduling, reliable intertask communication and synchronization, non-fragmenting dynamic memory allocation, and basic timer services.

The issue of timing determinism is important in differentiating general-computing operating systems from real-time operating systems. This issue crops up in many parts of operating system kernels, such as task schedulers, dynamic memory allocation and intertask message communication. While general-computing operating systems often offer non-deterministic services in these areas, fully deterministic solutions are needed for real-time and embedded systems. A number of real-time operating systems implement these solutions in their compact high-performance kernels.

GOALS AND FUNCTIONS

GOALS

Developing a single application for multiple platforms is a difficult task. The most significant issue is the need for a clean solution for developing Graphical User Interfaces [GUI's]. FOX aims to address this by providing a single GUI library that can run on different computer hardware and operating system environments. The benefits to application vendors and developers are clear:

Reducing Effort to Support Multiple Environments

After development, your FOX based application is only a compile away from running on other operating systems. When multiple hardware and software combinations are required by customers operating in a heterogeneous environment, using a single GUI system such as FOX is clearly the most cost-effective method to achieve the goal.

Availability of Software on other Platforms

Without the necessity of additional development work, the cost of which would have to be amortized over the number of sales, additional revenues can be engendered by having your software be available on multiple hardware and software environments.

Software development is a costly undertaking; because of this, software vendors typically limit the number of platforms to a small subset of the platforms being used by *all* customers, effectively leaving certain customers in the dark. FOX allows applications to be developed on one platform, then simply recompile the application on a number of other hardware/software systems. Because the cost of doing so is negligible, this approach will be able to generate positive cashflow even with low sales volumes.

Captive Audience

If the application you're developing is available on all platforms, you may be able to create a captive customer base on hardware/software systems where your competitor is absent; you may in fact even be able to charge premium prices. Using the additional revenues derived from these customers, your product will be able to derive a steady addional revenue stream which will allow you to compete more aggressively against your single-platform competitor.

Higher Quality

For programmers, the benefits of multi-platform development v.s. single platform development are the additional confidence and code quality that compiling under different environments will give. For example, I have compiled FOX on a number of different systems, and different compilers will discover different types of code bugs. By compiling on all these different systems, FOX has gotten quite a bit better in the course of time.

Control Your Destiny

Programmers understand it as a matter of course that they need to continually work to track the changes in a system's API's. But what if the system vendor is also your competitor? In such a case, you *will* loose, sooner or later. The FOX GUI Library provides a platform-independent escape hatch that relies only on core system facilities which can be expected to be present on any modern operating system.

Approach

FOX attains the goal of platform independence by eliminating all system dependencies from its public interfaces. In fact, a typical FOX application may not even need to include any system-specific header files at all! By not including e.g. X-Windows header files, applications can not even accidentally slip up and introduce platform dependencies.

This strategy is also carried out inside FOX itself. Thus, large parts of FOX are in fact defined entirely in FOX itself. The only dependencies are concentrated in a few select base classes where this couldn't be avoided. The following salient points highlight some fundamental benefits of FOX *vis-a-vis* other purported platform independent toolkits:

Eliminate all Platform Specific Header Files

Applications should only include header files from FOX, and a few header files for such basic system services as opening files etc.

Internal Layering

FOX itself relies largely on FOX base classes; and

therefore a large fraction of FOX itself is platform independent as well.

Rely only on Low-level System Facilities

FOX relies only on core system facilities, and does NOT wrap native GUI libraries or toolkits. This has the following benefits:

Identical Behaviour

The behaviour will be close to identical on all systems, as the behaviour is completely controlled by the FOX implementation, rather than some underlying library.

Identical Looks

FOX applications will look the same no matter what system you're running it on.

Ability to Subclass

Because FOX is written from the ground up in C++, and is NOT a C++ wrapper around some other legacy toolkit or library, FOX Controls may be subclassed and extended by application programmers. Moreover, if these additions can be done by calling upon FOX built-in facilities, those additions will be platform independent also.

Higher Quality

It is a given in software development that those facilities which are most frequently used are the ones which are most stable. Thus, by using core system facilities instead of higher-level transient API's, the impact of the underlying system's instability is minimized. A chain is as strong as the weakest link, and while I can not control the quality of the links, I can minimize the number of them.

Higher Speed

Eliminating layers between FOX and the underlying system not only increases the application's quality, it will also make it faster, and reduce memory overhead.

Go to the Bedrock

FOX's core facilities needed from the target system are things like mouse/keyboard event handling, and basic graphics facilities such as drawing of lines and rectangles [and some other system facilities]. In most operating systems, these are fairly mature API's and not subject to much change. If you want to build a big building, you need to go down to the solid bedrock. This is what FOX does.

FOX is Extensible

The FOX library is designed to be open-ended and extensible. What this means is that unlike other libraries which take the approach of wrapping legacy GUI toolkits, FOX may be extended with *Custom Controls* and Widgets which will set your application apart from the others. Building Custom Controls is extremely easy in FOX, as it is essentially just a matter of C++ subclassing.

FOX is Available Under Library GNU Public License

Since FOX is distributed in source form under LGPL, you have the ability to make changes or extensions to FOX to suit your needs. Having FOX inspected by 1000's of programmers all over the world will iron out any bugs it may have very quickly. This process is already under way.

I care a great deal about software quality; I imagine, so do you. In the course of my programming life, I have ran into many situations where the bugs I needed to fix were not in my own code, but in someone else's, and of course I didn't have the source.

Thus, the quality of my own software was limited by the quality of someone else's. Problem is, the developers of the libraries and software I depend on are frequently not motivated to make their software correct.

This has made me a firm believer in the *GPL* or *Open Source* model of software development. FOX was started in part because I didn't want to explain to our customers that the reason X or Y didn't work was because of the broken software or libraries on their machine. The only way one can create high-quality applications is to bring as much of the underlying system under one's control as possible. Hence the *Go to the Bedrock* philosophy.

FOX is not perfect. But as the source code is available under LGPL, it has the advantage that its imperfections can be addressed as soon as they are discovered.

Purpose

The purpose of this HOWTO is to describe a methodology for managing multiple operating systems on a single computer system. It is intended for Linux users who have a basic familiarity with both Linux and LILO installations. Nothing here is terribly complex however, considering the amount of time it takes to install some operating systems it can be relatively time consuming.

It is different from other methods in that it doesn't require multiple operating systems on the boot disk. Instead it uses a fixed internal disk containing a single primary operating system and a selection of removable disks with one or more operating systems installed on each of them. If you absolutely have to have two, three, or four different operating systems on a single disk and are trying to get them to behave with each other, this HOWTO is not for you.

Its specific goals are:

- A primary/operational disk that once configured and installed is rarely changed. This includes not having to repartition or otherwise modify the disk it resides on.
- Easy selection of multiple alternative operating systems at boot time without having to go through more than one or two menu selections.
- No need to modify the BIOS, LILO, or any other configuration to access an O/S once it is installed.
- Easy addition/removal of operating systems depending on requirements at the moment.
- Inexpensive and scalable to allow for an increasing number of operating systems and versions as time goes on.

OPERATING SYSTEM FUNCTIONS

Usually Operating system is there to manage all pieces of a complex system Imagine what will happen if three programmes running on a computer all try to print their output simultaneously on the same printer. The first few lines might be from programme one and the next few lines might be from programme two and so on with the result resulting in chaos. The operating system can bring order to potential chaos by buffering all the output destined for the printer on the disk. The primary task of operating system is to keep track of who is using which resource, to grant resource request, to account for usage, and to meditate conflicting request from different programmes and users.

When a computer has multiple users, the need for managing and protecting the memory, input/output devices and other resources are even more apparent. This need arises because it is usually necessary to share expensive resource such as tapes drives and phototypesetters. Operating systems perform basic tasks, such as recognizing input from the keyboard, sending output to the display screen, keeping track of files anddirectories on the disk, and controlling peripheral devices such as disk drives and printers.

For large systems, the operating system has even greater responsibilities and powers. It is like a traffic cop — it makes sure that different programme and usersrunning at the same time do not interfere with each other. The operating system is also responsible for security, ensuring that unauthorized users do not accessthe system. The set of software products that jointly controls the system resource using these resources on a computer system is known as operating system. Examples are Unix, Windows.

Idea

The operating system is the core software component of your computer. It performs many functions and is, in very basic terms, an interface between your computer and the outside world. In the section about hardware, a computer is described as consisting of several component parts including your monitor, keyboard, mouse, and other parts. The operating system provides an interface to these parts using what is referred to as "drivers". This is why sometimes when you install a new printer or other piece of hardware, your system will ask you to install more software called a driver.

Role of Driver

A driver is a specially written programme which understands the operation of the device it interfaces to, such as a printer, video card, sound card or CD ROM drive. It translates commands from the operating system or user into commands understood by the the component computer part it interfaces with. It also translates responses from the component computer part back to responses that can be understood by the operating system, application programme, or user. The below diagram gives a graphical depiction of the interfaces between the operating system and the computer component.

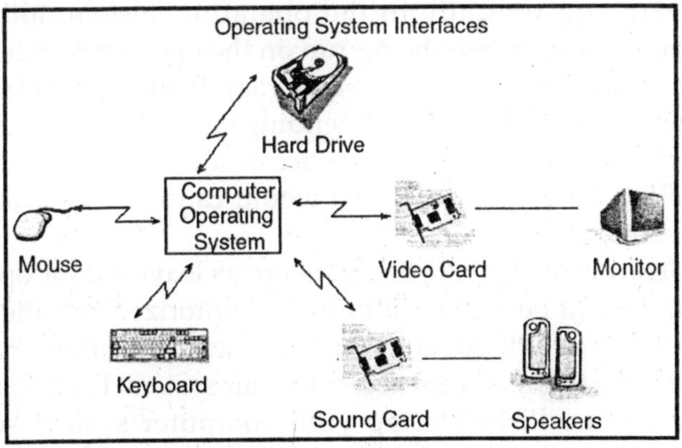

Operating System Functions

The operating system provides for several other functions including:

- System tools (programmes) used to monitor computer performance, debug problems, or maintain parts of the system.
- A set of libraries or functions which programmes

may use to perform specific tasks especially relating to interfacing with computer system components.

The operating system makes these interfacing functions along with its other functions operate smoothly and these functions are mostly transparent to the user.

Operating System Concerns

As mentioned previously, an operating system is a computer programme. Operating systems are written by human programmers who make mistakes. Therefore there can be errors in the code even though there may be some testing before the product is released. Some companies have better software quality control and testing than others so you may notice varying levels of quality from operating system to operating system.

Errors in operating systems cause three main types of problems:

System crashes and instabilities: These can happen due to a software bug typically in the operating system, although computer programmes being run on the operating system can make the system more unstable or may even crash the system by themselves. This varies depending on the type of operating system. A system crash is the act of a system freezing and becoming unresponsive which would cause the user to need to reboot.

Security flaws: Some software errors leave a door open for the system to be broken into by unauthorized intruders. As these flaws are discovered, unauthorized intruders may try to use these to gain illegal access to your system. Patching these flaws often will help keep your computer system secure. Sometimes errors in the operating system will cause the computer not to work correctly with some peripheral devices such as printers.

NECESSITY OF OPERATING SYSTEM

The evolution of software and hardware technology has also determined big changes in current operating systems, therefore constant development of newer versions. The big problems are when users try to install older software apps on the newest operating systems or when the latest software version does not have the same functionalities as the older ones. There are many situations where incompatibilities get in the way of proper functionality and where they cannot be repaired. The release of a new version of a certain software platform does not necessarily ask for an upgrade, because usually the latest versions of an application may require the presence of the newest operating system and the computer hardware might not support it. On the other hand, it is possible that the latest version of an application does not have the features of the previous version or shows a higher number of bugs than the older editions.

Web developers and generally programmers don't need the complexity of the graphical interface of a new operating system. Instead, what they are interested in is having their development tools functioning at full capacity on a compatible operating system.

Usually, software companies do not provide access to the older releases and if you reinstall the operating system, the software version you are used to work with might not be available anymore. As a consequence, the existence of older software databases is completely justified. These websites allow you to download both current versions of certain software apps, as well as various older versions. If you need to download older software editions, you could find them on existing databases, like OldVersion.com or OldApps.com for example.

Even if the trend is to update your applications constantly, chances are that you use a software app that, on a new release, would also require a higher processor speed or came bundled with unnecessary plugins. It is recommended to carefully select the development tools you are working with in order to avoid frequent software updates or changes of the operating system.

NECESSITY WITH WINDOWS XP AND VISTA

Why do we now have to deal with registry problems on the new operating systems, Windows XP and Vista when we didn't have to worry about our registries so much with Windows 98 and 95? Doesn't it seem like a new, improved operating system would give us less problems. In this article, we're going to discuss these things and see if we can make some sense of the irony that newer operating systems need more attention than older ones!

Hierarchal Structure

A Windows Operating System's registry is organized in a hierarchal structure exactly the same way your documents are arranged in your Word programme. There is one major directory in your registry which would be the equivalent of your MyDocuments folder. Under that directory, there are many, many, many directories and each one of these directories may or may not have files contained in them.

Certainly, way down at the bottom in the very lowest directory there are lots of files. Now, multiply this MyDocuments structure by 5 and you have something that looks very much like a Windows Registry.

A Long Trip

Many times, the command you give at your keyboard or mouse spans across many registry directories and needs to travel back and forth through the registry to carry out one command. So, you can see that one little keystroke needs to wend its way through a lot of files before it is executed. When these files become disorganized the trip can become much longer.

Tangible Programmes

When we add a programme or anything tangible to the computer, we add entries to the registry. When that tangible programme is removed, many of the entries are left behind. These entries that are no longer needed are known as registry corruption. There are other forms of registry corruption, but this is a common one. It is important to note viruses, spyware, adware and malware are all tangible programmes and most of us use spyware cleaners daily to remove these things from our computer. Since these parasites are a lot more prevalent now than they were in Windows 98's hay-day, and they are usually, a lot bigger and more complicated than they used to be, removing them leaves much more corruption nowadays than it used to. As time goes on, this registry corruption causes the computer to act up. The computer will probably slow down at first and after the corruption gets more plentiful, the computer is likely to suffer crashes.

Function

What all this means is in today's world, we have many more tangible programmes in the form of viruses/spyware and such that are being added and removed regularly from our operating system; probably thousands times more than 10 years ago. Add to this fact newer Windows operating systems and their tangible programmes are way larger than the early Windows operating systems and their tangible programmes and you can see how registry corruption has become a much bigger issue than it used to be!

It is easy enough to take care of registry corruption. Just install a good registry cleaner on your computer and run it periodically and your computer will be fine! The best time to run a registry cleaner is after spyware and/or viruses have been removed. By the way, you do have a good spyware cleaner installed on your computer.

TYPES OF OPERATING SYSTEM

There are many types of operating systems. The most common is the Microsoft suite of operating systems. They include from most recent to the oldest:

WINDOWS XP PROFESSIONAL EDITION

A version used by many businesses on workstations. It has the ability to become a member of a corporate domain.

WINDOWS XP HOME EDITION

A lower cost version of Windows XP which is for home use only and should not be used at a business.

WINDOWS 2000

A better version of the Windows NT operating system which works well both at home and as a workstation at a business. It includes technologies which allow hardware to be automatically detected and other enhancements over Windows NT.

WINDOWS ME

A upgraded version from windows 98 but it has been historically plagued with programming errors which may be frustrating for home users.

WINDOWS 98

This was produced in two main versions. The first Windows 98 version was plagued with programming errors but the Windows 98 Second Edition which came out later was much better with many errors resolved.

WINDOWS NT

A version of Windows made specifically for businesses offering better control over workstation capabilities to help network administrators.

WINDOWS 95

The first version of Windows after the older Windows 3.x versions offering a better interface and better library functions for programmes.

There are other worthwhile types of operating systems not made by Microsoft. The greatest problem with these operating systems lies in the fact that not as many application programmes are written for them. However if you can get the type of application programmes you are looking for, one of the systems listed below may be a good choice.

UNIX

A system that has been around for many years and it is very stable. It is primary used to be a server rather than a workstation and should not be used by anyone who does not understand the system. It can be difficult to learn. Unix must normally run an a computer made by the same company that produces the software.

UNIX is a multi-user and multi-tasking operating system. It is very popular operating system used in microcomputers to Supercomputer. It provides the command line interface. It was developed at AT&T Bell Laboratories of USA. It was specially developed at AT&T for their own minicomputers. Microsoft Company of USA also developed a version of UNIX, which is named as XENIX. It is mainly used in network environment because it has powerful security features

LINUX

Linux is similar to Unix in operation but it is free. It also should not be used by anyone who does not understand the system and can be difficult to learn.

APPLE MACINTOSH

Most recent versions are based on Unix but it has a good graphical interface so it is both stable (does not crash often or have as many software problems as other systems may have) and easy to learn. One drawback to this system is that it can only be run on Apple produced Hardware.

SINGLE USER

Single-user allows one single user to login at a time. There is no user account database which makes the level of security low and so users cannot protect their files from being viewed, copied or deleted. Examples of this type are DOS and Windows 98.

List of single user operating system

- MS-DOS
- Amiga OS
- Classic Mac OS (System 1 through Mac OS 9).
- Windows 1.0
- Windows 2.0
- Windows 3.0
- Windows 3.1x

- Windows 95
- Windows 98
- Windows ME

MULTI-USER

The Multi-user has a user database account which states the right that users have on certain resources. They are more secure than the single user since access is limited. Example of this is UNIX

In computing, an operating system that enables several users to access centrally stored data and programmes simultaneously over a network. Each user has a terminal, which may be local (connected directly to the computer) or remote (connected to the computer via a modem and a telephone line). The growth of the internet has given rise to new forms of application level multi-user systems. Multi-user online games and meeting software are examples of a growing range of collaboration and interaction systems.

Multi-access is usually achieved by time-sharing: the computer switches very rapidly between terminals and programmes so that each user has sole use of the computer for only a fraction of a second but can work as if she or he had continuous access.

Multi-user systems are becoming increasingly common in the workplace, and have many advantages – such as enabling employees to refer to and update a shared corporate database. The travel industry uses a multi-user system to manage bookings of airline tickets; travel agents around the world using the system can access information on available seats as readily as an airline's own office.

Networked/Work Alone/

Stand alone are usually not connected to a network and thus cannot access networked resources. They are usually more secured than and remote users cannot log into the computer. A network operating System uses a standard communication protocol for UNIX networks and over the internet(we have the TCP/IP). For Novell Netware internetwork Packet

Exchange /Sequenced Packet Exchange (IPX/SPX). They are less secure than Standalone and should be protected (most times by creating user accounts. More examples are Windows NT 5.0, Windows 98,

MULTI-TASKING/SINGLE TASKING:

Multitasking allows one or more programmes to run, at time. Each process is given a prioritised amount of time on the processor. Single-user allows are programmes to run at a time. It is usually faster than multi-tasking Systems +as some time is taken to in switching in multi-user. But multi-user is more efficient as they allow other tasks to run when a task is not performing any operation. Single-users are more robust, as multi-programmes are require to communicate with each other which can cause synchronization problems (deadlock)

Multi Processor/Single Processor: Some Operating System allows for more than one processor to use on the system. This allows more than one task to be run, at a time, on different processors. Windows NT/2000 supports multi processors (up to). Single Processor, Multitasking involves running each of the processor for a given time slice or a single processor where with multi processor, they can all run at the same.

TIME SHARING OF OPERATING SYSTEM

The last dozen years of computer usage have seen great strides. In the early 1950's, the problems solved were largely in the construction and maintenance of hardware; in the mid-1950's, the usage languages were greatly improved with the advent of compilers; now in the early 1960's, we are in the midst of a third major modification to computer usage: the improvement of man-machine interaction by a process called time-sharing.

Much of the time-sharing philosophy, expressed in this paper, has been developed in conjunction with the work of an MIT preliminary study committee, chaired by H. Teager, which examined the long range computational needs of the Institute, and a subsequent MIT computer working committee, chaired by J. McCarthy. However, the views and conclusions expressed in this paper should be taken as solely those of the present authors.

Before proceeding further, it is best to give a more precise interpretation to time-sharing. One can mean using different parts of the hardware at the same time for different tasks, or one can mean several persons making use of the computer at the same time.

The first meaning, often called multiprogramming, is oriented towards hardware efficiency in the sense of attempting to attain complete utilization of all components. The second meaning of time-sharing, which is meant here, is primarily concerned with the efficiency of persons trying to use a computer. Computer efficiency should still be considered but only in the perspective of the total system utility.

The motivation for time-shared computer usage arises out of the slow man-computer interaction rate presently possible with the bigger, more advanced computers. This rate has changed little (and has become worse in some cases) in the last decade of widespread computer use.

In part, this effect has been due to the fact that as elementary problems become mastered on the computer, more complex problems immediately become of interest. As a result, larger and more complicated programmes are written to take advantage of larger and faster computers. This process inevitably leads to more programming errors and a longer period of time required for debugging.

Using current batch monitor techniques, as is done on most large computers, each programme bug usually requires several hours to eliminate, if not a complete day. The only alternative presently available is for the programmer to attempt to debug directly at the computer, a process which is grossly wasteful of computer time and hampered seriously by the poor console communication usually available.

Even if a typewriter is the console, there are usually lacking the sophisticated query and response programmes which are vitally necessary to allow effective interaction. Thus, what is desired is to drastically increase the rate of interaction between the programmer and the computer without large economic loss and also to make each interaction more meaningful by extensive and complex system programming to assist in the man-computer communication.

To solve these interaction problems we would like to have a computer made simultaneously available to many users in a manner somewhat like a telephone exchange. Each user would be able to use a console at his own pace and with-out concern for the activity of others using the system.

This console could as a minimum be merely a typewriter but more ideally would contain an incrementally modifiable self-sustaining display. In any case, data transmission requirements should be such that it would be no major obstacle to have remote installation from the computer proper.

The basic technique for a time-sharing system is to have many persons simultaneously using the computer through typewriter consoles with a time-sharing supervisor programme sequentially running each user programme in a short burst or quantum of computation.

This sequence, which in the most straightforward case is a simple round-robin, should occur often enough so that each user programme which is kept in the high-speed memory is run for a quantum at least once during each approximate human reaction time (~.2 seconds).

In this way, each user sees a computer fully responsive to even single key strokes each of which may require only trivial computation; in the non-trivial cases, the user sees a gradual reduction of the response time which is proportional to the complexity of the response calculation, the slowness of the computer, and the total number of active users. It should be clear, however, that if there are n users actively requesting service at one time, each user will only see on the average 1/n of the effective computer speed.

During the period of high interaction rates while debugging programmes, this should not be a hindrance since ordinarily the required amount of computation needed for each debugging computer response is small compared to the ultimate production need.

Not only would such a time-sharing system improve the ability to programme in the conventional manner by one or two orders of magnitude, but there would be opened up several new forms of computer usage. There would be a gradual reformulation of many scientific and engineering applications so that programmes containing decision trees which currently must be specified in advance would be eliminated and instead the particular decision branches would be specified only as needed.

Another important area is that of teaching machines which, although frequently trivial computationally, could naturally exploit the consoles of a time-sharing system with the additional bonus that more elaborate and adaptive teaching programmes could be used. Finally, as attested by the many small business computers, there are numerous applications in business and in industry where it would be advantageous to have powerful computing facilities available at isolated locations with only the incremental capital investment of each console. But it is important to realise that even without the above and other new applications, the major advance in programming intimacy available from time-sharing would be of immediate value to computer installations in universities, research laboratories, and engineering firms where programme debugging is a major problem.

Implementation Problems

As indicated, a straightforward plan for time-sharing is to execute user programmes for small quantums of computation without priority in a simple round-robin; the strategy of time-sharing can be more complex as will be shown later, but the above simple scheme is an adequate solution. There are still many problems, however, some best solved by hardware, others affecting the programming conventions and practices. A few of the more obvious problems are summarized:

Hardware Problems

- Different user programmes if simultaneously in core

memory may interfere with each other or the supervisor programme so some form of memory protection mode should be available when operating user programmes.

- The time-sharing supervisor may need at different times to run a particular programme from several locations. (Loading relocation bits are no help since the supervisor does not know how to relocate the accumulator, etc.) Dynamic relocation of all memory accesses that pick up instructions or data words is one effective solution.
- Input-output equipment may be initiated by a user and read words in on another user programme. A way to avoid this is to trap all input-output instructions issued by a user's programme when operated in the memory protection mode.
- A large random-access back-up storage is desirable for general programme storage files for all users. Present large capacity disc units appear to be adequate.
- The time-sharing supervisor must be able to interrupt a user's programme after a quantum of computation. A programme-initiated one-shot multivibrator which generates an interrupt a fixed time later is adequate.
- Large core memories (e.g. a million words) would ease the system programming complications immensely since the different active user programmes as well as the frequently used system programmes such as compilers, query programmes, etc. could remain in core memory at all times.

Programming Problems

- The supervisor programme must do automatic user usage charge accounting. In general, the user should be charged on the basis of a system usage formula or algorithm which should include such factors as computation time, amount of high-speed memory required, rent of secondary memory storage, etc.

- The supervisor programme should coordinate all user input-output since it is not desirable to require a user programme to remain constantly in memory during input-output limited operations. In addition, the supervisor must coordinate all usage of the central, shared high-speed input-output units serving all users as well as the clocks, disc units, etc.
- The system programmes available must be potent enough so that the user can think about his problem and not be hampered by coding details or typographical mistakes. Thus, compilers, query programmes, post-mortem programmes, loaders, and good editing programmes are essential.
- As much as possible, the users should be allowed the maximum programming flexibility both in choices of language and in the absence of restrictions.

Usage Problems

- Too large a computation or excessive typewriter output may be inadvertently requested so that a special termination signal should be available to the user.
- Since real-time is not computer usage-time, the supervisor must keep each user informed so that he can use his judgment regarding loops, etc.
- Computer processor, memory and tape malfunctions must be expected. Basic operational questions such as "Which programme is running?" must be answerable and recovery procedures fully anticipated.

Experimental Time-Sharing System

Having briefly stated a desirable time-sharing performance, it is pertinent to ask what level of performance can be achieved with existent equipment. To begin to answer this question and to explore all the programming and operational aspects, an experimental time-sharing system has been developed. This system was originally written for the IBM 709 but has since been converted for use with the 7090 computer. The 7090 of the MIT Computation Centre has, in addition to three channels with 19 tape units, a fourth channel with the standard Direct Data Connection. Attached to the Direct Data Connection is a real-time equipment buffer and control rack designed and built under the direction of H. Teager and his group. [This group is presently using another approach (ref.9) in developing a time-sharing system for the MIT 7090.]

This rack has a variety of devices attached but the only ones required by the present systems are three flexowriter typewriters. Also installed on the 7090 are two special modifications (i.e. RPQ's): a standard 60 cycle accounting and interrupt clock, and a special mode which allows memory protection, dynamic relocation and trapping of all user attempts to initiate input-output instructions.

In the present system the time-sharing occurs between four users, three of whom are on-line each at a typewriter in a foreground system, and a fourth passive user of the background Fap-Mad-Madtran-BSS Monitor system similar to the Fortran-Fap-BSS Monitor System (FMS) used by most of the Centre programmers and by many other 7090 installations.

Significant design features of the foreground system are:

- It allows the user to develop programmes in languages compatible with the background system,
- Develop a private file of programmes,
- Start debugging sessions at the state of the previous session, and
- Set his own pace with little waste of computer time.

Core storage is allocated such that all users operate in the upper 27,000 words with the time-sharing supervisor (TSS) permanently in the lower 5,000 words. To avoid memory allocation clashes, protect users from one another, and simplify the initial 709 system organization, only one user was kept in core memory at a time. However, with the special memory protection and relocation feature of the 7090, more sophisticated storage allocation procedures are being implemented. In any case, user swaps are minimized by using 2-channel overlapped magnetic tape reading and writing of the pertinent locations in the two user programmes. The foreground system is organized around commands that each user can give on his typewriter and the user's private programme files which presently (for want of a disc unit) are kept on a separate magnetic tape for each user.

For convenience the format of the private tape files is such that they are card images, have title cards with name and class designators and can be written or punched using the off-line equipment. (The latter feature also offers a crude form of large-scale input-output.) The magnetic tape requirements of the system are the seven tapes required for the normal functions of the background system, a system tape for the time-sharing supervisor that contains most of the command programmes, and a private file tape and dump tape for each of the three foreground users.

The commands are typed by the user to the time-sharing supervisor (not to his own programme) and thus can be initiated at any time regardless of the particular user programme in memory. For similar coordination reasons, the supervisor handles all input-output of the foreground system typewriters. Commands are composed of segments separated by vertical strokes; the first segment is the command name and the remaining segments are parameters pertinent to the command.

Each segment consists of the last 6 characters typed (starting with an implicit 6 blanks) so that spacing is an easy way to correct a typing mistake. A carriage return is the signal which initiates action on the command. Whenever a command is received by the supervisor, "WAIT", is typed back followed by "READY." when the command is completed.

(The computer responses are always in the opposite colour from the user's typing.) While typing, an incomplete command line may be ignored by the "quit" sequence of a code delete signal followed by a carriage return. Similarly after a command is initiated, it may be abandoned if a "quit" sequence is given. In addition, during unwanted command typeouts, the command and output may be terminated by pushing a special "stop output" button. The use of the foreground system is initiated whenever a typewriter user completes a command line and is placed in a waiting command queue. Upon completion of each quantum, the time-sharing supervisor gives top priority to initiating any waiting commands.

The system programmes corresponding to most of the commands are kept on the special supervisor command system tape so that to avoid waste of computer time, the supervisor continues to operate the last user programme until the desired command programme on tape is positioned for reading.

At this point, the last user is read out on his dump tape, the command programme read in, placed in a working status and initiated as a new user programme. However, before starting the new user for a quantum of computation, the supervisor again checks for any waiting command of another user and if necessary begins the look-ahead positioning of the command system tape while operating the new user.

Whenever the waiting command queue is empty, the supervisor proceeds to execute a simple round-robin of those foreground user programmes in the working status queue. Finally, if both these queues are empty, the background user programme is brought in and run a quantum at a time until further foreground system actively develops.

Foreground user programmes leave the working status queue by two means. If the programme proceeds to completion, it can reenter the supervisor in a way which eliminates itself and places the user in dead status; alternatively, by a different entry the programme can be placed in a dormant status (or be manually placed by the user executing a quit sequence). The dormant status differs from the dead status in that the user may still restart or examine his programme.

User input-output is through each typewriter, and even though the supervisor has a few lines of buffer space available, it is possible to become input-output limited. Consequently, there is an additional input-output wait status, similar to the dormant, which the user is automatically placed in by the supervisor programme whenever input-output delays develop. When buffers become near empty on output or near full on input, the user programme is automatically returned to the working status; thus waste of computer time is avoided.

RESOURCE MANAGER

RULES

When programming in a GUI operating system, you allocate operating system resources for widgets, images, fonts, and other graphical objects. Since there is a platform limit on the amount of resources you can allocate, you must be careful to free any objects that you allocate in your application. If you allocate a resource and do not free it when you are done with it, your application is "leaking" resources. An application that repeatedly leaks resources will eventually consume all of the available resources, forcing the user to reboot the operating system.

Fortunately, SWT makes resource allocation and disposal a straightforward process. There are only two rules that you need to remember when allocating and freeing SWT resource-based objects:

Rule 1

This is a simple rule. SWT makes it easy for you to remember when operating system resources are allocated: *all* SWT resource-based objects (like *Colour, Cursor, Display, Font, GC, Image, Printer, Region, Widget and subclasses*) allocate any needed operating system resources in their constructor.

There are no exceptions to this rule. There are no methods in SWT (other than constructors) that allocate operating system resources that the programmer must manage. If you didn't call the constructor, then you don't need to free the resources, so don't call dispose on the object.

For example, in the following line of code, an operating system font is allocated: Font font = new Font (display, "Courier", 10, SWT.NORMAL); Since you called the *Font* constructor to create the resource, you must dispose the font when you are finished with it, as follows:

```
font.dispose();
```

In the following line of code, however, a constructor is not called:

```
Font font = control.getFont ();
```

Therefore, you must not call dispose. The font variable does contain an operating system font resource, but you did not allocate it. If you were to dispose of this font, you would be leaving the control without a font! The results are undefined.

So, if you are using *any* getter that returns an SWT resource-based object that you did not allocate, do not dispose the object. This rule occasionally leads to API that seems artificial. For example, GC.getClipping (Region) forces the programmer to create a *Region* in order to get the clipping region from a *GC*.

Although it might have been a bit "prettier" to provide GC.getClipping () that returned a *Region*, this would break the rule because it would have to allocate an operating system resource outside of a constructor. While it could be documented that the programmer needs to free the *Region* returned by GC.get Clipping (), programmers don't always read the documentation. Making the programmer call the constructor for the *Region* makes it clear that it is the *programmer's* responsibilit to free the resource.

Rule 2

When you dispose a *Shell*, its children are disposed. In fact, disposing any *Composite* will dispose all of the *Composite*'s children. Disposing a *Menu* disposes all menu items. Disposing a *Tree* or *TreeItem* disposes all child items.

Why does this make sense? Apart from the obvious burden of having to dispose each child if this were not the case, the fact that a widget cannot exist in the operating system without a parent implies that when the parent is disposed, the child *must* also be disposed.

What about the fonts and colours that you created and set into a *Widget*? Since they are not children of the widget, they are not disposed when the parent is disposed. A widget will never dispose a resource that you allocated. To do so would mean that the widget was breaking rule 1. Because fonts and colours can be shared by different widgets, disposing a resource in one widget would dispose it in another, leading to unpredictable results.

Extensions to Rule 2

There are two extensions to rule 2. These are places where a relationship exists that is not strictly a parent-child relationship, but where it still makes sense for rule 2 to apply.

MenuItem.setMenu

Disposing a cascade *MenuItem* that has a submenu set with setMenu (Menu) disposes the submenu. This is a natural extension of rule 2. It would be a burden to the programmer to dispose each individual submenu. It's also common behaviour in most operating systems to do this automatically. Both Windows® and X dispose submenus when a cascade menu item is disposed.

Control.setMenu

Disposing a *Control* that has a pop-up menu set with setMenu (Menu) disposes the pop-up menu. Many application programmers expected this behaviour, even though many operating systems don't do this automatically. Leaving the application programmer responsible for disposing a pop-up menu when disposing the *Control* led to temporary leaks. (The leak was only temporary because the pop-up menu is eventually disposed when the shell is disposed).

FREE

The operating system frees all of a program's resources when the programme exits. Why not just rely on this? Operating system resources are not infinite. If your programme doesn't free up resources as they are no longer needed, it can run out of resources.

It can also cause other programmes to run out of resources. So waiting until the programme exits to free up resources is generally a bad idea. Leak tools exist to help detect resource leaks. You can use the *Sleak* tool to look for leaks in your SWT application.

JAVA LANGUAGE A GARBAGE COLLECTION

The Java language successfully uses a garbage collector to manage the memory used by Java objects. Why doesn't SWT use the Java garbage collector to manage operating system resources too? Many Java programmers ask this question. We will answer it with the following discussion on finalization.

FINALIZATION

Most attempts to use the Java garbage collector to manage operating system resources involve finalization. When an object is about to become garbage, the garbage collector sends it the finalize message. This seems like a logical place to free the resource, right?

One of the main reasons that this statement is true is that there is no guarantee how soon after an object becomes garbage that the finalize method for the object will run. Even if you could predict this time interval for a particular VM, you certainly couldn't guarantee it for new versions of the VM. Worse still, if there is plenty of memory or if an exception occurs in an object's finalize method, there is no guarantee that the object will be finalized at all! All of this is stated right in *The Java Language Specification*: "The Java programming language does not specify how soon a finalizer will be invoked, except to say that it will happen before the storage for the object is reused. ... If an uncaught exception is thrown during the finalization, the exception is ignored and finalization of that object terminates."

Releasing operating system resources is critical to correct programme execution. Freeing resources at some unknown time in the future (or not at all) typically leads to programme failure.

Here are some examples of typical problems encountered when using finalization:

- If a non-garbage object references another object, that

object is not garbage and won't be collected. If the object has operating system resources that it frees in its finalize method, those resources will never be freed because finalize will never be called. This is a classic programming error because it's easy to hang on to objects accidentally in an inner class or a static variable.

- It is possible to starve other operating system processes by creating lots of "garbage resources" that have not yet been finalized. When another programme attempts to acquire a resource, it fails because it cannot run the Java finalizer. SWT could run the finalizer if it couldn't get a resource, but other programmes (i.e. non-Java programmes or even Java programmes running in a different VM) - and operating system calls that allocate and free resources internally - can't run the Java finalizer.
- *Some resources are very limited*: For example, only a small number of cached HDCs are available on Windows 98. It is essential to free these up right away, instead of waiting for finalization.
- Different types of resource are shared on the same operating system heap, so a failure to acquire one resource may be caused by failure to free another. For example, on Windows 98, HBRUSH and HFONT are both allocated from the GDI heap, so failure to create an HBRUSH can happen if too many HFONTs are awaiting finalization. This can cause applications to have some strange dependencies on the timing of finalizer runs.

The non-deterministic nature of finalization is sufficient reason to avoid using it to free resources, but even if we decided to go against conventional wisdom and implement a resource management scheme using finalization, we would still face many other problems.

The implementation would require the addition of some very complex, platform-specific code that would be difficult to get right, and tough to debug. Here are a few examples of some of the tricky issues that would need to be carefully coded around in each object's finalize method.

- Operating system objects can have subtle limitations on when particular objects can be disposed. For example in the X Window System, a GC can contain a Font. If you dispose the Font before the GC, you leave the operating system in an indeterminate state. The following quote from *The Java Language Specification* hints at the complexity of the code that would be required to handle such limitations for each object finalizer:

"The Java programming language imposes no ordering on finalize method calls. Finalizers may be called in any order, or even concurrently." Add to this that for some operating systems, subtle platform behaviour in this area may be undocumented and can change in future versions of the operating system.

- On some platforms, operating system resources need to be disposed in the UI thread. According to *The Java Language Specification*: "... the language does not specify which thread will invoke the finalizer for any given object." This means that SWT finalize methods would need to synchronize with the UI thread, which would mean that there would be a significant cost overhead for each dispose. In addition, given the previous point that disposal order is important for some resources, we think it is possible to get into a deadlock situation if we are trying to reorder multiple concurrent threads that are trying to synchronize with the UI thread.
- The Java objects that model operating system objects need to capture all of the subtle relationships between the operating system objects. For example, on Windows, an HBRUSH can be referenced in the operating system by an HDC, but not referenced in Java code. When the Java object representing the HBRUSH becomes garbage, freeing it will cause unexpected results. In fact, it's necessary to break

the reference from the HDC first before attempting to free the HBRUSH. If these relationships are not captured and managed, it is possible for a resource to be finalized when there are still references to it in the operating system.

- Freeing some resources automatically frees others. For example, on Windows, destroying a parent HWND automatically destroys the children HWNDs. On some operating systems, freeing a top level window also frees the icon associated with the window. Different rules for freeing resources need to be custom coded on a per platform basis.
- Freeing resources can be time consuming, so a critical memory allocation may need to wait until finalization is complete.
- Long waits in finalizers can also make it difficult to get good benchmarks when you are trying to performance tune your code.

Our final point against finalization is this: SWT keeps as much state in the operating system as possible to simplify the implementation (less code, smaller objects). If we were to use finalization, we could not store resources only in the operating system. We would have to hold on to them in Java code so that they would not get garbage collected.

For example, when you set a *Font* into a *Button,* SWT sets the font resource in the OS button. The *Button* doesn't keep a reference to the font resource, because it doesn't need to. The state is in the operating system. In order to determine the *Button*'s font, we query the OS. There is no point caching the font resource in Java code, because it just takes up space and complicates the *Button* code, which now has to make sure there are no stale cache problems.

Given that there are many problems when trying to use finalization to free resources, we think it's dangerous to offer it as a solution in SWT, which is designed to expose operating system functionality.

We believe it is reasonable to expect programmes to explicitly free operating system resources. We see this as simply a fact of life because the current generation of operating systems do not support garbage collection.

OS PROCESS

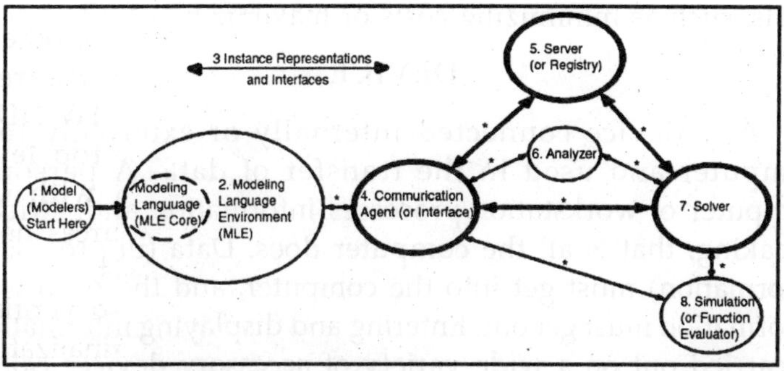

For our optimization system, there are mainly three categories of "human" customers:

- Application developers create and build system components such as modeling language environments and solvers as part of a larger optimization system. The components together take care of such generic functions as managing data, solving optimization problems, and presenting solutions nicely.
- Modelers work in a modeling language environment or GUI to build optimization models and get acceptable solutions.
- Users run application packages that perform optimization at some stage through the optimization system. Users are usually the ultimate customers of any optimization system.

Modelers and application developers may see optimization in different ways. For modelers, a mathematical programme is an abstract representation to be analyzed and understood; for application developers, a mathematical programme is a concrete instance to be represented, communicated and solved.

Modelers benefit most immediately from innovations that help people to choose and experiment with optimization software. Some application developers are also modelers, while others deal mainly with the inputs and outputs of optimization models set up by modelers. Users may not even realise that they are running optimization system components such as solvers, although they are often aware of optimization goals, such as minimizing costs or maximizing profits.

DEVICE

Any device connected internally or externally to a computer and used in the transfer of data. A personal computer or workstation processes information and, strictly speaking, that is all the computer does. Data (unprocessed information) must get into the computer, and the processed information must get out. Entering and displaying information is carried out on a wide variety of accessory devices called peripherals, also known as input/output (I/O) devices. Some peripherals, such as keyboards, are only input devices; other peripherals, such as printers, are only output devices; and some are both.

The monitor is the device on which images produced by the computer operator or generated by the programme are displayed on a cathode-ray tube (CRT). Electron guns—one in a monochromemonitor, three in a colour monitor—irradiate phosphors on the inside of the vacuum tube, causing them to glow. The flat-panel displays on most portable computers, known as liquid-crystal displays (LCDs), use two polarizing filters with liquid crystals between them to produce the image.

The computer keyboard, based on the typewriter keyboard, contains keys for entering letters, numbers, and punctuation marks, as well as keys to change the meaning of other keys. The function keys perform tasks that vary from programme to programme.

The mouse is a device that is rolled on the desktop to move the cursor on the screen. A ball on the bottom of the mouse translates the device's movements to sensors within the mouse and then through the connecting port to the computer. There are also mice that substitute optical devices for mechanical balls, and mice that use infrared rather than physical connections. The trackball is essentially an upside-down mouse, with the ball that is used to move the cursor located on the top rather than on the bottom. The joystick is a pointing device used principally for games.

The light pen performs the same functions as a mouse or trackball, but it is held up to the screen, where its sensors detect the presence of pixels and send a signal through a cable to the computer.The graphics, or digitizing, tablet is a pad with electronics beneath the surface which is drawn upon with a pointed device, called a stylus. The shapes drawn appear on the monitor's screen.

The most common input, or storage, device in personal computers or workstations is a hard disk drive, a stack of magnetized platters on which information is stored by heads generating an electrical current to represent either 1 or 0 in the binary number system. The device is called hard because the platters are inflexible, and is called a drive because it spins at 3600 revolutions or more a minute, within a sealed case. Diskettes, made of flexible film like that used in recording tape, are usually stored within a hard shell and are spun by their drives at about 360 revolutions per minute.

Data can also be stored and retrieved with light, the light of a laser beam reading a pattern of pits on an optical disk. The most familiar type of optical disk is the CD-ROM (compact disk-read only memory). Another kind of optical disk is the WORM (write once read many times).

As a consequence of their greater efficiency and speed, disk drives have quickly replaced tape drives as the primary means of data and programme storage. Tape drives are still in use for backup storage, copying the contents of a hard disk as insurance against mechanical failure or human error.

The scanner converts an image of something outside the computer, such as text, a drawing, or a photograph, into a digital image that it sends into the computer for display or further processing. The image is viewed as a graphics image, not a text image, so it can be altered with a graphics programme but cannot be edited with a word-processing programme, unless the scanner is part of a character-recognition system. To digitize photographs, a scanner may dither the image (put the dots a varying amount of space apart), or use the tagged image file format (TIFF), storing the image in 16 gray values. Some scanners can use standard video cameras to capture images for the computer.

The printer puts text or other images produced with a computer onto paper or other surfaces. Printers are either impact or nonimpact devices.

Daisy-wheel or thimble printers are so called from the shape of the elements bearing raised images of the characters. Their speed, perhaps 30 characters per second, is now considered unacceptably slow. Dot-matrix printers produce their images by striking a series of wire pins, typically, 9, 18, or 24, through the ribbon in the pattern necessary to form the letter, number, line, or other character.

Ink-jet printers carry their ink in a well, where it is turned into a mist by heat or vibration andsprayed through tiny holes to form the pattern of the character on paper. Laser printers are similar to photocopying machines. The quality of laser-printer output is the highest generally available. The modem connects one computer to another, ordinarily through the telephone lines, to exchange information.

COMPUTER STORAGE DEVICES

Computer storage devices can be classified into either primary storage, secondary storage, or tertiary storage. Each of these storage devices are used to store certain files and data and are accessed in different ways by the computer's CPU. Here's a brief explanation of the differences.

Primary Computer Storage Devices

Primary storage refers to the computer's memory, which connects directly to the computer's CPU. The computer's memory evolved into what is now known as random access memory (RAM) which is a volatile form of storage. Volatile storage means that you totally lose data when you switch the system off.

Aside from the RAM, two other primary storage areas can be found; these are on the CPU itself; the Processor registers and the Processor cache. The Processor register is some form of small storage which resides on the CPU and can contain data which can be accessed quickly. The processor registers are measured by the amount of data the can hold, that is either, 8 bit, 32 bit or 64 bit. Processor cache on the other hand is used by the CPU for reducing the time it takes to access the main memory. It stores data coming from the most frequently used applications of the CPU. During normal operations, the CPU checks the processor cache before checking the main memory, making the processing time faster.

Secondary Computer Storage Devices

These storage devices are external in nature and non-volatile as compared to primary storage devices. Secondary storage devices do not lose data even when they are turned off. Hence, they are the ideal back-upand data storage devices. Examples of secondary storage devices include; CD and DVD; flash memory; floppy disks; paper and magnetic tape; RAM disks, also called SSDs; ZIP drives; and punch cards.

Since secondary storage devices are not attached to the computer's CPU, it takes a longer time for the CPU to access them. Secondary storage devices need to be formated before they can store data. Secondary storage devices are formated based on a filesystem format data are organized into files and directories. It also includes other pertinent information about the data, which is described in what is called the metadata.

Tertiary Computer Storage Devices[SH]

This type of computer storage device is not as popular as the other two storage device types. Its main use is for storing data at a very large-scale. This includes optical jukeboxes and tape libraries. Tertiary storage devices require a database to organize the data that are stored in them, and the computer needs to go through the database to access those data.

Offline Storage

Aside from these three types of computer storage devices, there is also another type - offline or disconnected storage. It is not directly connected to the computer and is used as a transfer medium only. Offline storage devices are remotely located and accessed as per need only. This storage device also needs human intervention to be read properly by the main computer system.

Offline storage aside, from its use as a data transmission medium, can also serve as a good back-up device since it is remotely located, hence it will not be affected by any disaster that might hit the direct source of data. Offline storage also provides good security for data since you ca

COMPUTER STORAGE DEVICES

Awhile back, we covered the different types of hardware used with computers. You know, basic hardware and the extra hardware you can buy separately, etc. (You can read here for that article).

Knowing what kinds of storage devices are available can keep you from using up too much space on your computer's hard drive. They can also help keep your computer's hard drive from crashing, along with keeping it running at top speed. The most common storage devices are:

Floppy Disk

They are plastic square disks, usually with a silver or black sliding piece going across the top. These disks come in a variety of colours and they hold about 144 million bytes. (Bytes are characters, symbols and letters).

Zip Disk

They look like a floppy disk, but they are a little thicker. This disk also comes in a variety of colours and holds about 200 MB of data.

CD + RW Disc (Compact Disc Rewriteable)

This disc looks like a regular CD. The only difference is that you can write on this disc and erase it as many times as you want. It works just like a floppy disk or a zip disk. A CD + RW disc holds about 650 MB.

CD + R Disc (Compact Disc Recordable)

This one is a CD that you can record on. It's mostly used to record audio and once it's been written on, you cannot rewrite or erase anything off of it. This compact disc comes in different sizes, but they are usually silver in colour. (Some CDs are black in colour and they actually don't get as many scratches on them as the silver ones do. They are also a lot less fragile).

A DVD – R Disc (Digital Video Recordable)

These discs hold the space of about 4.7 GB and are used to record movies on.

Removable Hard Drive

This is a disk drive in which a plastic or metal case surrounds the hard drive. It can be inserted and removed just like a floppy disk. It holds about 2 GB of data.

Internet Hard Drive

This one is a service on the Internet that provides storage space to computer users. This service offers about 25 MB of space, but it could be more, depending on the service type.

Flash Drive

This a storage device that comes in many colours and has a stick shape to it. They are very small in size, but they can hold anywhere between 256 MB and 3 GB of material on them.

PC Card

This is a thin credit card size device that fits into a PC card slot, usually on a notebook computer. This card simply adds storage to most notebooks.

Smart Cards

These are the size of an ATM card. When inserted into a smart card reader, they can read and update data for you.

Storage Tape

This one is a magnetically coated ribbon of plastic, capable of storing large amounts of data at a very low cost. Usually, storage tapes are a little bigger than audio tapes.

Older computers used tape and tape drives, but even today, some people still back their systems up with storage tape. These tapes hold between 20 GB to about 110 GB of data. An external tape drive can be purchased separately as well, but those are even harder to find.

Miniature Mobile Storage Media

This is used mostly with handheld computers and digital cameras.

Memory Stick

This is a rectangular shaped disk that is used mostly with digital cameras and notebook computers. They hold approximately 128 MB as well.

Micro Drive

This is a square disk that has 1 GB of space and is used with digital cameras and handheld computers.

Smart Media Disc

This is a square disk that has 2 MB to about 128 MB of space on it. It's used with digital cameras, handheld computers and photo printers.

There you go! These are just some of the storage devices that are available today. So, the next time you want to save something that takes up a large amount of space on your hard drive, think twice about it and consider using one of these storage devices instead. One of these devices could save you a lot of space on your hard drive and keep your system running at its best!

MEMORY AND FILE MANAGEMENT

MEMORY

Memory is the electronic holding place for instructions and data that the computer's microprocessor can reach quickly. When the computer is in normal operation, its memory usually contains the main parts of the operating system and some or all of the application programmes and related data that are being used.

Memory is often used as a shorter synonym for random access memory (RAM). This kind of memory is located on one or more microchips that are physically close to the microprocessor in the computer.

Most desktop and notebook computers sold today include at least 16 megabytes of RAM, and are upgradeable to include more. The more RAM you have, the less frequently the computer has to access instructions and data from the more slowly accessed hard disk form of storage.

Memory is sometimes distinguished from storage, or the physical medium that holds the much larger amounts of data that won't fit into RAM and may not be immediately needed there. Storage devices include hard disks, floppy disks, CD-

ROM, and tape backup systems. The terms auxiliary storage, auxiliary memory, and secondary memory have also been used for this kind of data repository.

Additional kinds of integrated and quickly accessible memory are read-only memory (ROM), programmable ROM (PROMO), erasable programmable ROM (EPROM). These are used to keep special programmes and data, such as the basic input/output system, that need to be in the computer all the time.

The memory is a resource that needs to be managed carefully. Most computers have a memory hierarchy, with a small amount of very fast, expensive, volatile cache memory, some number of megabytes of medium-speed, medium-price, volatile main memory (RAM), and hundreds of thousands of megabytes of slow, cheap, non-volatile disk storage. It is the job of the operating system to coordinate how these memories are used.

The part of the operating system that manages the memory hierarchy is the memory manager. It keeps track of parts of memory that are in use and those that are not in use, to allocate memory to processes when they need it and de-allocate it when they are done, and to manage swapping between main memory and disk when main memory is too small to hold all the processes.

Systems for managing memory can be divided into two categories: the system of moving processes back and forth between main memory and disk during execution (known as swapping and paging) and the process that does not do so (that is, no swapping and ping).

Mono programming without Swapping or Paging

The most simple memory management scheme is to run one programme at a time, sharing the memory between that programme and the operating system.

As shown in the diagram bellow, there are three variations of this type. The operating system may be at the bottom of the memory in TAM (random access memory), as shown in the diagram 1, or it may be in ROM (read-only memory) at the top of the memory, as shown in diagram 2, or the device drivers may be at the top of the memory in a ROM and the rest of the system in RAM down below. With the system organised in this way, only one process at a time can be running.

As soon as the user types a command, the operating system copies the request programme from a disk to memory and executes it.

When the process finishes, the operating system displays a prompt character and waits for a new command. When it receives the command, it loads a new programme into memory overwriting the first one.

Mono Programming with Fixed Partitions

It is often desirable to allow multiple processes to run at the same time, even on simple operating systems in which multiprogramming is sometimes used. On time-sharing systems, having multiple processes in memory at once means that when one process is blocked waiting for the I/O to finish, another one can use the CPU.

This way, multiprogramming increases the CPU utilisation. It is however preferable to be able to run two or more programmes at once even on personal computers.

Swapping

The process of organising memory into fixed partitions on batch system is simple compared to time sharing systems or graphically oriented personal computers. On batch systems, each job is loaded into a partition when it gets to the head of the queue.

It stays in memory until it has finished. As long as enough jobs can be kept in memory to keep the CPU busy all the time, there is no reason to use anything more complicated.

On time-sharing machines, sometimes there is not enough main memory to hold all the currently active processes, therefore excess processes must be kept on disk and brought in to run dynamicallySwapping as an approach to memory management consists of bringing each process in its entirety, running it for a while, then putting it back on the disk.

THE SCENARIO

The problem we are trying to overcome is simply this: You want to develop some kind of file or text editor, and you want your programme to be able to load, edit and save files of any size. In fact, you want your programme to load and edit the largest sized file possible. Under 32bit Windows this is a 4Gb file. (Actually, Windows NT supports 18 exabyte files with its 64bit NTFS file system, but I will talk about this type of file later in the series. Your file editor needs be able to load a 4Gb file in a fraction of a second. In addition, insertions and deletions to and from the file must be as fast for a 4Gb file as they are for a 1Kb file.

This series of articles (I haven't decided exactly how many articles there will be yet) will take you through the design decisions and algorithms necessary to accomplish these goals. At the end of the series you will have enough information to develop your own file-handling functions, which will be as powerful and flexible as those used in my HexEdit application.

MEMORY MANAGEMENT

Let's forget about actually editing a large file for the moment, and concentrate just on loading a file into your application. So, your have a 4Gb file saved on your hard disk, and you want to load this file so you can preview any portion of it. Let's assume that our first application will be a simple hex file viewer, with no editing capabilities.

The first decision to take is what memory facilities we will use to gain access to the file's contents. To make this decision, we need to know what memory facilities are available to our programme, and base our decision on that. Because our file viewer will be a 32bit Windows programme capable of running under Windows 9x and NT / 2000, we have the following facilities at our disposal.

VIRTUAL MEMORY

Another strategy for managing memory is the virtual

memory, which allows programmes to run even when they are only partially in main memory. The basic idea behind this strategy is that the combine size of the programme, data, and stack may exceed the amount of physical memory available for it. The operating system keeps those parts of the programme currently in use in main memory, and the rest on the disk.

Virtual memory can also work in a multiprogramming system, with bits and pieces pf many programmes in memory at once. While a programme is waiting for a part of itself to be brought in, it is waiting for I/O and cannot run, so the CPU can be given to another process, the same way as for any other multiprogramming system. Most virtual memory systems use a technique called paging.

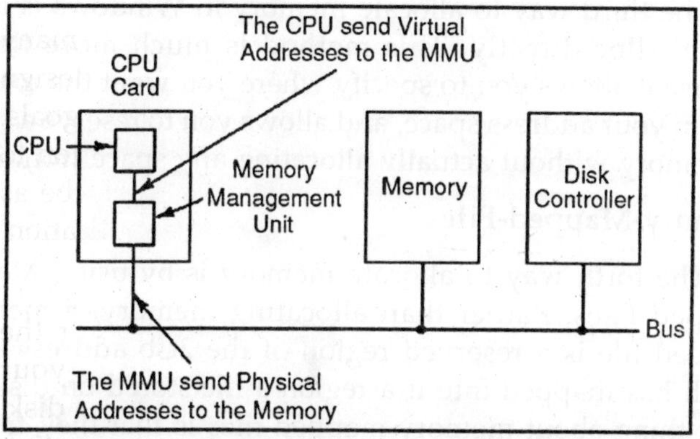

Every 32bit process in Windows has a 4Gb virtual address space, regardless of the amount of physical RAM you have installed. Of this total virtual space, only 2Gb is available for an application's private use. Actually, the available space slightly less than this - 128Kb less in WinNT and 4Mb less in Win9x). There are a variety of methods to allocate memory from this 2Gb region of space. All depend on how much memory needs to be allocated, and what its intended use is.

Malloc and new

The simplest is to use the standard C or C++ memory allocation routines (malloc and new[], respectively). Both of these methods use the memory allocation facilities provided by the operating system. In Visual C++ 6.0, malloc and new[] use VirtualAlloc internally. Anyway, malloc and new[] are only really meant for allocating lots of small objects, not one gigantic memory region.

HeapAlloc

The second method to allocate memory in Windows is to use the Heap function – HeapAlloc (or the older LocalAlloc and GlocalAlloc). These functions are also meant for allocating many small objects though - just like malloc and new[] - and are also implemented by calls to VirtualAlloc.

VirtualAlloc

The third way to allocate memory in Windows is to use VirtualAlloc directly. This method is much more flexible because it allows you to specify where you want the memory to be in your address space, and allows you to reserve a region of memory without actually allocating any space from it.

Memory-Mapped-Files

The forth way to allocate memory is by using Memory Mapped Files. Rather than allocating memory, a memory-mapped file is a reserved region of the 2Gb address space, which has mapped into it a region a file stored on disk. The great thing about memory-mapped-files is that they free the programmer from having to do any direct file reading or writing.

Simply reading and writing to the memory-mapped view causes the file's contents to be accessed. The operating system provides clever page caching to make memory-mapped files a very quick way to read/write to a file.

DOS

DEFINITION

DOS (Disk Operating System) was the first widely-installedo perating system for personal computers. (Earlier, the same name had been used for an IBM operating system for a line of business computers.) The first personal computer version of DOS, called PC-DOS, was developed for IBM by Bill Gates and his new Microsoft Corporation.

He retained the rights to market a Microsoft version, called MS-DOS. PC-DOS and MS-DOS are almost identical and most users have referred to either of them as just "DOS." DOS was (and still is) a non-graphical line-oriented command- or menu-driven operating system, with a relatively simple interface but not overly "friendly" user interface.

Its prompt to enter a command looks like this:

```
C:>
```

The first Microsoft Windows operating system was really an application that ran on top of the MS-DOS operating system. Today, Windows operating systems continue to support DOS (or a DOS-like user interface) for special purposes by emulating the operating system.

In the 1970s before the personal computer was invented, IBM had a different and unrelated DOS (Disk Operating System) that ran on smaller business computers. It was replaced by IBM's VSE operating system.

DOS stands for Disk Operating System. DOS controls the computer's hardware and provides an environment for programmes to run. Everything you can do with a GUI can be done at the DOS prompt. There are many flavours of *DOS operating system*like MS-DOS, PC DOS, DR DOS, FreeDOS, etc. There are two types of commands in DOS, internal and external.

Internal commands are part of the command processor, whereas external commands exist as executable files. The entire operating system is small enough to fit on a floppy disk.

Booting

To run DOS on a computer, it should be the first programme to be executed when the computer is switched on. This led to a problem for the designers: "How can DOS be loaded and executed when there is no DOS programme running to load and execute *it*??!!". Well, just as the fictional

Baron Munchausen managed to pull himself up by his own bootstraps, the computer manages this seemingly impossible trick, and the term "bootstrapping", or "booting up" is applied to this process.

Communicating with DOS

DOS is an entirely text based system. All it provides for the user is a prompt: "C:>" or "A:>", where the user can type in commands from the keyboard. The system is entirely case insensitive: so either "ForMAt C:" or "format c:" would erase your hard disk...

The latter example is of course a small warning: with DOS comes power, you can very easily mess up your system if you use powerful commands in the wrong way. The commands you should be careful of are: "Format", "Recover", and "Del". All of these perform useful functions, when used correctly, and all the others are pretty much safe to use.

Working of DOS

DOS works within a file, directory and disk drive structure. This means that all programme and data files are named, and grouped together in named directories on disks. 'Directories' are just lists of files.

Naming of Files

While newer versions of DOS support longer filenames, the standard DOS filename format remains: 1-8 letter name, period, 3 letter extension eg:

PROGRAMME.EXE **DATA.DAT** **LETTER.DOC**

The extension to a file's name is there to allow files of a similar type to be grouped together. Ie. all wordprocessor files might have the extension .DOC, while all picture files might have the extension .PIC While these extensions can be specified by the user, many programmes have used them to differentiate between formats, and so they have gradually become standardised.

For example you would expect a ".TXT" file to be a file containing unformatted text, or a ".BMP" file to be in a bit mapped graphics file format. To completely specify a file on your computer you must specify its drive and directory path, and its filename.

However a file does not always have to be specified in this complete form: If it is in the current directory, then you can just enter its filename.

Naming Directories

Every disk drive has a root directory which can have subdirectories which are named in the same format as filenames, (though generally without any extension). The subdirectories can have subdirectories and so on. Eg: a floppy disk might contain the following directory structure:

```
PICTURES
HOLIDAY
ITALY
FRANCE
FAMILY
PETS
TEXT
LETTERS
EMAIL
```

A directory path name includes the disk drive and all subdirectories needed to specify a directory on a disk. The disk drive is specified by a single letter. Eg: The floppy disk drive is A and the hard disk drive is C.

The drive letter, is followed by a colon, the directory path names are separated by backward slashes (\), (*Not* forward slashes like internet addresses). Eg. In the above example "A:\PICTURES\HOLIDAY\FRANCE" would be more than likely to contain pictures of a few baguettes and onions.

Uses of DOS

When you type anything at the DOS prompt, and press enter, you are telling DOS to run a programme. It will first look to see if there is an internal command programme which has that name, and if it does not find one, then it will look to see if there is a file on disk with that name. If it finds an external file with the extension.COM (command), or .EXE (executable), then the programme is loaded and run. At this point DOS looses control of the computer until the programme has ended. However parts of it are still used by the programmes as they are running, eg to load and save files etc.

Some very useful internal DOS commands:

- *A*: Change current directory path to the floppy disk drive
- C: Change current directory path to the hard disk drive
- *DIR*: Display current directory (show all files and sub-directories).
- *MD* Make a new directory, eg: MD C:\EMAIL
- *CD*: Change current directory, eg. CD C:\EMAIL
- *COPY*: Copy file(s) from one place to another.
- *Del*: Delete/erase a file

Any other text on the input line after the file name, is passed to the programme. This means that in the command "Copy help.txt help.bak", the text, "help.txt and help.bak" is passed to the copy programme which will in this case use it to specify source and destination files for a copy.

WINDOWS OPERATING SYSTEM

Microsoft first started developing the Interface Manager (later renamed Microsoft Windows) in September 1981. While the first prototypes used Multiplan and Word-like menus at the bottom of the screen, the interface was modified in 1982 to utilize pull-down menus and dialogues, as used on the Xerox Star.

On November 10, 1983, at the Plaza Hotel in New York City, Microsoft Corporation officially announced Microsoft Windows, a next-generation operating system that would supply a graphical user interface (GUI) and a multitasking environment for IBM computers.

This was after the release of the Apple Lisa, and prior to Digital Research announcing GEM, and DESQ from Quarterdeck and the Amiga Workbench , or GEOS/GeoWorks Ensemble, IBM OS/2, NeXTstep or even DeskMate from

Tandy. Windows assured an easy-to-use graphical interface, device-independent graphics and multitasking support. The development was held up several times, however, and the Windows 1.0 arrive at store shelves in November 1985. The selection of applications was thin, however, and Windows sales were moderate.

Windows 1.0 package, included: MS-DOS Executive, Calendar, Cardfile, Notepad, Terminal, Calculator, Clock, Reversi, Control Panel, PIF (Programme Information File) Editor, Print Spooler, Clipboard, RAMDrive, Windows Write, Windows Paint.

Microsoft Windows version 1.0 was viewed as buggy, rough, and sluggish. This bumpy start was made sorrier by a threatened lawsuit from Apple Computers. In September 1985, Apple lawyers warned Bill Gates that Windows 1.0 infringed on Apple copyrights and patents, and that his corporation had stolen Apple's trade secrets.

Microsoft Windows had similar drop-down menus, tiled windows and mouse support. Bill Gates and his head counsel Bill Neukom, chose to make an offer to license features of Apple's operating system. Apple concurred and a contract was drawn up.

The key to this is: Microsoft wrote the licensing agreement to include use of Apple features in Microsoft Windows version 1.0 and all future Microsoft software programmes. As it turned out, this move by Bill Gates was as intelligent as his decision to purchase QDOS from Seattle Computer Products and his persuading IBM to let Microsoft keep the licensing rights to MS-DOS.

Windows 1.0 fluttered on the market until January 1987, when a Windows-compatible programme called Aldus PageMaker 1.0 was brought out. PageMaker was the first WYSIWYG desktop-publishing programme for the PC. Later that year, Microsoft released a Windows-compatible spreadsheet called Excel.

Other popular and functional software like Microsoft Word and Corel Draw helped advance Windows, yet, Microsoft recognized that Windows required further development. Microsoft Windows version 2.0 came out in December 1987, and evidenced somewhat more popular than its predecessor. A great deal of the popularity for Windows 2.0 came through its inclusion as a "run-time version" with Microsoft's new graphical applications, Excel and Word for Windows.

They could be operated from MS-DOS, executing Windows for the length of their activity, and shutting down Windows upon exit.

Microsoft Windows incurred a major boost about this time when Aldus PageMaker came out in a Windows version, having previously run exclusively on Macintosh. Some computer historians date this, the introduction of a significant and non-Microsoft application for Windows, as the start of the success of Windows.

Versions 2.0x used the real-mode memory model, which held it to a maximum of 1 megabyte of memory. In such a form, it could run under a different multitasker like DESQview, which used the 286 Protected Mode. Subsequently, two new versions were published: Windows/286 2.1 and Windows/386 2.1.Like preceding versions of Windows, Windows/286 2.1 used the real-mode memory model, but was the first version to support the HMA.

Windows/386 2.1 had a protected mode kernel with LIM-standard EMS emulation, the predecessor to XMS which would at last shift the topology of IBM PC computing. All Windows and DOS-based applications at the time were real mode, running over the protected mode kernel by using the virtual 8086 mode, which was new with the 80386 processor. After Versions 2.0 and beyond were released, Apple began filing suit against IBM for various copyright infringements. In their defence, Microsoft claimed that their licensing agreement actually afforded them the rights to use Apple features.

Apple claimed that Microsoft had encroached on 170 of their copyrights. After a four-year court case, Microsoft won. The courts stated that the licensing agreement gave Microsoft the rights to use all but nine of the copyrights, and Microsoft later convinced the courts that the other nine copyrights shouldn't be covered by copyright law. Bill Gates asserted that Apple had acquired ideas from the graphical user interface developed by Xerox for Xerox's Alto and Star computers.

On June 1, 1993, Judge Vaughn R. Walker of the U.S. District Court of Northern California ruled in Microsoft's favour in the Apple vs. Microsoft & Hewlett-Packard copyright suit. The judge granted Microsoft's and Hewlett-Packard's motions to dismiss the last remaining copyright infringement claims against Microsoft Windows versions 2.03 and 3.0, as well as HP NewWave.

What would have occurred if Microsoft had lost the lawsuit? Microsoft Windows might never have become the predominant operating system that it is today.

FEATURES

Some individuals with disabilities require assistive technology (AT) in order to access computers. Hundreds of Windows AT third-party products are available, making it possible for almost anyone to use Windows® applications, regardless of their disabilities.

The Microsoft® Windows® operating systems also provides a core set of basic accessibility features and AT applications, which can be deployed on all computers in a computer lab or classroom without additional cost. These applications provide students with basic accessibility features from any workstation, maximizing the inclusiveness of the learning environment.

It should be noted that the AT applications that are bundled with Windows provide only a minimum level of accessibility, not the full set of features that many users require for equal access to the operating system, educational programmes, and other software applications.

Therefore, many educational entities deploy the standard set of Windows AT on all workstations by default, but addditionally 1) provide a small number of dedicated workstations that are equipped with commonly requested third party AT, and 2) are prepared to purchase and install additional AT as needed by specific students.

It should also be noted that the availability of AT does not itself guarantee accessibility. Software applications must be designed in a way that is compatible with AT and other accessibility features of the operating system. The following is a list of basic accessibility features that are included with Windows XP. Previous versions of Windows also included several of these same features.

Display and Readability

These features are designed to increase the visibility of items on the screen.

- Font style, colour, and size of items on the desktop—using the Display options, choose font colour, size and style combinations.
- Icon size—make icons larger for visibility, or smaller for increased screen space.
- Screen resolution—change pixel count to enlarge objects on screen.
- High contrast schemes—select colour combinations that are easier to see.
- Cursor width and blink rate—make the cursor easier to locate, or eliminate the distraction of its blinking.
- Microsoft Magnifier—enlarge portion of screen for better visibility.

Sounds and Speech

These features are designed to make computer sounds easier to hear or distinguish - or, visual alternatives to sound. Speech-to-text options are also available.

- *Sound Volume*: Turn computer sound up or down.
- *Sound Schemes*: Associate computer sounds with particular system events.
- *ShowSounds*: Display captions for speech and sounds.
- *SoundSentry*: Display visual warnings for system sounds.
- *Notification*: Get sound or visual cues when accessibility features are turned on or off.

- *Text-to-Speech*: Hear window command options and text read aloud.

Keyboard and Mouse

These features are designed to make the keyboard and mouse faster and easier to use.

Mouse Options:

- *Double-Click Speed*: Choose how fast to click the mouse button to make a selection.
- *ClickLock*: Highlight or drag without holding down the mouse button.
- *Pointer Speed*: Set how fast the mouse pointer moves on screen.
- *SnapTo*: Move the pointer to the default button in a dialog box.
- *Cursor Blink Rate*: Choose how fast the cursor blinks—or, if it blinks at all.
- *Pointer Trails*: Follow the pointer motion on screen.
- *Hide Pointer While Typing*: Keep pointer from hiding text while typing.
- Show Location of Pointer: Quickly reveal the pointer on screen.
- *Reverse the function of the right and left mouse buttons*: Reverse actions controlled by the right and left mouse buttons.
- *Pointer schemes*: Choose size and colour options for better visibility.

Keyboard Options

- *Character Repeat Rate*: Set how quickly a character repeats when a key is struck.
- *Dvorak Keyboard Layout*: Choose alternative keyboard layouts for people who type with one hand or finger.
- *Sticky Keys*: Allow pressing one key at a time (rather than simultaneously) for key combinations.
- *Filter Keys*: Ignore brief or repeated keystrokes and slow down the repeat rate.
- *Toggle Keys*: Hear tones when pressing certain keys.

- *MouseKeys*: Move the mouse pointer using the numerical keypad.
- *Extra Keyboard Help*: Get ToolTips or other keyboard help in programmes that provide it.

Accessibility Wizard

The Accessibility Wizard is designed to help new users quickly and easily set up groups of accessibility options that address visual, hearing and dexterity needs all in one place. The Accessibility Wizard asks questions about accessibility needs. Then, based on the answers, it configures utilities and settings for individual users. The Accessibility Wizard can be run again at any time to make changes, or changes can be made to individual settings through Control Panel.

LINUX

FUNDAMENTAL OF LINUX

If you truly enjoy working with computers, Linux is the operating system of your dreams. It is more fun than any other computer operating system around. Linux is a computer hobbyist's paradise. However, the reason why Linux is truly revolutionary is that it is Open Software. Our science and technology work owing to the free availability of information, peer review, public critique, and the capablitiy to pick up ideas and modify or extend them. Open Software is an implementation of the scientific method into the field of software development. The freedom to pick-up, modify and extend, that comes with the Linux licence, offers a promise that the software development under Linux licence will continue in the way that science does.

The making of horseshoes, good glass, or measuring time were once closely guarded trade secrets. Science and technology exploded 500 years ago thanks to the sharing of knowledge by the means of printing, and thus breaking the monopoly of the few on the know-how. Why were the science and technology relatively stagnant before the printing era? Because the "trade secret" approach to growth has its limits:

the development continues until the rate of learning equals the rate of forgetting. Moving the know-how to the public domain (printed on paper) shifted the position of the equilibrium to a higher level, which, after 500 years of turbulent development, we are still to achieve. For interested, I can present equations, borrowed from chemical equilibrium field, that describe this in a more formal way. The main point is that printing increased the audience, and allowed passing information across space and time.

In the early days of printing, many of those who dared to share were assassinated for revealing "trade secrets." Linux is for the computer age what Gutenberg was for writing. Hopefully there will be no assassinations this time :-) . Linux does clash, violently at times, with those who claim the "ownership" of information, trying to push time back 500 years. Open Source Linux has also implications for computer security. Imagine a plane based on secret "scientific laws" and built to an unreviewed design, a plane at internals of which nobody but the manufacturer could inspect.

Would you believe that this new, unique, completely proprietary plane, obviously built by clever and well-financed marketers in their basement, is any safer than one built in the open world, under the eyes of thousands of critical engineers and curious hobbyists with no association to the manufacturer? Then why would you trust a secret computer programme? Open-source Linux is ideally suited for a mission-critical application—its security and power are based on robust solutions which are reviewed with no restrictions whatsoever, and continuously improved upon.

Linux is quite different from MS Windows, so do not expect that if you can get around MS Windows, then Linux will be straightforward for you. You may need to learn. On the other hand, if you come from UNIX, Linux will be easy for you.

BENEFITS OF LINUX

Linux can give you:

- A modern, very stable, multi-user, multitasking

environment on your inexpensive PC hardware, at no (or almost no) monetary cost for the software. Linux is a rich and powerful platform—don't think of it as a "poor people" operating system. Out-of-box Linux has as much capability as MS Windows NT with $5000 in software add-ons, is more stable, and requires less powerful hardware for comparable tasks.

- *Standard platform*: Linux is VERY standard—it is essentially a POSIX compliant UNIX. (Yes, Linux is a best-of-the-breed UNIX. The word "UNIX" is not used in conjunction with Linux because "UNIX" is a registered trademark of "The Open Group".) Linux includes all the tools and utilities typically associated with UNIX, plus more, significantly more than even the most expensive commercial UNIX implementations. To run Linux software, UNIX vendors these days implement "Linux compatiblity layers" into their platforms.
- Unsurpassed computing power, portability, flexibility, and customizibility. A Linux cluster recently (April 1999) beat a Cray supercomputer in a standard benchmark. Linux is most popular on Intel-based PCs (price of the hardware), but it runs very well on numerous other hardware platforms, from toy-like to mainframes. One distribution (Debian) expresses the idea like this: "Linux, The Universal Operating System." Linux can be customised to perform almost any computing task.
- Advanced graphical user interface. Linux uses a standard, network-transparent X-windowing system with a "window manager" (typically KDE or GNOME). The graphical desktop under Linux can be made to look like MS Windows (or probably ANY other graphical user interface of your choice).
- Dozens of excellent, free, general-interest desktop applications. These include a range of web browsers, email programmes, word processors, spreadsheets,

bitmap and vector graphics programmes, file managers, audio players, CD writers, some good games, etc.

- Thousands of free applets, tools, and smaller programmes. "Small is beautiful" goes well with Linux philosophy. The small Linux tools and applets often work in tandem to perform more complex tasks.
- Hundreds of specialized applications built by researchers around the world (astronomy, information technology, chemistry, physics, engineering, linguistics, biology, ...). In many fields, Linux seems like "the only" operating system in existence (try to find out what your friend astronomer runs on her computer). The software in this category is typically not very easy to use, but if you want the power, it is the best software that humanity has in these areas.
- Scores of top-of-the line commercial programmes including all the big databases (e.g., Oracle, Sybase, but no Microsoft's). Many (most?) of these are offered free for developers and for personal use.
- *A truly great learning platform*: If you are a parent, you should be really glad your daughter/son does Linux—s/he will surely learn something of lasting value. If you are a teacher, you should consider the installation of Linux at your school. "It is indeed a strange world when educators need to be convinced that sharing information, as opposed to concealing information, is a good thing". You select Linux if you care to provide education, not training. The better the university, the greater the chance their computer department uses Linux in teaching. For example, under Linux, you can immediately begin modifying and compiling for yourself a spreadsheet application which is in every bit as advanced and capable as MS Excel. Linux puts you right on the cutting edge (in technology, project management, QA, methodology

of science). Many teachers won't use Linux in schools because they are lacking in computer education themselves.

- Excellent networking capability built into your operating system. You think you don't need a network? Once you try home networking, you will never be able to live without it! How about connecting the two or more computers that you have at home and sharing your hard drives, CDROM(s), sound card(s), modem, printer(s), etc.? How about browsing the net on two or more machines at the same time using a single Internet connection? How about playing a game with your son over your home network? Even your old 386 with Win3.11 may become useful again when connected to your Linux Pentium server and when it is able to use your network resources. All necessary networking software comes with standard Linux, free, just setup is required. And it is not second-rate shareware—it is exactly the same software that runs most of the Internet (the Apache software runs more than 50% of all Internet web servers and Sendmail touches some 70% of all e-mail). The pleasure of home networking is something I was able to discover only owing to Linux.
- Connectivity to Microsoft, Novel, and Apple proprietary networking. Reading/writing to your DOS/MS Windows and other disk formats. This includes "transparent" use of data stored on the legacy MS Windows partition of your hard drive(s).
- State-of-the-art development platform with many best-of-the-kind programming languages and tools coming free with the operating system. Access to all the operating system source codes, should you require it, is also free. The "C" compiler that comes standard with Linux can compile code for more platforms than (probably) any other compiler on earth. Perl, Python, Guile, Tcl, Ruby, powerful "shell"

The Major Differences

Linux is free, whereas MS Windows costs money. Same for applications. If MS Windows or Office comes preinstalled with the computer it is unlikely it is free. Ask in the store to take it off your computer and you are likely to obtain a discount, at least in smaller stores.

- Linux file formats are free, so you can access them in a variety of ways. On MS Windows, the common practice is to make you lock your own data in secret formats that can only be accessed with tools leased to you at the vendor's price. How corrupt (or incompetent?) must be the politicians who lock our public records into these formats! "What we will get with Microsoft is a three-year lease on a health record we need to keep for 100 years" [http://news.bbc.co.uk/hi/english/health/newsid_1694000/1694372.stm].
- With Linux, you are unlikely to violate any licence agreement—all the software is happily yours. With MS Windows you likely already violate all kinds of licenses and you could be pronounced a computer pirate if only a smart lawyer was after you (don't worry, most likely none is after you).
- MS Windows tries to be the "lowest-common-denominator" operating system (for better or worse), whereas Linux is built for more sophisticated, feature-hungry computer users (for better or worse).
- *MS Windows is based on DOS*: Linux is based on UNIX. MS Windows Graphical User Interface (GUI) is based on Microsoft-owned specifications. Linux GUI is based on an industry-standard network-transparent X-Windowing system.
- Linux beats Windows hands down on network features, as a development platform, in data processing capabilities, and as a scientific workstation. MS Windows desktop has a more polished appearance, smoother general business

applications, and many more games for kids (these are not better games though—Linux games tend to be more sophisticated).

- Linux is more feature-rich than you could imagine. Heard on the Internet: "Two big products came from the University of California: UNIX and LSD. And I don't think it's a coincidence." MS Windows is simpler.

LINUX IS A GOOD

The Linux community has repeatedly been labeled "religious zealots" by journalists whose well-established computer magazines received massive feedback after they had published highly unfair articles on Linux. So yes, the Linux community is numerous, literate, and willing to express its opinions. And many computer journalists/magazines know that Linux means less money for them (users pay less for their computing and the associated advertisement, while expecting more). Does this explain the "zealots"?

Face it, you salespeople pretending to be journalists. There is hardly any integrity left in the computing press. How many words on Linux did your PC Magazine (or any other IT magazine) publish by 1999-01-01? Wasn't Linux at least an interesting technology by that time? It surely was, yet you conspired to keep your readership in the dark, selling your journalistic integrity for a few dollars. And now, after Linux has surfaced in the mainstream (non-computer) media, you keep writing misleading articles about it saying "yah, but it will/cannot/may ...." whatever (trying the "fear, uncertainty and doubt" tactics to kill it).

And adding "Microsoft is already ...", continuing to write about the vaporware and the future paradise in the face of the increasingly stealthy, unstable, pricey, architecturally unsound computer platform, whose greatest achievement has been exhorting unheard-of-before money by denying inter-operatibility, and killing any existing or proposed standard (by "embracing" and then proprietary-extending it). Whom do you serve? Surely not your readers.

You think "self-serving" is OK in business? How pathetic must your business be then! I always thought that business was a social contract in which we exchange good values, for a mutual benefit. As I read history, societies use to hang / guillotine / electrocute those members who really persisted in their self-serving business. Well, times have changed. A bit for the better, a bit for the worse :)) To be fair, there seems to be a number of hard-core devotees around any computer programme/platform, and Linux might have accummulated a fair share of them. Oh, well, you may be religious about whatever you like.

COMPARISON OF LINUX WITH MS-DOS AND WINDOWS

LINUX VS MS-DOS

DOS was the first operating system I learned to use. I remember a test by my tutor in which one had to create a hierarchical set of directories. This probably sounds trivial to anyone familiar with graphical user interfaces, but then the scenario was very different. It even looks ancient by today's standards. Windows 95 hadn't been released at that time, and Linux was unheard of in India. I liked DOS much better than Windows 3.1, which looked quite flimsy and unstable, not to mention that it was a big memory hog. DOS is quite different from Linux in many ways.

DOS does not provide any graphical user interface and you have to learn at least a dozen commands with its numerous options to do some basic tasks like copying a file or moving between the directories. Even a minor spelling mistake can result in a "Bad command or file name" error.

DOS does not support the concept of multi-users; each and every user has to customise the system according to his need every time he wants to work on it. It was also not a multitasking system. This meant that you could not check out the value of a calculation when typing a letter without closing that application first. DOS also does not have any in built security features. This was acceptable as long as you did not want a networking system. There was other variants of MS-DOS, like PC-DOS from IBM and some others, which tried to add the missing features. Some of the deficiencies have been resolved using third party utilities but basic limitations like the arcane 640kb-memory limit and single-tasking were not acceptable to many.

Now in case you are wondering why anyone would care to use DOS, I will point out some advantages. Basically DOS has had very different goals from that of Linux. It was a very cheap system (as far as cost is concerned) and it was quite usable with its minimalist set of features. It was a simple system to work with. There weren't too many complications to worry about if you didn't want to develop anything on it. It was arguably the world's most popular operating system and it had a comfortable number of applications for common tasks.

Files and Directories

The files in Linux can be very long, up-to 255 characters like Windows, and they do not always have extensions. The executable files are identified through an attribute rather than the extension. File extensions are less important to Linux than for DOS and Windows, since Linux usually identifies files by a unique identification code called the magic number that depends on the file type. Directories are similar to that of DOS and follow a hierarchical structure. The path names are separated by forward slashes (/)in Linux whereas DOS and Windows uses back slashes (\). *For example*:

```
% cd /mnt/cdrom
```

A / denotes the root and .. stands for the parent directory, similar to DOS.

In bash shells, the ~ symbol maybe used to jump to the home directory quickly. *For example*:

```
% cd ~
```

Linux Shell

Several of the DOS commands have Linux equivalents. The Linux shell is similar to the DOS command line but is far more powerful, and I found that it was also more workable with features like colour highlighting and friendlier navigation capabilities, depending on the particular shell you are using.

Most Linux distributions come with the Bash (Bourne Again SHell) as the default. There are several others, like the Korn shell and the C shell. They are usually similar. It's recommended that you learn to work with one shell completely before trying out the others. Things usually get complicated if you want to run shell scripts, which are similar to batch files (files with the .bat extension) under DOS.

Running DOS Programmes Under Linux

There is a DOS emulator called dosemu www.dosemu.org for Linux that is capable of running DOS programmes under the Linux operating system. This software is still under development; you may wish to try it out though. It is known to be fairly usable at least for some applications. If you are looking for Linux just to use DOS programmes for free then try using FreeDOS www.freedos.org. That should be much better than Linux.

LINUX VS. WINDOWS

As I have said before Windows is more or less similar to Linux. When people are introduced to Linux they are at first intimidated by the system. It has different kinds of graphical interfaces and things don't always work as they are expected to. When users look at me in a puzzled manner I demonstrate in some easy ways how common tasks like changing the desktop wallpaper or playing a song is similar to Windows. The problem with this kind of approach is that the users complain very soon that Linux doesn't offer them much more than Windows does :-).

I agree with them to a certain extent on this. There are some limitations to what you can expect from an operating system. You just can't expect Linux to work like a 3D-shooter game or something. Of course, there are many differences in the shell, the choice of user interfaces and the philosophy and goals of the operating system. Linux is developed as a open system in which the source code of the core Linux system (kernel) is available for anyone for free but how this could affect the end user is difficult to explain initially.

The user interface is probably the first thing you notice when you begin to use the Linux system. Windows offers a single, monolithic user interface, which is more or less the same across all the versions. In contrast, Linux has two major desktop environments called KDE and Gnome. KDE has a built-in window manager, while Gnome is supported by many, such as Sawfish and Enlightenment.

The decision of choosing one among the desktop environments and windows managers is left to you. Some of them can run efficiently in a system with low amounts of memory and some of them are designed to look like a game console. KDE would be more similar to Windows, and Gnome with the Enlightenment window manager was fancy enough for me. Try out some of the popular ones before making the decision. Let's take a look at Windows in more detail so that you can clearly make out the differences.

Versions of Windows

Windows has two major series, a desktop oriented series (Windows 9x) And a network oriented series Windows.There are also other versions like Windows CE for embedded systems.

Windows 9x Series

Before Windows 95 was released, all versions of Windows until version 3.1 were graphical platforms on top of DOS. This offered limited capability for multitasking and the Programme Manager interface was cluttered with no distinct hierarchy. Windows 95 was a 32-bit operating system and a major improvement in user interface with its "Desktop" concept adapted from the Macintosh user interface.

It also offered limited compatibility with previous versions of Windows and DOS. Stability was also improved Windows 98 and Windows ME offered some more features though nothing major was added. The more recent version called Windows XP is considerably more stable due to incorporating the Windows 2000 kernel, and is comparatively friendlier and easier due to an attractive interface.

Windows NT Series

Windows NT is considerably stable but demands more resources. It supports the Intel architecture, and at one time the Digital alpha and MIPS processors, but I believe those have been dropped now. It managed to replace UNIX in small-scale networks due to the similarity to the popular Windows 95 interface. The latest incarnation called Windows 2000 provides a few more administrative utilities and services.

Chapter 5

Computer Memory

Computer memory can refer to many types of memory within a computer, but, typically, it refers to random access memory (RAM). It is physically found on computer chips that are inserted onto the computer's motherboard. RAM is electionic, rather than mechanical; that is, it does not have moving parts and therefore data access to it is very fast. Modern computers often have somewhere between 256 MB (megabytes) and 2 GB (gigabytes) of RAM, although there are, of course, computers with more or less RAM.

RAM is also volatile, meaning that it gets lost when the computer is switched off. The expensive nature of RAM spurred the creation of another type of computer memory called virtual memory. With virtual memory, a slow down in performance is observed only when you try to operate a programme whose files are in the virtual memory. In essence, this slow down is only observed when shifting between programmes. In this way, virtual memory often provides a cheaper alternative to RAM.

A third type of computer memory is cache. There are two types of cache. Primary cache, or level 1 cache, is built right into the central processing unit (CPU) and ensures instant availability of data that the CPU frequently needs. Secondary cache, or level 2 cache, is usually built on a memory chip, is located very close to the CPU, and has a direct connection to the CPU through a dedicated circuit. Secondary cache is bigger in capacity than primary cache. Cache basically speeds up the rate at which data moves from the main memory to the CPU. The registers form a fourth type of computer memory. These are units within the CPU that contain specific types of data, especially for the Arithmetic and Logic Unit (ALU). A final group of computer memory is called flash. This is a solid-state, rewritable type of memory. Examples of flash memory include BIOS and memory cards. Just like the RAM, they are electronic and not mechanical. They are also non-volatile, and are therefore suitable for digital cameras, mobile phones and other miniaturized computers

OVERVIEW

The system memory is the place where the computer holds current programmes and data that are in use. There are various levels of computer memory (memory), including ROM, RAM, cache, page and graphics, each with specific objectives for system operation. This section focusses on the role of computer memory, and the technology behind it.

Although memory is used in many different forms around modern PC systems, it can be divided into two essential types: RAM and ROM. ROM, or Read Only Memory, is relatively small, but essential to how a computer works. ROM is always found on motherboards, but is increasingly found on graphics cards and some other expansion cards and peripherals. Generally speaking, ROM does not change. It forms the basic instruction set for operating the hardware in the system, and the data within remains intact even when the computer is shut down. It is possible to update ROM, but it's only done rarely, and at need. If ROM is damaged, the computer system simply cannot function.

RAM, or Random Access Memory, is "volatile." This means that it only holds data while power is present. RAM changes constantly as the system operates, providing the storage for all data required by the operating system and software. Because of the demands made by increasingly powerful operating systems and software, system RAM requirements have accelerated dramatically over time. For instance, at the turn of the millennium a typical computer may have only 128Mb of RAM in total, but in 2007 computers commonly ship with 2Gb of RAM installed, and may include graphics cards with their own additional 512Mb of RAM and more. Clearly, modern computers have significantly more memory than the first PCs of the early 1980s, and this has had an effect on development of the PC's architecture. The trouble is, storing and retrieving data from a large block of memory is more time-consuming than from a small block. With a large amount of memory, the difference in time between a register access and a memory access is very great, and this has resulted in extra layers of cache in the storage hierarchy.

When accessing memory, a fast processor will demand a great deal from RAM. At worst, the CPU may have to waste clock cycles while it waits for data to be retrieved. Faster memory designs and motherboard buses can help, but since the 1990s "cache memory" has been employed as standard between the main memory and the processor. Not only this, CPU architecture has also evolved to include ever larger internal caches. The organization of data this way is immensely complex, and the system uses ingenious electronic controls to ensure that the data the processor needs next is already in cache, physically closer to the processor and ready for fast retrieval and manipulation. Read on for a closer look at the technology behind computer memory, and how developments in RAM and ROM have enabled systems to function with seemingly exponentially increasing power.

CLASSIFICATION OF MEMORY

RAM

Random access memory or RAM most commonly refers to computer chips that temporarily store dynamic data to enhance computer performance. By storing frequently used or active files in random access memory, the computer can access the data faster than if it to retrieve it from the far-larger hard drive. Random access memory is also used in printers and other devices. Random access memory is volatile memory, meaning it loses its contents once power is cut. This is different from non-volatile memory such as hard disks and flash memory, which do not require a power source to retain data.

When a computer shuts down properly, all data located in random access memory is committed to permanent storage on the hard drive or flash drive. At the next boot-up, RAM begins to fill with programmes automatically loaded at startup, and with files opened by the user.

There are several different types of random access memory chips which come several to a "stick." A stick of RAM is a small circuit board shaped like a large stick of gum. Sticks of RAM fit into "banks" on the motherboard. Adding one or more sticks increases RAM storage and performance. Random access memory is categorized by architecture and speed. As technology progresses, RAM chips become faster and employ new standards so that RAM must be matched to a compatible motherboard. The motherboard will only support certain types of random access memory, and it will also have a limit as to the amount of RAM it can support.

For example, one motherboard may support dual-channel Synchronous Dynamic Random Access Memory (SDRAM), while an older motherboard might only support Single In-line Memory Modules (SIMMS) or Dual In-line Memory Modules (DIMMS). Since random access memory can improve performance, the type and amount of RAM a motherboard will support becomes a major factor when considering a new computer. If there is a faster, better random access memory chip on the market, the buyer will want to consider purchasing a motherboard capable of using it. A year down the road, that 'new' RAM might be standard, while the buyer may be stuck with an old style motherboard. A new variety of non-volatile random access memory made with nanotubes or other technologies will likely be forthcoming in the near future.

These RAM chips would retain data when powered down. Memory, which is commonly referred to as RAM (Random Access Memory), is a temporary (Volatile) storage area utilized by the CPU. Before a programme can be run, the programme is loaded into the memory which allows the CPU direct access to the programme. Memory is a necessity for any computer and it is recommend that you have at least 64MB of memory for your IBM or Macintosh. Memory is commonly confused with Hard Drive Space. There are two types of memory; the first type of memory is the memory explained in the above paragraph, this memory is available in computer chips; the other type of memory is actually Hard Drive Space which is stored on the computer Hard Disk Drive. The Hard drive is actually a physical drive which contains several parts and is generally larger than the amount of memory found in your computer. The below explanation wil help in describing the most commonly found types of RAM in computers.

SINGLE IN-LINE MEMORY MODULE (SIMM)

A slender circuit board dedicated to storing memory chips. Each chip is capable of holding 8 to 9 chips per board, the ninth chip usually an error-checking chip (parity / non parity). The typical bus from the chip to the motherboard is 32-bits wide. When upgrading a Pentium motherboard you will be required to upgrade 2 of the same type of chips at the same time to accommodate the Pentium processor.

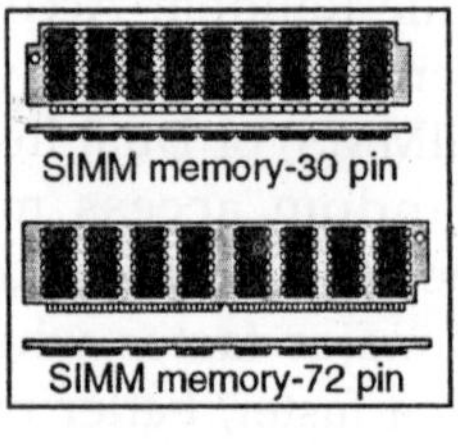

SPEED

Can determine the size amount of the chip by looking at the part number of each chip on the SIMM board. For 2-, 8- and 9- chip SIMMs, all the chips should have the same part numbers. Look at the number that ends with a dash and a digit such as "-7". This is the rate speed or nanoseconds of the chip. With "-7" this would indicate that the memory is 70ns.

SIZE

Look at the four digits to the left of this number; these often carry information about the number of bits in the chip. A 4256 indicates 256K bits arranged in sets of four, for a total of 1Mb. "1000" indicates 1MB of bits arranged in one set. With some types of memory, the last one or two digits may be changed to indicate different kinds of memory; there are 1MB chips that end with 4256, 4257, and 4258. In this case, round the last digits to an even 256 or thousand. Three-chip SIMMs will typically have two larger chips that are four times the capacity of the third chip (because 4 plus 4 plus 1 makes 9, which is the number of bits needed per byte including parity).

PARITY / NON PARITY

To determine if the SIMM is Parity / Non Parity, look for x36 / x9 which indicate that the chip is parity (Error checking). x36 is used with 72-pin SIMMs and x9 is for 30-pin SIMMs. If x32 / x8 this would be an indication that the chip in Non Parity (Non Error checking) x32 is used with 72-pin SIMMs and x8 is used with 30-pin SIMMs. Another method: count the chips. If you see three or nine discrete chips, the SIMM probably includes a parity. If there are two or eight chips, the SIMM probably does not include parity bit. In this case, divide the number of bits by 8 to determine bytes.

SIMM Memory and Pentium Computers

When updating the computer's memory with a Pentium processor, ensure that you purchase two SIMMs rather than one. Such as if planning to upgrade to 32 MB of RAM that you use two 16 MB SIMMs rather than one. This must be done to allow the memory to work properly with the Pentium processor.

DUAL IN-LINE MEMORY MODULE (DIMM)

Type of Circuit board that holds memory chips. DIMMS have a 64-bit path because of the Pentium Processor requirements. Because of the new bit path, DIMMS can be installed one at a time un-like SIMMs which on a Pentium would require two be added.

Some of the Advantages DIMMs Have Over SIMMs

DIMMs have separate contacts on each side of the board, thereby providing twice as much data as a single SIMM. The command address and control signals are buffered on the DIMMs. With heavy memory requirements this will reduce the loading effort of the memory.

STATIC RAM (SRAM)

Static RAM is a type of RAM that holds its data without external refresh, for as long as power is supplied to the circuit. This is contrasted to dynamic RAM (DRAM), which must be refreshed many times per second in order to hold its data contents. SRAMs are used for specific applications within the PC, where their strengths outweigh their weaknesses compared to DRAM:

- *Simplicity*: SRAMs don't require external refresh circuitry or other work in order for them to keep their data intact.
- *Speed*: SRAM is faster than DRAM.

In contrast, SRAMs have the following weaknesses, compared to DRAMs:

- *Cost*: SRAM is, byte for byte, several times more expensive than DRAM.
- *Size*: SRAMs take up much more space than DRAMs (which is part of why the cost is higher).

These advantages and disadvantages taken together obviously show that performance-wise, SRAM is superior to DRAM, and we would use it exclusively if only we could do so economically.

Unfortunately, 32 MB of SRAM would be prohibitively large and costly, which is why DRAM is used for system memory. SRAMs are used instead for level 1 cache and level 2 cache memory, for which it is perfectly suited; cache memory needs to be very fast, and not very large. SRAM is manufactured in a way rather similar to how processors are: highly-integrated transistor patterns photo-etched into silicon. Each SRAM bit is comprised of between four and six transistors, which is why SRAM takes up much more space compared to DRAM, which uses only one (plus a capacitor). Because an SRAM chip is comprised of thousands or millions of identical cells, it is much easier to make than a CPU, which is a large die with a non-repetitive structure.

DYNAMIC RAM (DRAM)

Dynamic RAM is a type of RAM that only holds its data if it is continuously accessed by special logic called a refresh circuit. Many hundreds of times each second, this circuitry reads the contents of each memory cell, whether the memory cell is being used at that time by the computers or not.

Due to the way in which the cells are constructed, the reading action itself refreshes the contents of the memory. If this is not done regularly, then the DRAM will lose its contents, even if it continues to have power supplied to it. This refreshing action is why the memory is called dynamic. All PCs use DRAM for their main system memory, instead of SRAM, even though DRAMs are slower than SRAMs and require the overhead of the refresh circuitry.

It may seem weird to want to make the computer's memory out of something that can only hold a value for a fraction of a second. In fact, DRAMs are both more complicated and slower than SRAMs.

The reason that DRAMs are used is simple: they are much cheaper and take up much less space, typically 1/4 the silicon area of SRAMs or less. To build a 64 MB core memory from SRAMs would be very expensive. The overhead of the refresh circuit is tolerated in order to allow the use of large amounts of inexpensive, compact memory.

The refresh circuitry itself is almost never a problem; many years of using DRAM has caused the design of these circuits to be all but perfected. DRAMs are smaller and less expensive than SRAMs because SRAMs are made from four to six transistors (or more) per bit, DRAMs use only one, plus a capacitor.

The capacitor, when energized, holds an electrical charge if the bit contains a "1" or no charge if it contains a "0". The transistor is used to read the contents of the capacitor. The problem with capacitors is that they only hold a charge for a short period of time, and then it fades away. These capacitors are tiny, so their charges fade particularly quickly.

This is why the refresh circuitry is needed: to read the contents of every cell and refresh them with a fresh "charge" before the contents fade away and are lost. Refreshing is done by reading every "row" in the memory chip one row at a time; the process of reading the contents of each capacitor re-establishes the charge.

DRAM is manufactured using a similar process to how processors are: a silicon substrate is etched with the patterns that make the transistors and capacitors (and support structures) that comprise each bit. DRAM costs much less than a processor because it is a series of simple, repeated structures, so there isn't the complexity of making a single chip with several million individually-located transistors.

DDR-SDRAM

The DDR-SDRAM (Double Data Rate SDRAM) is a memory, based on the SDRAM technology, which doubles the transfer rate of the SDRAM using the same frequency. Data are read or written into memory based on a clock. Standard DRAM memories use a method known as SDR (Single Data Rate) involving reading or writing a piece of data at each leading edge.

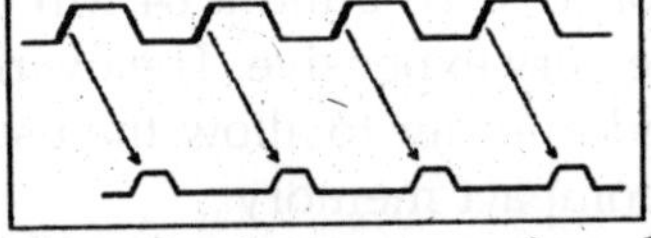

The DDR doubles the frequency of reading/writing, with a clock at the same frequency, by sending data to each leading edge and to each trailing edge.

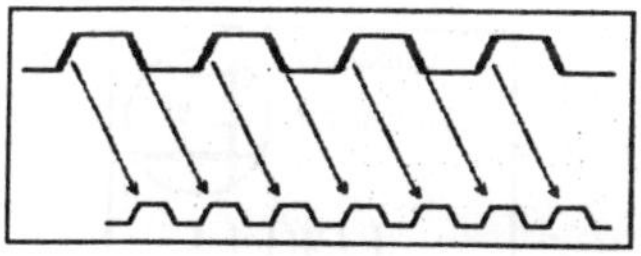

DDR memories generally have a product name such as PCXXXX where "XXXX" represents the speed in Mo/s.

DDR2-SDRAM

DDR2 (or DDR-II) memory achieves speeds that are twice as high as those of the DDR with the same external frequency. QDR (Quadruple Data Rate or quad-pumped) designates the reading and writing method used. DDR2 memory in fact uses two separate channels for reading and writing, so that it is able to send or receive twice as much data as the DDR.

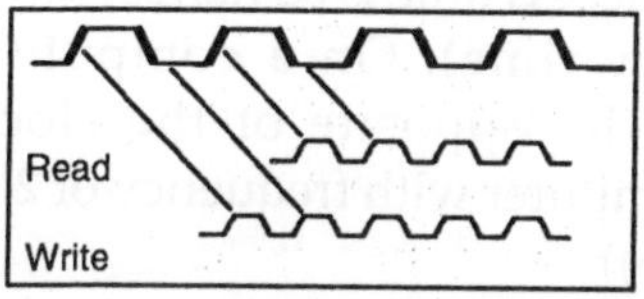

DDR2 also has more connectors than the classic DDR (240 for DDR2 compared with 184 for DDR).

OPERATION OF RANDOM ACESS MEMORY

The random access memory comprises hundreds of thousands of small capacitors that store loads. When loaded, the logical state of the capacitor is equal to 1, otherwise it is 0, meaning that each capacitor represents one memory bit.

Given that the capacitors become discharged they must be constantly recharged (the exact term is refresh) at regular intervals, known as the refresh cycle. DRAM memories for example require refresh cycles of around 15 nanoseconds (ns).

Each capacitor is coupled with a transistor (MOS-type) enabling "recovery" or amendment of the status of the capacitor. These transistors are arranged in the form of a table (matrix) thus we access a memory box (also called memory point) via a line and a column..

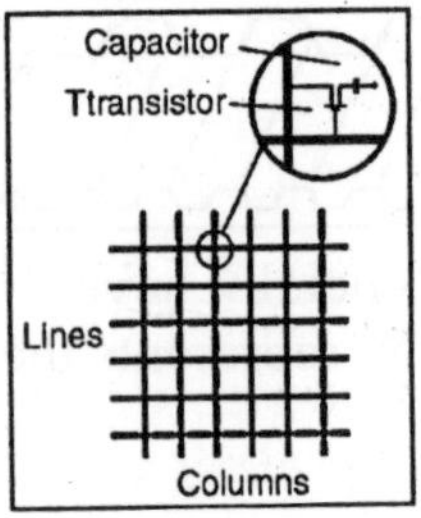

Each memory point is thus characterised by an address which corresponds to a row number and a column number. This access is not instant and the access time period is known as latency time.

Consequently, time required for access to data in the memory is equal to cycle time plus latency time. Thus, for a DRAM memory, access time is 60 nanoseconds (35ns cycle time and 25ns latency time). On a computer, the cycle time corresponds to the opposite of the clock frequency; for example, for a computer with frequency of 200 MHz, cycle time is 5 ns (1/200*106)).

Consequently a computer with high frequency using memories with access time much longer than the processor cycle time must perform wait states to access the memory. For a computer with frequency of 200 MHz using DRAM memories (and access time of 60ns), there are 11 wait states for a transfer cycle. The computer's performance decreases as the number of wait states increases, therefore we recommend the use of faster memories.

READ ONLY MEMORY

DEFINITION

ROM is an integrated-circuit memory chip that contains configuration data. ROM is commonly called firmware because its programming is fully embedded into the ROM chip. As such, ROM is a hardware and software in one.

Because data is fully incorporated at the ROM chip's manufacture, data stored can neither be erased nor replaced. This means permanent and secure data storage. However, if a mistake is made in manufacture, a ROM chip becomes unusable. The most expensive stage of ROM manufacture, therefore, is creating the template. If a template is readily available, duplicating the ROM chip is very easy and affordable.

A ROM chip is also non-volatile so data stored in it is not lost when power is turned off. There is a type of memory that stores data without electrical current; it is the ROM (Read Only Memory) or is sometimes called non-volatile memory as it is not erased when the system is switched off.

This type of memory lets you stored the data needed to start up the computer. Indeed, this information cannot be stored on the hard disk since the disk parameters (vital for its initialisation) are part of these data which are essential for booting.

Different ROM-type memories contain these essential start-up data, that is:

- The BIOS is a programme for controlling the system's main input-output interfaces, hence the name BIOS ROM which is sometimes given to the read-only memory chip of the mother board which hosts it.
- *The bootstrap loader*: a programme for loading (random access) memory into the operating system and launching it. This generally seeks the operating system on the floppy drive then on the hard disk, which allows the operating system to be launched from a system floppy disk in the event of malfunction of the system installed on the hard disk.
- The CMOS Setup is the screen displayed when the computer starts up and which is used to amend the system parameters (often wrongly referred to as BIOS).
- The Power-On Self Test (POST), a programme that runs automatically when the system is booted, thus allowing the system to be tested (this is why the system "counts" the RAM at start-up).

Given that ROM are much slower than RAM memories (access time for a ROM is around 150 ns whereas for SDRAM it is around 10 ns), the instructions given in the ROM are sometimes copied to the RAM at start-up; this is known as shadowing, though is usually referred to as shadow memory). One major type of memory that is used in PCs is called read-only memory, or ROM for short. ROM is a type of memory that normally can only be read, as opposed to RAM which can be both read and written.

There are two main reasons that read-only memory is used for certain functions within the PC:

- *Permanence*: The values stored in ROM are always there, whether the power is on or not. A ROM can be removed from the PC, stored for an indefinite period of time, and then replaced, and the data it contains will still be there. For this reason, it is called non-volatile storage. A hard disk is also non-volatile, for the same reason, but regular RAM is not.
- *Security*: The fact that ROM cannot easily be modified provides a measure of security against accidental (or malicious) changes to its contents. You are not going to find viruses infecting true ROMs, for example; it's just not possible. (It's technically possible with erasable EPROMs, though in practice never seen.)

Read-only memory is most commonly used to store system-level programmes that we want to have available to the PC at all times. The most common example is the system BIOS programme, which is stored in a ROM called (amazingly enough) the system BIOS ROM.

Having this in a permanent ROM means it is available when the power is turned on so that the PC can use it to boot up the system. Remember that when you first turn on the PC the system memory is empty, so there has to be something for the PC to use when it starts up.

While the whole point of a ROM is supposed to be that the contents cannot be changed, there are times when being able to change the contents of a ROM can be very useful. There are several ROM variants that can be changed under certain circumstances; these can be thought of as "mostly read-only memory" :^)

TYPES OF ROMS

There are types of ROMs with a description of their relative modifiability.

ROM

A regular ROM is constructed from hard-wired logic, encoded in the silicon itself, much the way that a processor is. It is designed to perform a specific function and cannot be changed. This is inflexible and so regular ROMs are only used generally for programmes that are static (not changing often) and mass-produced. This product is analagous to a commercial software CD-ROM that you purchase in a store.

Programmable ROM (PROM)

This is a type of ROM that can be programmed using special equipment; it can be written to, but only once. This is useful for companies that make their own ROMs from software they write, because when they change their code they can create new PROMs without requiring expensive equipment. This is similar to the way a CD-ROM recorder works by letting you "burn" programmes onto blanks once and then letting you read from them many times. In fact, programming a PROM is also called burning, just like burning a CD-R, and it is comparable in terms of its flexibility.

Erasable Programmable ROM (EPROM)

An EPROM is a ROM that can be erased and reprogrammed. A little glass window is installed in the top of the ROM package, through which you can actually see the chip that holds the memory. Ultraviolet light of a specific frequency can be shined through this window for a specified period of time, which will erase the EPROM and allow it to be reprogrammed again. Obviously this is much more useful than a regular PROM, but it does require the erasing light. Continuing the "CD" analogy, this technology is analogous to a reusable CD-RW.

Electrically Erasable Programmable ROM (EEPROM)

The next level of erasability is the EEPROM, which can

be erased under software control. This is the most flexible type of ROM, and is now commonly used for holding BIOS programmes.

When you hear reference to a "flash BIOS" or doing a BIOS upgrade by "flashing", this refers to reprogramming the BIOS EEPROM with a special software programme. Here we are blurring the line a bit between what "read-only" really means, but remember that this rewriting is done maybe once a year or so, compared to real read-write memory (RAM) where rewriting is done often many times per second!

SECONDARY STORAGE DEVICES

DEFINITION

Storage Devices are the data storage devices that are used in the computers to store the data. The computer has many types of data storage devices. Some of them can be classified as the removable data Storage Devices and the others as the non removable data Storage Devices. The data Storage Devices come in many sizes and shapes. And more over the technology used for the storage of the data over them is also altogether different.

The storage devices are one of the most important components of the computer system. The memory is of two types; one is the primary memory and the other one is the secondary memory. The primary memory is the volatile memory and the secondary memory is the non volatile memory. The volatile memory is the kind of the memory that is erasable and the non volatile memory is the one where in the contents cannot be erased.

Basically when we talk about the data storage devices it is generally assumed to be the secondary memory. The secondary memory is used to store the data permanently in the computer. The secondary storage devices are usually as follows: hard disk drives - this is the most common type of storage device that is used in almost all the computer systems. The other ones include the floppy disk drives, the CD ROM, and the DVD ROM. The flash memory, the USB data card etc.

The storage devices are used to record the data over any storage surface. The memories may also be of different types depending upon the architecture and the design like the optical data storage memory, magnetic media storage and the mechanical storage media etc and also the flash memory devices etc. The storage devices are actually defined as the peripheral unit which holds the data like the tape, disk, or flash memory card etc.

The most of the drives that are used for the purpose of data storage are fragile and the data can be easily corrupted in them. The data storage devices are the ones that are also used for the backup and the archiving of the data. The data storage devices were at a time in the past used to be too costly and expensive. But these days the data storage devices are becoming cheap day by day. Hence the data storage devices price is falling. So, we are in a position to get a storage device for a comparatively cheaper price than the earlier drive. The technology is improving a lot and now the memory storage capacity has gone up TB.

The data in the storage devices can be in the form of the files, data bases, digital video and the audio etc. The storage devices that are called as the non volatile can store the data permanently until otherwise erased purposely. This is in the case of the hard disk drives or the floppy disk drives. The other kinds of the storage media like for example the CD and the DVD can even have again two types of the storage; the first one is that in which the data once written cannot be erased.

It is stored permanently over it. While the second type of the CD's or the DVD's are called as the rewritable; where in the data that is once written can be erased completely and the same storage device can be used again for storing the different data. The storage devices are used to record the data over any storage surface.

The memories may also be of different types depending upon the architecture and the design like the optical data storage memory, magnetic media storage and the mechanical storage media etc and also the flash memory devices etc. The storage devices are actually defined as the peripheral unit which holds the data like the tape, disk, or flash memory card etc. The most of the drives that are used for the purpose of data storage are fragile and the data can be easily corrupted in them. The data storage devices are the ones that are also used for the backup and the archiving of the data. The data storage devices were at a time in the past used to be too costly and expensive.

But these days the data storage devices are becoming cheap day by day. Hence the data storage devices price is falling. So, we are in a position to get a storage device for a comparatively cheaper price than the earlier drive. The technology is improving a lot and now the memory storage capacity has gone up TB. The data in the storage devices can be in the form of the files, databases, digital video and the audio etc. The storage devices that are called as the non volatile can store the data permanently until otherwise erased purposely. This is in the case of the hard disk drives or the floppy disk drives.

The other kinds of the storage media like for example the CD and the DVD can even have again two types of the storage; the first one is that in which the data once written cannot be erased. It is stored permanently over it. While the second type of the CD's or the DVD's are called as the rewritable; where in the data that is once written can be erased completely and the same storage device can be used again for storing the different data.

TYPES OF STORAGE DEVICES

REMOVABLE DATA STORAGE DEVICES

The Removable Storage Media are the types of storage devices that are used for the storage of the data. The main reason for using the removable storage media is the ease of portability. That is the ease with which the data can be transferred. The data is of importance and is necessary for the movement in some cases. Here the case of portability of the storage device comes into the picture. The removable storage media serves the same purpose. More over there are many application of the storage of the data over the removable media. The first and the foremost is the portability that is already discussed above. The next is the issue of the backup and archiving of the data that is important and also sensitive in nature. The backup of data is as important as the storage of data is important.

The CD and the DVD are key players in the removable storage types that are used for the purpose of backup and archiving of the data. The main reason for storing the data over the removable devices is that the data can be easily moved physically from one place to another at the time of any disaster or any other casualty.

The floppy disk drive was the removable storage media that was used for the purpose of storing the data over the disk for the backup. This was the case in the 80's; but as the pace has increased in the technology the CD's and the DVD's had gained momentum for the purpose of providing backup to the data. The floppy disk drives that are available even today do not provide enough memory capacity. And now the concept of the flash memory devices is doing rounds for providing data transfer from place to another.

There are some situations where in the normal data transfer through the networking is not possible. But as in the case of the removal storage media the data transfer can be easily done. Hence the main advantage regarding the removal storage media is the data transfer from the computers to the other computers where there is no existence of the network. The data transfer facility is important even in case; when the network actually exists but there is a failure of the network. In such situations the external data transfer is quite useful.

Also in some cases the data from one system is required to be used through the other system. Here the network connections are not at all possible. Hence the data has to be physically moved from one place to the other. The example for this may be the regular video or the audio. If it is so desired that the video or the audio is to be used through the mode of the large panel television; but the digital video or the audio is in the computer. Hence in such a situation it is not possible to connect the two different types of systems that are the computer and the television. In such a situation the removable data storage devices come into the play.

The solution to this problem is that the digital video or the audio should be burned over the CD or the DVD in the format that is supported by the VCD player associated with the television. And after that is done the video could be used through the television. Similar is the case with the audio also. The removable storage media has one more example of the Zip drives.

NON REMOVABLE DATA STORAGE DEVICES

The storage media is generally referred to the secondary memory devices such as the hard disk and the floppy disk drive, CD drive, DVD disk drive, USB drives and the flash memory devices and also to the Zip drives. But apart from the hard disk, none of them are the devices that are non removable in nature. It means that the hard disk is the only mentioned device that is considered as the Non-Removable Storage Media. All the rest are the removable storage media.

Another example that can be used for the Non-Removable Storage Media is the RAM. But it is a volatile memory that cannot be used for permanently storing the data. It is just the primary memory that is of utmost importance to the system but at the same time cannot be used for the backup or the archiving of the data.

The non removable storage media is fixed permanently in to the computer case and can also be used for the backup or the archiving of the data. The hard disk drives are the best suitable example for this type of storage media.

It also important to mention here that the hard disk drive can also either be internal or the external disk drive. In the internal hard disk; the drive is fixed permanently to the computer case. Where as, in the case of the external disk drive the hard drive can be moved from one place to another. Such a drive has a hard casing made over the normal disk drive. It is made to with stand the shocks in case of any physical damage. The external hard disk drive's case acts as shield and a shock absorber in case of any physical damage. The external hard drive is provided with a USB cable that is plugged into the computer case for the ease of usage. Hence this type of the external hard disk becomes the removal type of data storage. The discussion matters here only with the non removable storage media. Hence the internal hard disks and its types can be discussed elaborately.

The internal hard disk drive is usually fixed in the computer case. The type of hard disk controller gives the name for the different types of the hard disks. The IDE hard disk is the normal hard disk that is used in the regular computers. The IDE controller is used for the purpose of providing connections to this type of the hard disk drive.

The SCSI controllers are used to provide the connections for the SCSI hard disk. The other technology that can be implemented by the internal hard disk drives is the RAID. The RAID is the Redundant Array of Independent (or Inexpensive) disks. In the regular cases the hard disk or mostly the internal hard disk is connected to the motherboard. The motherboard has the IDE connector where in the bus from the hard disk drive is to be plugged in.

If two or more than two hard disk drives are used, then in such case the hard disk drive should clearly be specified as which one is used as the master drive and the other one should also clearly be specified as the slave. The hard disk drive has the jumper settings, by which it can be determined or specified. The internal hard disk is specifically used as the secondary memory. And most importantly the secondary memory that is used in the computer is the non removable storage media. The removal storage media is not used as the secondary memory.

SECONDARY STORAGE DEVICES

Secondary Storage refers to non-volatile data storage which is not directly accessible by the CPU and only accessible via primary storage devices using I/O (Input/Output) channels or device drivers. Typical examples of Secondary Storage are hard disks, floppy disks, optical storage devices (such as CD

, DVD drives), magnetic tape data storage devices, RAM drives, and flash memory (such as USB sticks /keys.) The secondary storage helps in securing the data on media types and storage categories, as data is vulnerable to network attacks, administrative access and media theft. There are many organizations who are working with third parties and disaster recovery efforts. Often data goes offsite and is in the hands of employees that are not authorized to see critical company data. And storage consolidation opens the door to greater administrative access. All of these trends drive the need to ensure the data at rest is secure.

Secondary storage devices hold files that are not currently being used. For a file to be used it must first be copied to main memory first. After any modifications files must be saved to secondary storage. It is advisable to save your data files at the regular intervals as you work on them as data can be lost unexpectedly because of various reasons like interruption in power supply, memory management problems, freezing keyboard, etc.

Compared to main memory, secondary memory is slower, bigger, and cheaper (per unit storage.) Any method for secondary storage must involve two physical parts: a peripheral device (the component of the computer which 'reads' in or 'writes' out the information to/from the system unit,) and an input/output medium, on which the information is actually stored.

Diskettes and cassettes are types of media. The medium has to be 'in' a corresponding peripheral device for information transfer to take place. In most methods of secondary storage, this transfer is realized by passing the medium by a read/write head, which is capable of sensing/writing information from/ to that type of medium.

Secondary storage media may be removable (easily separable from the computer) like your diskettes, or fixed, like hard disks, which, for example, can be found in relatively expensive PCís. A fixed medium generally has much greater capacity (and is faster) compared to a removable one of the same type. On the other hand, by replacing your removable medium by another one when it is full, you can attain a virtually unlimited storage capacity. Another nice feature of removable media is that they allow backup copies of important material to be taken and kept away from the computer, so that they do not get corrupted if some disaster strikes the computer.

The act of retrieving pieces of stored information is called access. There may be two kinds of access to data stored as a sequence of items: Sequential access, where the items are traversed one by one from the beginning of the sequence to the desired one, and direct access (or random access), where any item can be accessed relatively independently of its location in the sequence. Different types of secondary memory media support one or more of these different methods, depending on their nature. Cassette tapes, for example, are sequential access media: You have to 'go through' the first 10 minutes if you want to listen to a piece which begins at the 11th minute of the tape.

The most common type of secondary storage medium is the magnetic disk. Diskettes (small disks made of flexible plastic) and hard disks (made of rigid metal) are the two different kinds of magnetic disks. Magnetic disks are coated with a magnetizable substance, the spots on which mean '0' or '1', depending on whether they are magnetized or not.

Each surface of the disk is subdivided into concentric rings called tracks. Disks with bigger capacity have more tracks than others. In larger computers, one stores the same amount of data in each track and keeps several disks mounted on a shaft on top of each other as a disk pack. The group of tracks which are at the same position in their respective disks on a disk pack is called the disk cylinder for that position. The associated peripheral device is called the disk unit.

At least one read-write head is assigned for each surface. The read-write heads are mounted on a device called the access mechanism, which positions them on the cylinder in which the appropriate data item is to be located. The time for the read-write head to move from its initial location to the appropriate track is called seek time. In larger computers, the shaft on which the disk is mounted continuously rotates at a great speed, and the time required for the relevant portion of the track to come near the head is called rotational delay. The time needed for the actual information transfer between head and disk is called data movement time. Disk access time is the sum of these three components. In larger computers, the read/write head never touches the disk.

Diskettes, on the other hand, rotate only when a read/write is taking place. Furthermore, the head actually touches the diskette. Diskettes usually come in one of two diameters: 3.5 inches or 5.25 inches. 3.5-inch diskettes are products of a newer technology and can store more than 5.25-inch diskettes. Different types of computers employ different methods of data organization on a diskette.

For this reason, a new diskette has to be formatted before it is used on a particular computer. Formatting a disk involves designating parts of each track as individually addressable (directly accessible) sectors.

Each diskette contains a file directory, in which the names, lengths and starting addresses of the files (collections of related data) stored on it are listed. People with many files to store in the same disk are encouraged to use a tree-like directory structure in which related files are kept in separate subdirectories.

If a computer system has enough main memory and a programme designed to read/write data from/to a disk is to be executed, one can transfer the contents of the disk to main memory and then use a method called disk emulation (or RAM disk) to 'trick' the computer into thinking that it is accessing the disk, while it actually deals with the much faster main memory.

An older type of secondary storage medium is magnetic tape. Characters of data are represented in byte form across the tracks which go along the length of the tape. Other types of secondary storage media include mass storage units, which are combinations of spools of magnetic tape that can be automatically retrieved from a huge 'library' and read to disk. These store enormous amounts of information and do not require the intervention of a human operator, note that some disk packs and tapes need this kind of intervention. Optical disks employ a relatively new technology. They use laser beams for the read/write operations.

Most optical disks are of the CD-ROM (Compact Disk/ Read-Only Memory) type; whose vendor-determined contents cannot be changed by the user. Because of their great capacity, these are used for storing multimedia (i.e. mixed text, graphics, sound, etc.) applications of great size. Their speed is low, compared to magnetic hard disks.

As secondary storage media can be damaged and files on them become corrupted, it is suggested to make back-up copies of valuable files on a regular basis. Lots of people skip the last but very important step in the backup procedure - check that the backup copy of files is not damaged.

TYPES OF SECONDARY STORAGE DEVICES

It is important to know the difference between secondary storage and a computer's main memory. Secondary storage is also called auxiliary storage and is used to store data and programmes when they are not being processed.

Secondary storage is more permanent than main memory, as data and programmes are retained when the power is turned off. The needs of secondary storage can vary greatly between users.

A personal computer might only require 20,000 bytes of secondary storage but large companies, such as banks, may require secondary storage devices that can store billions of characters. Because of such a variety of needs, a variety of storage devices are available. The two most common types of secondary storage are magnetic tapes and magnetic disks.

Magnetic Tape Storage

Magnetic tape is a one-half inch or one-quarter inch ribbon of plastic material on which data is recorded. The tape drive is an input/output device that reads, writes and erases data on tapes. Magnetic tapes are erasable, reusable and durable. They are made to store large quantities of data inexpensively and therefore are often used for backup. Magnetic tape is not suitable for data files that are revised or updated often because it stores data sequentially.

Magnetic Disk Storage

Magnetic disks are the most widely used storage medium for computers. A magnetic disk offers high storage capacity, reliability, and the capacity to directly access stored data. Magnetic disks hold more data in a small place and attain faster data access speeds. Types of magnetic disks include diskettes, hard disks, and removable disk cartridges.

Diskettes and hard disks are magnetic media; that is, they are based on a technology of representing data as magnetized spots on the disk with a magnetized spot representing a 1 bit and the absence of such a spot representing a 0 bit.

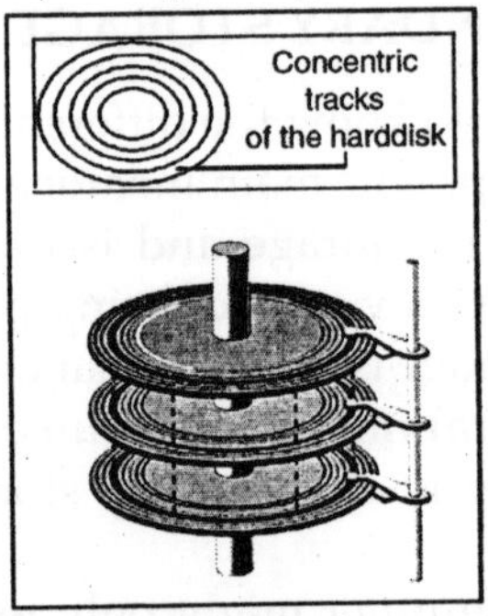

Reading data from the disk means converting the magnetized data to electrical impulses that can be sent to the processor. Writing data to disk is the opposite: sending electrical impulses from the processor to be converted to magnetized spots on the disk. The surface of each disk has concentric tracks on it. The number of tracks per surface varies with the particular type of disk.

Diskettes

Made of flexible Mylar, a diskette can record data as magnetized spots on tracks on its surface. Diskettes became popular along with the personal computer.

The older diskette, 5-1/4 inches in diameter, is still in use, but newer computers use the 3-1/2 inch diskette.

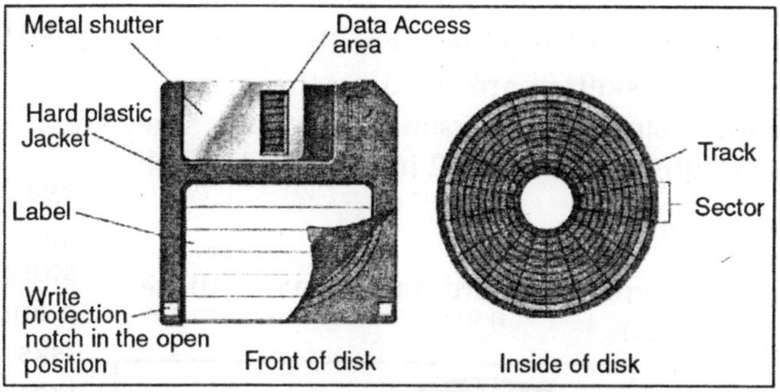

The 3-1/2 inch diskette has the protection of a hard plastic jacket, a size to fit conveniently in a shirt pocket or purse, and the capacity to hold significantly more data than a 5-1/4 inch diskette. Diskettes offer particular advantages, which, as you will see, are not readily available with hard disk:

Portability.

Diskettes easily transport data from one computer to another. Workers, for example, carry their files from office computer to home computer and back on a diskette instead of in a briefcase. Students use the campus computers but keep their files on their own diskettes.

Backup

It is convenient to place an extra copy of a hard disk file on a diskette.

New Software

Although, for convenience, software packages are kept on hard disk, new software out of the box may come on diskettes (new software also may come on CD-ROM disks, which we will discuss shortly). The end of the diskettes useful life-time may be upon us. In 1998 Macintosh introduced its new computer, the IMAC, without a floppy disk drive.

Alternatives such as Zip disks (discussed later), or transferring data via networks are making the low-capacity diskette become obsolete. The diskette was introduced in the early 1970s by IBM as a new type of secondary storage.

Originally they were eight inches in diameter and were thin and flexible which gave them the name floppy disks, or floppies. Diskettes are used as the principle medium of secondary storage for personal computers. They are available in two different sizes: 3 1/2 inch and 5 1/4 inch.

Storage Capacity

Before you can store data on your diskette, it must be formatted (G).

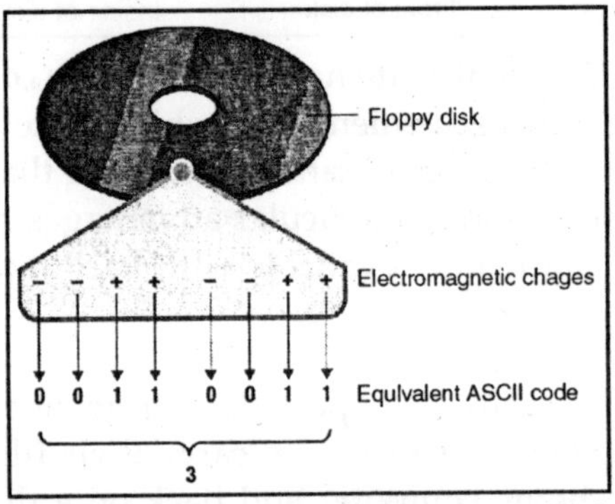

The amount of data you can store on a diskette depends on the recording density and the number of tracks on the diskette. The recording density is the number of bits (G) that can be recorded on one inch of track on the diskette, or bits per inch (bpi).

The second factor that influences the amount of data stored on a diskette is the number of tracks on which the data can be stored or tracks per inch (tpi). Commonly used diskettes are referred to as either double-density or high-density (single-density diskettes are no longer used). Double-density diskettes (DD) can store 360K for a 5 1/4 inch diskette and 720K for a 3 1/2 inch diskette. High-density diskettes (HD) can store 1.2 megabytes (G) on a 5 1/4 inch diskette and 1.44 megabytes on a 3 1/2 inch diskette.

Care Of Diskettes

You should keep diskettes away from heat, cold, magnetic fields (including telephones) and contaminated environments such as dust, smoke, or salt air. Also keep them away from food and do not touch the disk surface.

Hard Disks

A hard disk is a metal platter coated with magnetic oxide that can be magnetized to represent data. Hard disks come in a variety of sizes.

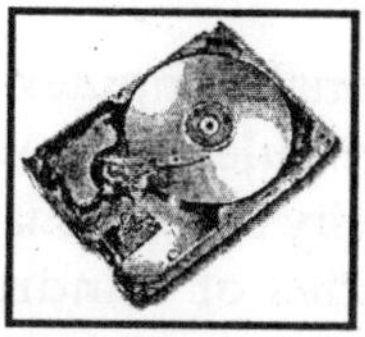

Hard disk for mainframes and minicomputers may be as large as 14 inches in diameter. Several disks can be assembled into a disk pack. There are different types of disk packs, with the number of platters varying by model.

Each disk in the pack has top and bottom surfaces on which to record data. Many disk devices, however, do not record data on the top of the top platter or on the bottom of the bottom platter.

A disk drive is a machine that allows data to be read from a disk or written on a disk. A disk pack is mounted on a disk drive that is a separate unit connected to the computer. Large computers have dozens or ever hundreds of disk drives. In a disk pack all disks rotate at the same time although only one disk is being read or written on at any one time.

The mechanism for reading or writing data on a disk is an access arm; it moves a read/write head into position over a particular track. The read/write head on the end of the access arm hovers just above the track but does not actually touch the surface. When a read/write head does accidentally touch the disk surface, this is called a head crash and all data is destroyed.

Data can also be destroyed if a read/write head encounters even minuscule foreign matter on the disk surface. A disk pack has a series of access arms that slip in between the disks in the pack. Two read/write heads are on each arm, one facing up for the surface above it and one facing down for the surface below it. However, only one read/write head can operate at any one time. In some disk drives the access arms can be retracted; then the disk pack can be removed from the drive. Most disk packs, however, combine the disks, access arms, and read/write heads in a sealed module called a Winchester disk. Winchester disk assemblies are put together in clean rooms so even microscopic dust particles do not get on the disk surface.

Hard disks for personal computers are 5-1/4 inch or 3-1/2 inch disks in sealed modules and even gigabytes are not unusual. Hard disk capacity for personal computers has soared in recent years; capacities of hundreds of megabytes are common and gigabytes are not unusual. Although an individual probably cannot imagine generating enough output-letters, budgets, reports, and so forth-to fill a hard disk, software packages take up a lot of space and can make a dent rather quickly.

Furthermore, graphics images and audio and video files require large file capacities. Perhaps more important than capacity, however, is the convenience of speed. Personal computer users find accessing files on a hard disk is significantly faster and thus more convenient than accessing files on a diskette.

Hard disks provide larger and faster secondary storage capabilities than diskettes. Usually hard disks are permanently mounted inside the computer and are not removable like diskettes.

On minicomputers (G) and mainframes (G), hard disks are often called fixed disks. They are also called direct-access storage devices (DASD). Most personal computers have two to four disk drives. The input/output device that transfers data to and from the hard disk is the hard disk drive.

Hard Disk Storage Capacity

Like diskettes, hard disks must be formatted before they can store information. The storage capacity for hard drives is measured in megabytes. Common sizes for personal computers range from 100MB to 500MB of storage. Each 10MB of storage is equivalent to approximately 5,000 printed pages (with approximately 2,000 characters per page).

Hard Disks in Groups

A concept of using several small disks that work together as a unit is called a redundant array of inexpensive disks, or simply RAID.

The group of connected disks operates as if it were just one large disk, but it speeds up reading and writing by having multiple access paths. The data file for, say, aircraft factory tools, may be spread across several disks; thus, if the computer is used to look up tools for several workers, the computer need not read the data in turn but instead read them at the same time in parallel.

Furthermore, data security is improved because if a disk fails, the disk system can reconstruct data on an extra disk; thus, computer operations can continue uninterrupted. This is significant data insurance.

How Data Is Organized on a Disk

There is more than one way of physically organizing data on a disk. The methods we will consider here are the sector method and the cylinder method.

The Sector Method

In the sector method each track is divided into sectors that hold a specific number of characters. Data on the track is accessed by referring to the surface number, track number, and sector number where the data is stored. The sector method is used for diskettes as well as disk packs.

Zone Recording

The fact that a disk is circular presents a problem: The distances around the tracks on the outside of the disk are greater than that of the tracks or the inside.

A given amount of data that takes up 1 inch of a track on the inside of a disk might be spread over several inches on a track near the outside of a disk. This means that the tracks on the outside are not storing data as efficiently. Zone recording involves dividing a disk into zones to take advantage of the storage available on all tracks, by assigning more sectors to tracks in outer zones than to those in inner zones. Since each sector on the disk holds the same amount of data, more sectors mean more data storage than if all tracks had the same number of sectors.

The Cylinder Method

A way to organize data on a disk pack is the cylinder method. The organization in this case is vertical. The purpose is to reduce the time it takes to move the access arms of a disk pack into position. Once the access arms are in position, they are in the same vertical position on all disk surfaces. To appreciate this, suppose you had an empty disk pack on which you wished to record data.

You might be tempted to record the data horizontally-to start with the first surface, fill track 000, then fill track 001, track 002, and so on, and then move to the second surface and again fill tracks 000, 001, 002, and so forth.

Each new track and new surface, however, would require movement of the access arms, a relatively slow mechanical process. Recording the data vertically, on the other hand, substantially reduces access arm movement.

The data is recorded on the tracks that can be accessed by one positioning of the access arms-that is, on one cylinder. To visualize cylinder organization, pretend a cylindrically shaped item, such as a tin can, were figuratively dropped straight down through all the disks in the disk pack.

All the tracks thus encountered, in the same position on each disk surface, comprise a cylinder. The cylinder method, then, means all tracks of a certain cylinder on a disk pack are lined up one beneath the other, and all the vertical tracks of one cylinder are accessible by the read/write heads with one positioning of the access arms mechanism.

Tracks within a cylinder are numbered according to this vertical perspective: A 20-surface disk pack contains cylinder tracks numbered 0 through 19, top to bottom.

Removable Storage: Zip Disks

Personal computer users, who never seem to have enough hard disk storage space, may turn to a removable hard disk cartridge. Once full, a removable hard disk cartridge can be replaced with a fresh one. In effect, a removable cartridge is as portable as a diskette, but the disk cartridge holds much more data. Removable units also are important to businesses concerned with security, because the units can be used during business hours but hidden away during off hours. A disadvantage of a removable hard disk is that it takes longer to access data than a built-in hard drive.

Fig. Zip Disk

The most popular removable disk media is the Zip drive as shown in Figure. Over 100's of millions have been sold, making it the de facto standard. The disk cartridges look like a floppy disk, but are slightly bigger in all dimensions. Older Zip disks hold 100MB, newer ones hold 250MB and cost $8-$10 a piece (Floppies hold 1.4MB and cost around $2). The drive sells for around $80- $125. Many new PCs come with Zip drives built in addition to floppy drives. Zip disks are a great way to store large files and software programmes.

Disk Cartridges

Removable disk cartridges are another form of disk storage for personal computers. They offer the storage and fast access of hard disks and the portability of diskettes. They are often used when security is an issue since, when you are done using the computer, the disk cartridge can be removed and locked up leaving no data on the computer.

Backup

Backup means creating a copy of important programmes and data. To backup diskettes, copy the data from one to the other. Diskettes are frequently used to backup important files on hard drives of personal computers.

Data Recovery

There does exist certain software programmes that, under special circumstances, can recover data and programmes that have been "lost." Often your operating system (G) will be able to do this, or applications such as Norton Utilities.

Optical Disk Storage

The explosive growth in storage needs has driven the computer industry to provide cheaper, more compact, and more versatile storage devices with greater capacity. This demanding shopping list is a description of the optical disk, like a CD. The technology works like this: A laser hits a layer of metallic material spread over the surface of a disk.

When data is being entered, heat from the laser produces tiny spots on the disk surface. To read the data, the laser scans the disk, and a lens picks up different light reflections from the various spots. Optical storage technology is categorized according to its read/write capability. Read-only media are recorded on by the manufacturer and can be read from but not written to by the user.

Such a disk cannot, obviously, be used for your files, but manufacturers can use it to supply software. Applications software packages sometimes include a dozen diskettes or more; all these could fit on one optical disk with plenty of room to spare. The most prominent optical technology is the CD-ROM, for compact disk read-only memory.

CD-ROM has a major advantage over other optical disk designs: The disk format is identical to that of audio compact disks, so the same dust-free manufacturing plants that are now stamping out digital versions of Mozart or Mary Chapin Carpenter can easily convert to producing anything from software to an encyclopedia. Furthermore, CD-ROM storage is large -up to 660 megabytes per disk, the equivalent of over 400 3-1/2 inch diskettes.

When buying a computer the speed of the CD-ROM drive is advertised using an "X" factor, like 12X, or 24X. This indicates the speed at which the CD can transfer data to the CPU - the higher the X factor, the faster the CD. Modern computers now offer a write CD drive or, CD-RW as an option. CD-RW is a write-once, read-many media. With a CD-RW drive, you can create your own CDs. This offers an inexpensive, convenient, safe way to store large volumes of data such as favourite songs, photographs, etc.

DVDs

Digital Versatile Disk (DVD) drives are now widely available in computers as well as home entertainment centres. DVD-ROM drives can read data, such as stored commercial videos for playing. DVD-RW allow DVDs to be created on a computer.

The DVD is a flat disk, the size of a CD - 4.7 inches diameter and .05 inches thick. Data are stored in a small indentation in a spiral track, just like in the CD. DVD disks are read by a laser beam of shorter wave-length than used by the CD ROM drives. This allows for smaller indentations and increased storage capacity.

The data layer is only half as thick as in the CD-ROM. This opens the possibility to write data in two layers. The outer gold layer is semi transparent, to allow reading of the underlying silver layer. The laser beam is set to two different intensities, strongest for reading the underlying silver layer.

A 4.7 GB side of a DVD can hold 135 minutes top quality video with 6 track stereo. This requires a transmission rate of 4692 bits per second. The 17 GB disk holds 200 hours top quality music recording.

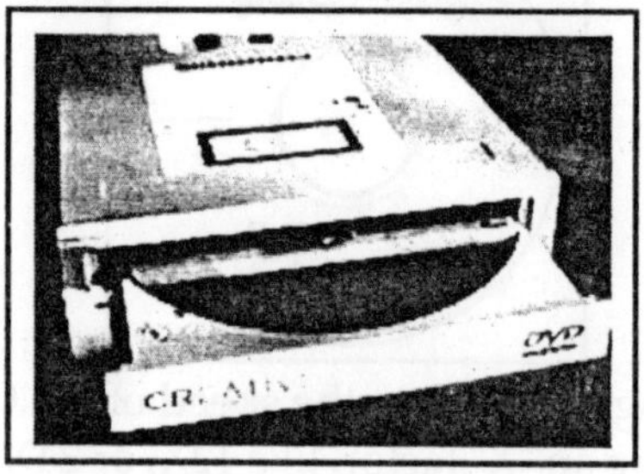

Fig. DVD Disk and Drive

DVD movies are made in two "codes." Region one is USA and Canada, while Europe and Asia is region two. When you play movies, your hardware (MPEG decoder. MGEG is the data coding for movies similar to JPEG for pictures.) must match the DVD region. The movies are made in two formats, each with their own coding. The DVD drives come in 2X, 4X, etc. versions, like the CD-ROM's.

The DVD drives will not replace the magnetic hard disks. The hard disks are being improved as rapidly as DVD, and they definitely offer the fastest seek time and transmission rate (currently 5-10 MB/second). No optic media can keep up with this. But the DVD will undoubtedly gain a place as the successor to the CD ROM and is playing an important role in the blending of computers and entertainment centres.

Magnetic Tape Storage

We saved magnetic tape storage for last because it has taken a subordinate role in storage technology. Magnetic tape looks like the tape used in music cassettes plastic tape with a magnetic coating. As in other magnetic media, data is stored as extremely small magnetic spots.

Tapes come in a number of forms, including l/2-inch-wide tape wound on a reel, l/4-inch- wide tape in data cartridges and cassettes, and tapes that look like ordinary music cassettes but are designed to store data instead of music. The amount of data on a tape is expressed in terms of density, which is the number of characters per inch (cpi) or bytes per inch (bpi) that can be stored on the tape.

The highest-capacity tape is the digital audio tape, or DAT, which uses a different method of recording data. Using a method called helical scan recording, DAT wraps around a rotating read/write head that spins vertically as it moves. This places the data in diagonal bands that run across the tape rather than down its length. This method produces high density and faster access to data.

Two reels are used, a supply reel and a take-up reel. The supply reel, which has the tape with data on it or on which data will be recorded, is the reel that is changed. The take-up reel always stays with the magnetic tape unit. Many cartridges and cassettes have the supply and take-up reels built into the same case.

Tape now has a limited role because disk has proved the superior storage medium. Disk data is quite reliable, especially within a sealed module. Furthermore, as we will see, disk data can be accessed directly, as opposed to data on tape, which can be accessed only by passing by all the data ahead of it on the tape. Consequently, the primary role of tape today is as an inexpensive backup medium.

Backup Systems

Although a hard disk is an extremely reliable device, a hard disk drive is subject to electromechanical failures that cause loss of data. Furthermore, data files, particularly those accessed by several users, are subject to errors introduced by users. There is also the possibility of errors introduced by software. With any method of data storage, a backup system a way of storing data in more than one place to protect it from damage and errors is vital. As we have already noted, magnetic tape is used primarily for backup purposes. For personal computer users, an easy and inexpensive way to back up a hard disk file is to simply copy it to a diskette whenever it is updated. But this is not practical for a system with many files or many users. Personal computer users have the option of purchasing their own tape backup system, to be used on a regular basis for copying all data from hard disk to a high-capacity tape. Data thus saved can be restored to the hard disk later if needed. A key advantage of a tape backup system is that it can copy the entire hard disk in minutes, saving you the trouble of swapping diskettes in and out of the machine.

A rule of thumb among computer professionals is to estimate disk needs generously and then double that amount. But estimating future needs is rarely easy. Many users, therefore, make later adjustments like adding a removable hard disk cartridge to accommodate expanding storage needs.

BENEFITS OF SECONDARY STORAGE DEVICES

Secondary storage, sometimes called auxiliary storage, is storage separate from the computer itself, where you can store software and data on a semi permanent basis. Secondary storage is necessary because memory, or primary storage, can be used only temporarily. If you are sharing your computer, you must yield memory to someone else after your programme runs; if you are not sharing your computer, your programmes and data will disappear from memory when you turn off the computer.

However, you probably want to store the data you have used or the information you have derived from processing; that is why secondary storage is needed. Furthermore, memory is limited in size, whereas secondary storage media can store as much data as necessary.

Capacity: Organizations may store the equivalent of a roomful of data on sets of disks that take up less space than a breadbox. A simple diskette for a personal computer holds the equivalent of 500 printed pages, or one book. An optical disk can hold the equivalent of approximately 400 books.

Reliability: Data in secondary storage is basically safe, since secondary storage is physically reliable. Also, it is more difficult for unscrupulous people to tamper with data on disk than data stored on paper in a file cabinet. Convenience. With the help of a computer, authorized people can locate and access data quickly. Cost. Together the three previous benefits indicate significant savings in storage costs. It is less expensive to store data on tape or disk (the principal means of secondary storage) than to buy and house filing cabinets. Data that is reliable and safe is less expensive to maintain than data subject to errors. But the greatest savings can be found in the speed and convenience of filing and retrieving data.

These benefits apply to all the various secondary storage devices but, as you will see, some devices are better than others. We begin with a look at the various storage media, including those used for personal computers, and then consider what it takes to get data organized and processed.

Chapter 6

Internet

DEFINITION

The Internet is a global network of computers. Every computer that is connected to the Internet is considered a part of that network. This means even your home computer. It's all a matter of degrees, you connect to your ISP's network, then your ISP connects to a larger network and so on. At the top of the tree is the high-capacity backbones, all of these interconnect at 'Network Access Points' 'NAPs' at important regions around the world. The entire Internet is based on agreements between these backbone providers who set in place all the fibre optics lines and other technical aspects of the Internet. The first high speed backbone was created by the 'National Science Foundation' in 1987.

The Internet was first created by the Advanced Research Projects Agency (ARPA) of the U.S. government in 1960's, and was first known as the ARPANet. At this stage the Internet's first computers were at academic and government institutions. They were mainly used for accessing files and to send email. From 1983 onwards the Internet as we know it today started to form with the introduction of the communication protocol TCP/IP to ARPANet.

Since 1983 the Internet has accommodated alot of changes and continues to keep developing. The last two decades has seen the Internet accommodate such things as network LANs and ATM and frame switched services. The Internet continues to evolve with it becoming available on mobile phones and pagers and possibly on televisions in the future.

The actual term "Internet" was finally defined in 1995 by FNC (The Federal Networking Council). The resolution created by the The Federal Networking Council (FNC) agrees that the following language reflects our definition of the term "Internet". "Internet" refers to the global information system that,

EVOLUTION

The underpinnings of the Internet are formed by the global interconnection of hundreds of thousands of otherwise independent computers, communications entities and information systems. What makes this interconnection possible is the use of a set of communication standards, procedures and formats in common among the networks and the various devices and computational facilities connected to them.

The procedures by which computers communicate with each other are called "protocols." While this infrastructure is steadily evolving to include new capabilities, the protocols initially used by the Internet are called the "TCP/IP" protocols, named after the two protocols that formed the principal basis for Internet operation.

On top of this infrastructure is an emerging set of architectural concepts and data structures for heterogeneous information systems that renders the Internet a truly global information system. In essence, the Internet is an architecture, although many people confuse it with its implementation. When the Internet is looked at as an architecture, it manifests two different abstractions.

One abstraction deals with communications connectivity, packet delivery and a variety of end-end communication services. The other abstraction deals with the Internet as an information system, independent of its underlying communications infrastructure, which allows creation, storage and access to a wide range of information resources, including digital objects and related services at various levels of abstraction.

Interconnecting computers is an inherently digital problem. Computers process and exchange digital information, meaning that they use a discrete mathematical "binary" or "two-valued" language of 1s and 0s. For communication purposes, such information is mapped into continuous electrical or optical waveforms. The use of digital signaling allows accurate regeneration and reliable recovery of the underlying bits.

We use the terms "computer," "computer resources" and "computation" to mean not only traditional computers, but also devices that can be controlled digitally over a network, information resources such as mobile programmes and other computational capabilities.

The telephone network started out with operators who manually connected telephones to each other through "patch panels" that accepted patch cords from each telephone line and electrically connected them to one another through the panel, which operated, in effect, like a switch. The result was called circuit switching, since at its conclusion, an electrical circuit was made between the calling telephone and the called telephone.

Conventional circuit switching, which was developed to handle telephone calls, is inappropriate for connecting computers because it makes limited use of the telecommunication facilities and takes too long to set up connections. Although reliable enough for voice communication, the circuit-switched voice network had difficulty delivering digital information without errors.

For digital communications, packet switching is a better choice, because it is far better suited to the typically "burst" communication style of computers. Computers that communicate typically send out brief but intense bursts of data, then remain silent for a while before sending out the next burst. These bursts are communicated as packets, which are very much like electronic postcards. The postcards, in reality packets, are relayed from computer to computer until they reach their destination.

The special computers that perform this forwarding function are called variously "packet switches" or "routers" and form the equivalent of many bucket brigades spanning continents and oceans, moving buckets of electronic postcards from one computer to another. Together these routers and the communication links between them form the underpinnings of the Internet.

Without packet switching, the Internet would not exist, as we now know it. Going back to the postcard analogy, postcards can get lost. They can be delivered out of order, and they can be delayed by varying amounts. The same is true of Internet packets, which, on the Internet, can even be duplicated. The Internet Protocol is the postcard layer of the Internet. The next higher layer of protocol, TCP, takes care of re-sending the "postcards" to recover packets that might have been lost, and putting packets back in order if they have become disordered in transit.

Of course, packet switching is about a billion times faster than the postal service or a bucket brigade would be. It also has to operate over many different communications systems, or substrata. The authors designed the basic architecture to be so simple and undemanding that it could work with most communication services.

Many organizations, including commercial ones, carried out research using the TCP/IP protocols in the 1970s. Email was steadily used over the nascent Internet during that time and to the present. It was not until 1994 that the general public began to be aware of the Internet by way of the World Wide Web application, particularly after Netscape Communications was formed and released its browser and associated server software.

Thus, the evolution of the Internet was based on two technologies and a research dream. The technologies were packet switching and computer technology, which, in turn, drew upon the underlying technologies of digital communications and semiconductors. The research dream was to share information and computational resources. But that is simply the technical side of the story.

Equally important in many ways were the other dimensions that enabled the Internet to come into existence and flourish. This aspect of the story starts with cooperation and far-sightedness in the U.S. Government, which is often derided for lack of foresight but is a real hero in this story. It leads on to the enthusiasm of private sector interests to build upon the government funded developments to expand the Internet and make it available to the general public.

Perhaps most important, it is fueled by the development of the personal computer industry and significant changes in the telecommunications industry in the 1980s, not the least of which was the decision to open the long distance market to competition. The role of workstations, the Unix operating system and local area networking (especially the Ethernet) are themes contributing to the spread of Internet technology in the 1980s into the research and academic community from which the Internet industry eventually emerged.

Many individuals have been involved in the development and evolution of the Internet covering a span of almost four decades if one goes back to the early writings on the subject of computer networking by Kleinrock, Licklider, Baran, Roberts, and Davies. The ARPANET, described below, was the first wide-area computer network. The NSFNET, which followed more than a decade later under the leadership of Erich Bloch, Gordon Bell, Bill Wulf and Steve Wolff, brought computer networking into the mainstream of the research and education communities. It is not our intent here to attempt to attribute credit to all those whose contributions were central to this story, although we mention a few of the key players

ROLE OF DARPA

Modern computer networking technologies emerged in the early 1970s. In 1969, The U.S. Defence Advanced Research Projects Agency (variously called ARPA and DARPA), an agency within the Department of Defence, commissioned a wide-area computer network called the ARPANET.

This network made use of the new packet switching concepts for interconnecting computers and initially linked computers at universities and other research institutions in the United States and in selected NATO countries. At that time, the ARPANET was essentially the only realistic wide-area computer network in existence, with a base of several dozen organizations, perhaps twice that number of computers and numerous researchers at those sites. The programme was led at DARPA by Larry Roberts. The packet switches were built by Bolt Beranek and Newman (BBN), a DARPA contractor. Others directly involved in the ARPANET activity included the authors, Len Kleinrock, Frank Heart, Howard Frank, Steve Crocker, Jon Postel and many many others in the ARPA research community.

Back then, the methods of internetworking (that is interconnecting computer networks) were primitive or non-existent. Two organizations could interwork technically by agreeing to use common equipment, but not every organization was interested in this approach. Absent that, there was jury-rigging, special case development and not much else. Each of these networks stood on its own with essentially no interaction between them - a far cry from today's Internet.

In the early 1970s, ARPA began to explore two alternative applications of packet switching technology based on the use of synchronous satellites (SATNET) and ground-based packet radio (PRNET). The decision by Kahn to link these two networks and the ARPANET as separate and independent networks resulted in the creation of the Internet programme and the subsequent collaboration with Cerf. These two systems differed in significant ways from the ARPANET so as to take advantage of the broadcast and wireless aspects of radio communications.

The strategy that had been adopted for SATNET originally was to embed the SATNET software into an ARPANET packet switch, and interwork the two networks through memory-to-memory transfers within the packet switch. This approach, in place at the time, was to make SATNET an "embedded" network within the ARPANET; users of the network would not even need to know of its existence. The technical team at Bolt Beranek and Newman (BBN), having built the ARPANET switches and now building the SATNET software, could easily produce the necessary patches to glue the programmes together in the same machine. Indeed, this is what they were under contract with DARPA to provide. By embedding each new network into the ARPANET, a seamless internetworked capability was possible, but with no realistic possibility of unleashing the entrepreneurial networking spirit that has manifest itself in modern day Internet developments. A new approach was in order.

The Packet Radio (PRNET) programme had not yet gotten underway so there was ample opportunity to change the approach there. In addition, up until then, the SATNET programme was only an equipment development activity. No commitments had been obtained for the use of actual satellites or ground stations to access them. Indeed, since there was no domestic satellite industry in the U.S. then, the only two viable alternatives were the use of Intelsat or military satellites. The time for a change in strategy, if it was to be made, was then.

INTERNET ARCHITECTURE

The authors created architecture for interconnecting independent networks that could then be federated into a seamless whole without changing any of the underlying networks. This was the genesis of the Internet, as we know it today.

In order to work properly, the architecture required a global addressing mechanism (or Internet address) to enable computers on any network to reference and communicate with computers on any other network in the federation. Internet addresses fill essentially the same role as telephone numbers do in telephone networks. The design of the Internet assumed first that the individual networks could not be changed to accommodate new architectural requirements; but this was largely a pragmatic assumption to facilitate progress.

The networks also had varying degrees of reliability and speed. Host computers would have to be able to put disordered packets back into the correct order and discard duplicate packets that had been generated along the way. This was a major change from the virtual circuit-like service provided by ARPANET and by then contemporary commercial data networking services such as Tymnet and

Telenet. In these networks, the underlying network took responsibility for keeping all information in order and for re-sending any data that might have been lost. The Internet design made the computers responsible for tending to these network problems.

A key architectural construct was the introduction of gateways (now called routers) between the networks to handle the disparities such as different data rates, packet sizes, error conditions, and interface specifications. The gateways would also check the destination Internet addresses of each packet to determine the gateway to which it should be forwarded.

These functions would be combined with certain end-end functions to produce the reliable communication from source to destination. A draft paper by the authors describing this approach was given at a meeting of the International Network Working Group in 1973 in Sussex, England and the final paper was subsequently published by the Institute for Electrical and Electronics Engineers, the leading professional society for the electrical engineering profession, in its Transactions on Communications in May, 1974.

DARPA contracted with Cerf's group at Stanford to carry out the initial detailed design of the TCP software and, shortly thereafter, with BBN and University College London to build independent implementations of the TCP protocol (as it was then called - it was later split into TCP and IP) for different machines. BBN also had a contract to build a prototype version of the gateway.

These three sites collaborated in the development and testing of the initial protocols on different machines. Cerf, then a professor at Stanford, provided the day-to-day leadership in the initial TCP software design and testing. BBN deployed the gateways between the ARPANET and the PRNET and also with SATNET. During this period, under Kahn's overall leadership at DARPA, the initial feasibility of the Internet Architecture was demonstrated.

The TCP/IP protocol suite was developed and refined over a period of four more years and, in 1980, it was adopted as a standard by the U.S. Department of Defence. On January 1,

1983 the ARPANET converted to TCP/IP as its standard host protocol. Gateways (or routers) were used to pass packets to and from host computers on "local area networks." Refinement and extension of these protocols and many others associated with them continues to this day by way of the Internet Engineering Task Force.

RUNNING THE INTERNET

The Domain Name System

The Internet evolved as an experimental system during the 1970s and early 1980s. It then flourished after the TCP/IP protocols were made mandatory on the ARPANET and other networks in January 1983; these protocols thus became the standard for many other networks as well.

Indeed, the Internet grew so rapidly that the existing mechanisms for associating the names of host computers (e.g. UCLA, USC-ISI) to Internet addresses (known as IP addresses) were about to be stretched beyond acceptable engineering limits. Most of the applications in the Internet referred to the target computers by name.

These names had to be translated into Internet addresses before the lower level protocols could be activated to support the application. For a time, a group at SRI International in Menlo Park, CA, called the Network Information Centre (NIC), maintained a simple, machine-readable list of names and associated Internet addresses which was made available on the net.

Hosts on the Internet would simply copy this list, usually daily, so as to maintain a local copy of the table. This list was called the "host.txt" file (since it was simply a text file). The list served the function in the Internet that directory services (e.g. 411 or 703-555-1212) do in the US telephone system - the translation of a name into an address.

As the Internet grew, it became harder and harder for the NIC to keep the list current. Anticipating that this problem would only get worse as the network expanded, researchers at USC Information Sciences Institute launched an effort to design a more distributed way of providing this same information. The end result was the Domain Name System (DNS) which allowed hundreds of thousands of "name servers" to maintain small portions of a global database of information associating IP addresses with the names of computers on the Internet.

The naming structure was hierarchical in character. For example, all host computers associated with educational institutions would have names like "stanford.edu" or "ucla.edu". Specific hosts would have names like "cs.ucla.edu" to refer to a computer in the computer science department of UCLA, for example. A special set of computers called "root servers" maintained information about the names and addresses of other servers that contained more detailed name/ address associations. The designers of the DNS also developed seven generic "top level" domains, as follows:

- *Education*: EDU
- *Government*: GOV
- *Military*: MIL
- *International*: INT
- *Network*: NET
- *(non-profit) Organization*: ORG
- *Commercial*: COM

Under this system, for example, the host name "UCLA" became "UCLA.EDU" because it was operated by an educational institution, while the host computer for "BBN" became "BBN.COM" because it was a commercial organization. Top-level domain names also were created for every country: United Kingdom names would end in ".UK," while the ending ".FR" was created for the names of France.

The Domain Name System (DNS) was and continues to be a major element of the Internet architecture, which contributes to its scalability. It also contributes to controversy over trademarks and general rules for the creation and use of domain names, creation of new top-level domains and the like. At the same time, other resolution schemes exist as well. One of the authors (Kahn) has been involved in the development of a different kind of standard identification and resolution scheme that, for example, is being used as the base technology by book publishers to identify books on the Internet by adapting various identification schemes for use in the Internet environment.

For example, International Standard Book Numbers (ISBNs) can be used as part of the identifiers. The identifiers then resolve to state information about the referenced books, such as location information (e.g. multiple sites) on the Internet that is used to access the books or to order them. These developments are taking place in parallel with the more traditional means of managing Internet resources. They offer an alternative to the existing Domain Name System with enhanced functionality.

The growth of Web servers and users of the Web has been remarkable, but some people are confused about the relationship between the World Wide Web and the Internet. The Internet is the global information system that includes communication capabilities and many high level applications. The Web is one such application.

The existing connectivity of the Internet made it possible for users and servers all over the world to participate in this activity. Electronic mail is another important application. As of today, over 60 million computers take part in the Internet and about 3.6 million web sites were estimated to be accessible on the net. Virtually every user of the net has access to electronic mail and web browsing capability. Email remains a critically important application for most users of the Internet, and these two functions largely dominate the use of the Internet for most users.

INTERNET STANDARDS PROCESS

Internet standards were once the output of research activity sponsored by DARPA. The principal investigators on the internetting research effort essentially determined what technical features of the TCP/IP protocols would become common. The initial work in this area started with the joint effort of the two authors, continued in Cerf's group at Stanford, and soon thereafter was joined by engineers and scientists at

BBN and University College London. This informal arrangement has changed with time and details can be found elsewhere. At present, the standards efforts for Internet are carried out primarily under the auspices of the Internet Society (ISOC). The Internet Engineering Task Force (IETF) operates under the leadership of its Internet Engineering Steering Group (IESG), which is populated by appointees approved by the Internet Architecture Board (IAB) which is, itself, now part of the Internet Society.

The IETF comprises over one hundred working groups categorized and managed by Area Directors specializing in specific categories. There are other bodies with considerable interest in Internet standards or in standards that must interwork with the Internet.

Examples include the International Telecommunications Union Telecommunicationsstandards group (ITU-T), the International Institute of Electrical and Electronic Engineers (IEEE) local area network standards group (IEEE 801), the Organization for International Standardization (ISO), the American National Standards Institute (ANSI), the World Wide Web Consortium (W3C), and many others.

As Internet access and services are provided by existing media such as telephone, cable and broadcast, interactions with standards bodies and legal structures formed to deal with these media will become an increasingly complex matter. The intertwining of interests is simultaneously fascinating and complicated, and has increased the need for thoughtful cooperation among many interested parties.

MANAGING THE INTERNET

Perhaps the least understood aspect of the Internet is its management. In recent years, this subject has become the subject of intense commercial and international interest, involving multiple governments and commercial organizations, and recently congressional hearings. At issue is how the Internet will be managed in the future, and, in the process, what oversight mechanisms will insure that the public interest is adequately served. In the 1970s, managing the Internet was easy. Since few people knew about the Internet, decisions about almost everything of real policy concern were made in the offices of DARPA. It became clear in the late 1970s, however, that more community involvement in the decision-making processes was essential.

In 1979, DARPA formed the Internet Configuration Control Board (ICCB) to insure that knowledgeable members of the technical community discussed critical issues, educated people outside of DARPA about the issues, and helped others to implement the TCP/IP protocols and gateway functions. At the time, there were no companies that offered turnkey solutions to getting on the Internet. It would be another five years or so before companies like Cisco Systems were formed, and while there were no PCs yet, the only workstations available were specially built and their software was not generally configured for use with external networks; they were certainly considered expensive at the time.

In 1983, the small group of roughly twelve ICCB members was reconstituted (with some substitutions) as the Internet Activities Board (IAB), and about ten "Task Forces" were established under it to address issues in specific technical areas. The attendees at Internet Working Group meetings were invited to become members of as many of the task forces as they wished.

The management of the Domain Name System offers a kind of microcosm of issues now frequently associated with overall management of the Internet's operation and evolution. Someone had to take responsibility for overseeing the system's general operation. In particular, top-level domain names had to be selected, along with persons or organizations to manage each of them. Rules for the allocation of Internet addresses had to be established. DARPA had previously asked the late Jon Postel of the USC Information Sciences Institute to take on numerous functions related to administration of names, addresses and protocol related matters.

With time, Postel assumed further responsibilities in this general area on his own, and DARPA, which was supporting the effort, gave its tacit approval: This activity was generally referred to as the Internet Assigned Numbers Authority (IANA). In time, Postel became the arbitrator of all controversial matters concerning names and addresses until his untimely death in October 1998.

It is helpful to consider separately the problem of managing the domain name space and the Internet address space. These two vital elements of the Internet architecture have rather different characteristics that colour the management problems they generate.

Domain names have semantics that numbers may not imply; and thus a means of determining who can use what names is needed. As a result, speculators on Internet names often claim large numbers of them without intent to use them other than to resell them later. Alternate resolution mechanisms, if widely adopted, could significantly change the landscape here.

The rapid growth of the Internet has triggered the design of a new and larger address space (the so-called IP version 6 address space); today's Internet uses IP version 4. However, little momentum has yet developed to deploy IPv6 widely. Despite concerns to the contrary, the IPv4 address space will not be depleted for some time.

Further, the use of Dynamic Host Configuration Protocol (DHCP) to dynamically assign IP addresses has also cut down on demand for dedicated IP addresses. Nevertheless, there is growing recognition in the Internet technical community that expansion of the address space is needed, as is the development of transition schemes that allow interoperation between IPv4 and IPv6 while migrating to IPv6.

In 1998, the Internet Corporation for Assigned Names and Numbers (ICANN) was formed as a private sector, non-profit, organization to oversee the orderly progression in use of Internet names and numbers, as well as certain protocol related matters that required oversight.

The birth of this organization, which was selected by the Department of Commerce for this function, has been difficult, embodying as it does many of the inherent conflicts in resolving discrepancies in this arena. However, there is a clear need for an oversight mechanism for Internet domain names and numbers, separate from their day-to-day management. Many questions about Internet management remain.

They may also prove difficult to resolve quickly. Of specific concern is what role the U.S. government and indeed governments around the world need to play in its continuing operation and evolution. This is clearly a subject for another time.

ADVANTAGES OF INTERNET

There are many advantages of using the Internet, such as:

Global Audience

Content published on the World Wide Web is immediately available to a global audience of users. This makes the World Wide Web a very cost-effective medium to publish information. Reaching more than 190 countries.

Operates 24 hours and 365 days

You don't need to wait until resources are available to conduct business. From a consumer's perspective as well as a provider's business can be consummated at any time. The fact that the Internet is operational at all times makes it the most efficient business machine to date.

Relatively Inexpensive

It is relatively inexpensive to publish information on the Internet. At a fraction of the cost to publish information by traditional methods, various organizations and individuals can now distribute information to millions of users. It costs only a few thousand dollars to establish an Internet presence and publish content on the Internet.

Product Advertising

You can use the World Wide Web to advertise various products. Before purchasing a product, customers will be able to look up various product specification sheets and find out additional information. You can use the multimedia capabilities of the World Wide Web to make available not only various product specification sheets but also audio files, images, and even video clips of products in action. The beauty of the Web is that it allows customers to explore products in as much detail as they desire.

If the client just wants a general overview, he or she can look at the advertising information. For those wanting more in depth information, you can provide white papers and product descriptions for download. The Web allows a business to provide timely information, you can simply place the information on the Web page and it is available immediately for your customers.

Distribute Product Catalogs

The World Wide Web is a very effective medium for distributing product catalogs. In the old days, putting together a product catalog used to be very costly in terms of time and money needed to publish and distribute it.

The World Wide Web changes all this by allowing content developers to put together a sales catalog and make it available to millions of users immediately. Furthermore, unlike printed product catalogs that are usually updated around once a month, product catalogs on the World Wide Web can be updated as needed to respond to various changing market conditions.

Online Surveys

Traditional methods of performing surveys are often relatively slow and expensive compared to online surveys conducted on the Internet. For example, in order to fill out various needs of customers or what they would like to see in a future product, it's often necessary to compile a list of address and mail a questionnaire to many customers.

The success of such an attempt is not always guaranteed and can be very costly in terms of mailing the questionnaires and entering responses to a databases and analyzing it. On the other hand, you can use the World Wide Web to automate the whole process. For example, you can set up a CGI script to conduct online surveys. Results of such a survey can be automatically updated to a database. This database can then be used to keep a pulse on various opinions and needs of customers.

Announcements

With the World Wide Web, you can distribute various announcements to millions of users in a timely manner. Because there is virtually no time lag from the time it takes to publish information to making the information available to users, the Web is an ideal medium to publicize announcements.

As more people discover the virtues of the Web and get connected to the Internet, the Web will become the medium of choice for many organizations and individuals to publicize various announcements.

Provide Technical Support

You can also use Web site to provide technical support to users. Because Web pages can be updated immediately with new information, various technical support literature can be immediately modified in light of new findings and developments.

This can be accomplished without having to distribute changes to all users affected by any changes using traditional mediums of information distribution, which are often quite costly compared to the World Wide Web.

Create Online Discussion Forums

By using applications such as WebBoard, it's possible to set up online discussion forums on the Web.

Obtain Customer Feedback

The interactive nature of the World Wide Web is ideal for obtaining customer feedback. You can easily set up a CGI script to obtain customer feedback about a product or service. Because customer feedback submitted by customers can be read immediately, it's possible to respond to various customer concerns in a timely manner, increasing customer satisfaction and quality of customer service.

Immediate Distribution of Information

When information is added to a Web site, it's immediately available for browsing by millions of Internet users. The World Wide Web is an ideal medium of information distribution because it takes away the time lag associated with publishing content and actually making it available to users

Easy Integration with Internal Information Systems

Internet information systems deployed on the Internet can be easily integrated with internal information systems managed with office productivity applications such as Microsoft Office.

Powerful Content Publishing Tools

A new breed of Internet aware applications will start emerging in software stores by the time you read this. These applications will enable users to develop content for the World Wide Web by simply saving as an HTML file.

In addition to software developers making existing applications Internet aware, various new, powerful, and easy-to use Internet content publishing applications are also being developed. These applications will make the task of publishing content on the Internet even easier. Most of these applications are developed for Windows users.

Multimedia

The capability to incorporate multimedia into Web pages is a major advantage of using World Wide Web to publish information. For example, many Web sites use sounds and video clips to make the content easier and more interesting to browse.

Formatting Capabilities

Content published on the World Wide Web can be richly formatted by using various HTML tags and graphic formats.

The capability to do this is a major reason for the success of the World Wide Web. In addition to using HTML tags and various multimedia formats in Web pages, various interactive controls can also be added to a web page.

This capability allows Web site content developers to create "active" Web sites. For example, before a user sends some information to a Web server for processing, a VBScript or JavaScript subroutine can be used to verify information typed in by the user. Various formatting capabilities, along with technologies such as Java and VBScript, make the World Wide Web a richly interactive medium that you can use to distribute information to millions of users.

DISADVANTAGES OF INTERNET

Many fear the Internet because of its disadvantages. They claim to not use the Internet because they are afraid of the possible consequences or are simply not interested. People who have yet connected to the Internet claim they are not missing anything . Today's technological society must realise, it is up to them to protect themselves on the Internet .

Children using the Internet has become a big concern. Most parents do not realise the dangers involved when their children log onto the Internet. When children are online, they can easily be lured into something dangerous. When children talk to others online, they do not realise they could actually be talking to a harmful person. In addition, children may also receive pornography online by mistake; therefore, causing concern among parents everywhere.

Whether surfing the Web, reading newsgroups, or using email, children can be exposed to extremely inappropriate material. Pornographic sites tend to make sure they are the first sites to be listed in any search area. Some critics say that parents are responsible for their own children on the Internet because there are available services to protect children.

To keep children safe, parents and teachers must be aware of the dangers. They must actively guide and guard their children online.There are a number of tools available today that may help keep the Internet environment safer for children.

Musicians are also concerned with disadvantages to the Net such as, accessibility and freedom. They are upset because the Internet provides their music online at no charge to consumers. File-sharing software, such Kazaa, Emule and may others provides copyrighted songs to all Internet users. The main concern is - the music is free! Musicians feel "they are not getting paid for their work". It is almost impossible to close down all file-sharing services; there are too many of them to count. Another major disadvantage of the Internet is privacy. Electronic messages sent over the Internet can be easily snooped and tracked, revealing who is talking to whom and what they are talking about.

As people surf the Internet, they are constantly giving information to web sites. People should become aware that the collection, selling, or sharing of the information they provide online increases the chances that their information will fall into the wrong hands. When giving personal information on the Internet, people should make sure the Web site is protected with a recognizable security symbol. On the other hand, this does not mean they are fully protected because anyone may obtain a user's information. Today, not only are humans getting viruses, but computers are also.

Computers are mainly getting these viruses from the Internet; yet, viruses may also be transmitted through floppy disks. However, people should mainly be concerned about receiving viruses from the Internet. Some of these dangerous viruses destroy the computer's entire hard drive, meaning that the user can no longer access the computer. Virus protection is highly recommended. In conclusion, today's society is in the middle of a technological boom. People can either choose to take advantage of this era, or simply let it pass them by. The Internet is a very powerful tool. It has many advantages; however, people need to be extremely aware of the disadvantages as well.

Chapter 7

Networking

NETWORK

For such an extensive and involved subject, which includes so many different technologies, hardware devices and protocols, the definition of networking is actually quite simple. A network is simply a collection of computers or other hardware devices that are connected together, either physically or logically, using special hardware and software to allow them to exchange information and cooperate. Networking is the term that describes the processes involved in designing, implementing, upgrading, managing and otherwise working with networks and network technologies.

Networks are used for an incredible array of different purposes. In fact, the definitions above are so simple for the specific reason that networks can be used so broadly, and can allow such a wide variety of tasks to be accomplished. While most people learning about networking focus on the interconnection of PCs and other "true" computers, you use various types of networks every day. Each time you pick up a phone, use a credit card at a store, get cash from an ATM machine, or even plug in an electrical appliance, you are using some type of network.

In fact, the definition can even be expanded beyond the world of technology altogether: I'm sure you've heard the term "networking" used to describe the process of finding an employer or employee by talking to friends and associates. In this case too, the idea is that independent units are connected together to share information and cooperate. The widespread networking of personal computers is a relatively new phenomenon. For the first decade or so of their existence, PCs were very much "islands unto themselves", and were rarely connected together. In the early 1990s, PC networking began to grow in popularity as businesses realized the advantages that networking could provide. By the late 1990s, networking in homes with two or more PCs started to really take off as well.

This interconnection of small devices represents, in a way, a return to the "good old days" of mainframe computers. Before computers were small and personal, they were large and centralized machines that were shared by many users operating remote terminals. While having all of the computer power in one place had many disadvantages, one benefit was that all users were connected because they shared the central computer.

Individualized PCs took away that advantage, in favour of the benefits of independence. Networking attempts to move computing into the middle ground, providing PC users with the best of both worlds: the independence and flexibility of personal computers, and the connectivity and resource sharing of mainframes. in fact, networking is today considered so vital that it's hard to conceive of an organization with two or more computers that would not want to connect them together!

TYPES OF NETWORKING

The word "networking" strikes fear into legions of otherwise intrepid job hunters. It conjures up one of three images: calling everyone in your address book to see whether anyone knows anyone who may know anyone who may give you an informational interview, attending club meetings with other job hunters or having your friends come up with ideas and contacts instead of advising you to get out there and network.

But there is no need to fear because there are many different types of networking techniques you can use to help with your job search and references. Obviously number three doesn't always work. But the other two aren't so appealing either. Who enjoys calling total strangers and asking them to meet with you when there's nothing in it for them? If they're successful in what they do - and why else would you want to meet with them? - they're likely to be busy doing it.

STRONG-CONTACT NETWORKS

Structured explicitly to pass business referrals among members, they allow only one member per profession. Strong-contact networks are particularly good for developing in-depth relationships because you see the same members week after week and pass referrals as a part of each meeting.

CASUAL-CONTACT NETWORKS

Bring businesspeople together in a less-structured context than strong-contact networks, but for many they are a primary source of referrals; membership is not limited by profession. These groups are good for developing breadth in your network, but deep, long-lasting relationships can be formed as well.

SERVICE ORGANIZATIONS

Associations that exist to provide and support humanitarian efforts and good works in the community and larger venues. They also bring people together in settings that facilitate referral and knowledge networking. Like casual-contact groups, they help you add breadth and diversity to your network.

PROFESSIONAL ASSOCIATIONS

Established to exchange information and ideas among those in a given industry, as well as to promote and support that industry. These networks often include direct competitors, but they also provide contacts in related, non-competing businesses as well.

SOCIAL/BUSINESS ORGANIZATIONS

Combine social activities with business networking and can provide a variety of networking opportunities; many tend to resemble singles bars.

WOMEN'S NETWORKING GROUPS

Still important networking organizations, but are slowly disappearing as women enter the business mainstream, especially as professionals, entrepreneurs, and small-business owners.

ONLINE NETWORKS

A new phenomenon covering a wide range of interests.

TYPES OF COMPUTER NETWORKS

A computer network is two or more computers connected together using a telecommunication system for the purpose of communication and sharing resources". Ask any computer network expert to simplify this definition to you and you will start a debate on how it should not be just two computers but three. Simply put a network is a means of communication between computers. Within a given network, computers can send files, emails and other correspondence to each other. Even things like instant messaging, is set up within a computer's network. There are two basic types of computer Networks.

LAN

LAN or Local Area Network is the most common kind of network set up. There are two ways to connect a LAN network. The simplest and easiest way is the peer-to-peer connection network. This is when two or more computers are directly connected to each other. For example if there were four computers in the network, computer 1 would be connected to computer 2, computer 2 would be connected to computer 3 and computer 3 would be connected to computer 4.

This means each computer is dependent on the other. And if there were a network problem with any one computer, all of them would be affected. The other type if the client server connection. This is the type of connection where all the computers in a given network are connected to one central computer. This is a more complicated network but one that is much more efficient that peer-to-peer. A local area network, or LAN, is a network of connected computers in a room, building, or set of buildings. Local area networks have been around since the beginning of computer use. A LAN is defined as a user network whereby data is sent at high rates between people located relatively close to each other. LANs do not usually make use of leased communication lines, but only means of communication that are provided by the installer of the network.

The Internet is a wide area network, or WAN, which is distinct from a LAN. In contrast to the term Internet, local area networks are often called intranets, though sometimes this term refers to a cluster of LANs associated with a particular company or organization but not connected to the larger Internet.

A local area network uses a hub or router to connect computers together. The means of communication is the omnipresent Ethernet cable or wireless wi-fi technology. These technologies offer data transfer rates running between 10 to 10000 Mbit/s.

Larger, more important LANs have redundant lines or other backup protocols. In networked computers, the most popular communication protocol is TCP/IP. Smaller LANs may be temporary and used between friends to play computer games over the network. Over a network, users can share files, view files, make changes to data on other computers if permitted, play movies or music on multiple computers at once, chat with instant messaging, send emails to each other, play games, and so on.

All the advantages of the Internet apply, although they only include others on the LAN, and the data transfer rates are high. Perhaps the most frequently employed use of a LAN is to connect users to the Internet with only one connected router.

In modern times, we use broadband cable or DSL modems to connect to the Internet, and it would be clumsy to have a modem associated with every computer, so we simply plug the modem into a router and link the router to computers with Ethernet cables. Configuring a LAN can be intimidating at first, but contemporary operating systems have programmes that do most of the necessary configurations automatically, so setting up a local area network is pretty easy. A local area network (LAN) supplies networking capability to a group of computers in close proximity to each other such as in an office building, a school, or a home. A LAN is useful for sharing resources like files, printers, games or other applications. A LAN in turn often connects to other LANs, and to the Internet or other WAN.

Most local area networks are built with relatively inexpensive hardware such as Ethernet cables, network adapters, and hubs. Wireless LAN and other more advanced LAN hardware options also exist.

Examples

The most common type of local area network is an Ethernet LAN. The smallest home LAN can have exactly two computers; a large LAN can accommodate many thousands of computers.

Many LANs are divided into logical groups called subnets. An Internet Protocol (IP) "Class A" LAN can in theory accommodate more than 16 million devices organized into subnets.

The High Performance Network

The HPN is used for the exchange of large amounts of operational data. Two Force10 E600 Routers, interconnected via 4-way 10-Gigabit Ethernet aggregated links, provide connectivity between the High Performance Computing Facility (HPCF) and the Data-Handling System (DHS). The HPCF network nodes are connected via 10-Gigabit Ethernet and all DHS nodes via Gigabit Ethernet aggregated links.

The General Purpose Network

The GPN is used for all other traffic. It has at its core two Foundry BigIron RX-16 routers and at the edge seven Foundry Super-X switches. The core routers are interconnected via 4-way 10-Gigabit Ethernet aggregated links and have multiple Gigabit Ethernet uplinks to the edge routers. The core also includes two further Super-X switches that are dual-attached to the RX-16s via 10-Gigabit Ethernet.

The GPN provides connectivity to:

- The HPCF, the DHS and additional servers via Gigabit Ethernet ports in the core.
- The user desktops and laptops via Gigabit Ethernet ports on the edge switches.
- The firewalls (for the Wide Area Network and the Demilitarized Zone (DMZ) via Gigabit Ethernet ports in the core. The DMZ includes ECaccess, web servers, the mail gateway and DNS (Domain Name Servers).

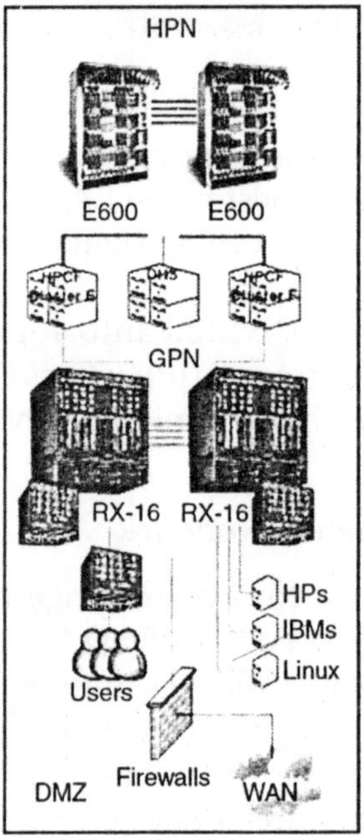

The Hardware

Both the Force10 E600 chassis are populated with 24 10-Gigabit-Ethernet and 144 Gigabit Ethernet ports. For resiliency there are four power supplies, two CPU modules and nine switching fabric modules. Both the RX-16 chassis are populated with 8 10-Gigabit Ethernet ports and 144 Gigabit Ethernet ports. For resiliency there are seven power supplies, two CPU modules and four switching fabric modules. The Super-X chassis each contain up to 156 Gigabit Ethernet ports and dual power-supplies.

WAN

DEFINITION

The wide area network, often referred to as a WAN, is a communications network that makes use of existing technology to connect local computer networks into a larger working network that may cover both national and international locations. This is in contrast to both the local area network and the metropolitan area network, which provides communication within a restricted geographic area. Here is how the wide area network functions, and why it is so important to communications today.

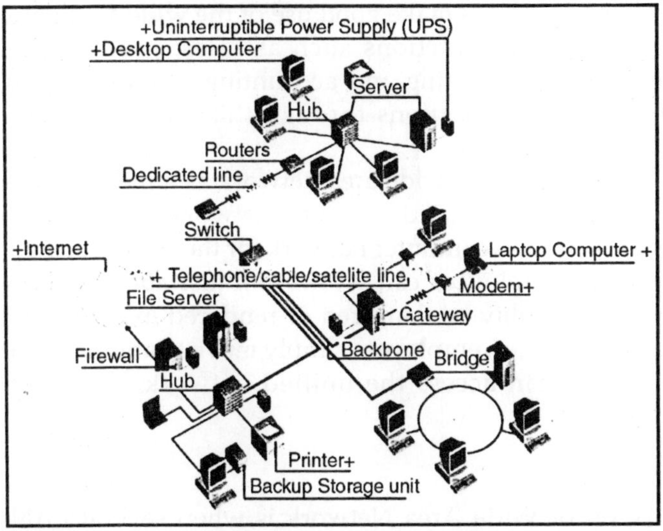

The concept of linking one computer network with another is often desirable, especially for businesses that operate a number of facilities. Beginning with the local area network and going up to the wide area network, this is most easily accomplished by using existing telephony technology. Essentially, fibre optics are used to create the link between networks located in different facilities. Often, this means using standard phone lines, referred to as POTS, or employing PSTN (public switched telephone network) technology. During the 1990s, a third option, that of ISDN (integrated services digital network) solutions for creation a wide area network gained a great deal of popularity, mainly because the concept made it more cost effective to extend the network beyond national boundaries.

With coverage in a broad area, a wide area network allows companies to make use of common resources in order to operate. For example, many retail drugstores make use of a wide area network as part of their support to customers who fill prescriptions with one of their stores. Once in the common customer database for the pharmacy, the client is free to fill a prescription at any of the company's locations, even while vacationing in another state.

Companies also make good use of the wide area network as well. Internal functions such as sales, production and development, marketing and accounting can also be shared with authorized locations through this sort of broad area network application.

The concept of a wide area network as a means of taking individual location based computer networks and using them to create a unified computer network for the entire corporation means that employees can work from just about anywhere. Should one facility be damaged or rendered inaccessible due to natural disaster, employees simply move to another location where they can access the unified network, and keep on working.

OVERVIEW

WAN or Wide Area Network is when several LANs or independent computers are connected to a single, wider network. The Internet is the perfect example of WAN. Emails, Chat Rooms and IMs all connect to the WAN of the Internet.

WAN is much more complex and requires connecting devices or hubs from all over the world. The term Wide Area Network (WAN) usually refers to a network which covers a large geographical area, and use communications circuits to connect the intermediate nodes. A major factor impacting WAN design and performance is a requirement that they lease communications circuits from telephone companies or other communications carriers.

Transmission rates are typically 2 Mbps, 34 Mbps, 45 Mbps, 155 Mbps, 625 Mbps (or sometimes considerably more). Numerous WANs have been constructed, including public packet networks, large corporate networks, military networks, banking networks, stock brokerage networks, and airline reservation networks.

Some WANs are very extensive, spanning the globe, but most do not provide true global coverage. Organizations supporting WANs using the Internet Protocol are known as Network Service Providers (NSPs). These form the core of the Internet. Wide Area Networks, or WANs, connect a geographically diverse group of computers within a state, country, or even across several states or countries.

WANs typically are connected by telephone lines, other types of communication lines, or radio waves. Quite often, smaller local area networks (LANs) are linked together to form a WAN. This is accomplished via dedicated private lines, leased from telecommunications firms like Sprint and AT&T, or by Switched Multi-Megabit Data Services (SMDS) technology, developed in 1995 to eliminate the need for a leased line. WAN technology has been refined over a period of several decades. It first emerged in the mid-twentieth century with the advent of networks like ARPAnet. Developed in 1969 by the Department of Defence, ARPAnet and several other networks eventually evolved into the Internet, the largest WAN in the world.

The packet switching technology most commonly used with WANs surfaced in the 1960s, and standard packet switching protocol, known as X.25, was developed in 1976. To increase network speed, packet switching allows for the parceling of data into smaller chunks, known as packets, prior to transmission. These packets can travel independently via alternate routes, and they are reassembled once they reach their target. Although X.25 remained the most popular WAN packet switching protocol for years, other packet switching protocols used with increasing frequency by WAN developers and administrators include the Internet standard, Transmission Control Protocol/Internet Protocol (TCP/IP), and Frame Relay, used most often by WANs connected via high speed T-1 and T-3 lines.

WANs are used for a variety of purposes. A corporation with offices in several locations may use a WAN to form an intranet. Quite often, the individual offices will use their own LANs for things like internal messaging, data processing functions, and hardware and software sharing. When these LANs are joined together to form a WAN, similar data sharing and messaging capabilities become possible across a much broader geographic area.

Businesses wanting to link up with their suppliers or distributors may create a WAN as a means of establishing an extranet. For example, an extranet could provide a sales representative with electronic access to information in about the time it might take to deliver a product, or the availability of a product. Some WANs bring together various types of communications, such as data, video, and voice. Some organizations, including companies, universities, research centres, hospitals, and libraries, use WANs to connect to the Internet.

By connecting the NSP WANs together using links at Internet Packet Interchanges (sometimes called "peering points") a global communication infrastructure is formed. NSPs do not generally handle individual customer accounts (except for the major corporate customers), but instead deal with intermediate organizations whom they can charge for high capacity communications.

They generally have an agreement to exchange certain volumes of data at a certain "quality of service" with other NSPs. So practically any NSP can reach any other NSP, but may require the use of one or more other NSP networks to reach the required destination. NSPs vary in terms of the transit delay, transmission rate, and connectivity offered.

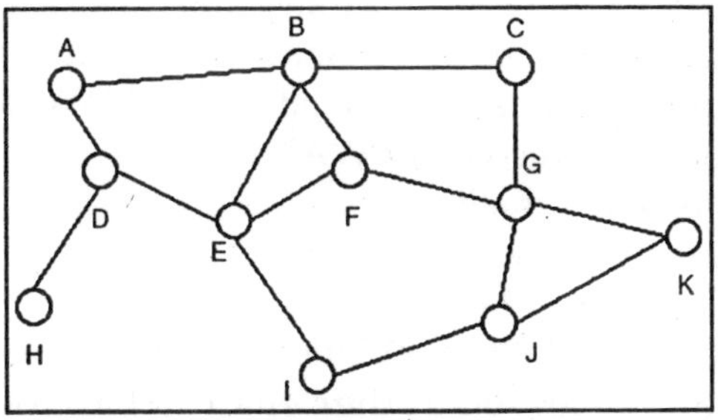

Fig. Typical "Mesh" Connectivity of a Wide Area Network

A typical network is shown in the figure above. This connects a number of End Systems (ES) (e.g. A, C, H, K) and a number of Intermediate Systems (IS) (e.g. B, D, E, F, G, I, J) to form a network over which data may be communicated between the End Systems (ES). The characteristics of the transmission facilities lead to an emphasis on efficiency of communications techniques in the design of WANs.

Controlling the volume of traffic and avoiding excessive delays is important. Since the topologies of WANs are likely to be more complex than those of LANs, routing algorithms also receive more emphasis. Many WANs also implement sophisticated monitoring procedures to account for which users consume the network resources. This is, in some cases, used to generate billing information to charge individual users.

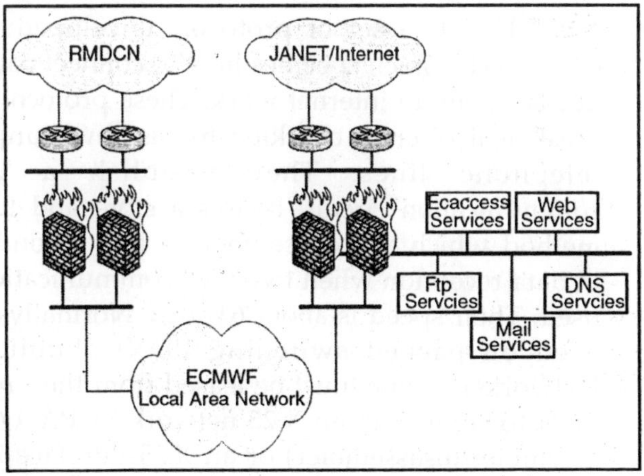

The size of a network is limited due to size and distance constraints. However networks may be connected over a high-speed communications link (called a WAN link) to link them together and thus becomes a WAN.

WAN links are usually:

- Dial up connection
- Dedicated connection - It is a permanent full time connection. When a dedicated connection is used, the cable is leased rather than a part of the cable bandwidth and the user has exclusive use.
- Switched network - Several users share the same line or the bandwidth of the line.

There are two types of switched networks:

- *Circuit switching*: This is a temporary connection between two points such as dial-up or ISDN.
- *Packet switching*: This is a connection between multiple points. It breaks data down into small packets to be sent across the network.

A virtual circuit can improve performance by establishing a set path for data transmission. This will shave some overhead of a packet switching network. A variant of packet switching is called cell-switching where the data is broken into small cells with a fixed length.

WAN CONNECTION TECHNOLOGIES

- X.25: This is a set of protocols developed by the CCITT/ITU which specifies how to connect computer devices over an internet work. These protocols use a great deal of error checking for use over unreliable telephone lines. They establish a virtual communication circuit. It uses a store and forward method which can cause about a half second delay in data reception when two way communications are used. Their speed is about 64Kbps. Normally X.25 is used on packed switching PDNs (Public Data Networks). A line must be leased from the LAN to a PDN to connect to an X.25 network. A PAD (packet assembler/disassembler) or an X.25 interface is used on a computer to connect to the X.25 network. CCITT is an abbreviation for International Telegraph and Telephone Consultative Committee. The ITU is the International Telecommunication Union.

- *Frame Relay*: Devices at both sides of the connection handle Error checking. Frame relay uses frames of varying length and it operates at the data link layer of the OSI model. A permanent virtual circuit (PVC) is established between two points on the network. Frame relay speed is between 56Kbps and 1.544Mbps. Frame relay networks provide a high-speed connection up to 1.544Mbps using variable-length packet switching over digital fibre-optic media. Frame relay does not store data and has less error checking than X.25.
- Switched Multi-megabit Data Service (SMDS) - Uses fixed length cell switching and runs at speeds of 1.533 to 45Mbps. It provides no error checking and assumes devices at both ends provide error checking.
- Telephone connections
  - Dial up
  - *Leased lines*: These are dedicated analog lines or digital lines. Dedicated digital lines are called digital data service (DDS) lines. A modem is used to connect to analog lines, and a Channel Service Unit/Data Service Unit or Digital Service Unit(CSU/DSU) is used to connect to digital lines. The DSU connects to the LAN and the CSU connects to the line.
  - *T Carrier lines*: Multiplexors are used to allow several channels on one line. The T1 line is basic T Carrier service. The available channels may be used separately for data or voice transmissions or they may be combined for more transmission bandwidth. The 64Kbps data transmission rate is referred to as DS-0 (Digital Signal level 0) and a full T1 line is referred to as DS-1.

Signal	System	Total Kbps	Channels	Number of equivalent T1 lines
DS-1	T1	1544	24	1
DS-2	T2	6312	96	4
DS-3	T3	44736	672	28
DS-4	T4	274760	4032	3668

- T1 and T3 lines are the most common lines in use today. T1 and T2 lines can use standard copper wire. T3 and T4 lines require fibre-optic cable or other high-speed media. These lines may be leased partially called fractional T1 or fractional T3, which means a customer, can lease a certain number of channels on the line. A CSU/ DSU and a bridge or router is required to connect to a T1 line.
- *Integrated Services Digital Network (ISDN)*: Comes in two types and converts analog signals to digital for transmission. It is a dial up service

- *Basic Rate ISDN (BRI)*: Two 64Kbps B-channels with one 16Kbps D channel. The D-channel is used tor call control and setup.
- *Primary Rate ISDN (PRI)*: 23 B-channels and one D channel. A device resembling a modem (called an ISDN modem) is used to connect to ISDN. The computer and telephone line are plugged into it.
  - *Switched-56*: A switched line similar to a leased line where customers pay for the time they use the line. Speed is 56Kbps. It is not dedicated and will not work to connect a WAN.
- *Asynchronous Transfer Mode (ATM)*: May be used over a variety of media with both baseband and broadband systems.

It is used for audio, video, and data. It uses fixed length data packets of 53 8 bit bytes called cell switching. 5 bytes contain header information. The cell contains path information that the packet is to use. It uses hardware devices to perform the switching of the data. Speeds from 155Mbps to 622 Mbps are achieved. Error checking is done at the receiving device, not by ATM. A permanent virtual connection or circuit (PVC) is established.

It may also use a switched virtual circuit (SVC). Service classes:

- Constant bit rate for data.
- Variable bit rate for audio or video.
- Connection less for data.
- Connection oriented for data.

ATM can be embedded in other protocols such as ATM-25, T1, T3, OC-1, OC-3, OC-12, and OC-48. Some ATM technologies include:

- *ATM*-25: 25Mbps speed.
- *STS*-3: 155Mbps on fibre or category 5 cable.
- *STS*-12: 620 Mbps on fibre cable for campus wide network.
- *STS*-48: 2.2 Gbps on fibre cable on a MAN.
- *STS*-192: 8.8 Gbps on fibre cable on intercity long distance. Phone companies normally use this.

Synchronous Optical Network (SONET) - A physical layer standard that defines voice, data, and video delivery methods over fibre optic media. It defines data rates in terms of optical carrier (OC) levels. The transmission rate of OC-1 is 51.8 Mbps. Each level runs at a multiple of the first. The OC-5 data rate is 5 times 51.8 Mbps which is 259 Mbps.

SONET also defines synchronous transport signals (STS) for copper media which use the same speed scale of OC levels. STS-3 runs at the same speed of OC-3. Mesh or ring topology is used to support SONET. SONET uses multiplexing. The ITU has incorporated SONET into their Synchronous Digital Hierarchy (SDH) recommendations.

NETWORKING TOPOLOGIES

DEFINITION

Network topology refers to the way that your computer network is arranged. The network can have a physical or a logical topology. The physical topology describes the layout of computers and where the workstations are positioned. The logical network topology describes how the information flows through the network.

Choosing your physical topology is important because if it is not chosen correctly, this could cause your network to not operate properly. There are several terms that describe the type of physical topology that a network can have. The most common topologies are bus, ring, star, and mesh.

In a bus topology, all of the computers are attached to a single cable using terminators. The terminators work to absorb the energy from the signals in the network. The bus topology is easy to install, but it is not reliable because a single default can bring down your network.

In a ring topology, each computer is connected directly to two other computers on the network. As with a bus topology, a single fault can disrupt a ring network. This type of network does have advantages, however, and does not require a network server.

In a star topology, each computer is connected using its own separate cable. This set up is more reliable than a bus topology because its design makes it fault tolerant and susceptible to errors. The information on the network is transmitted from one system to another and the data flows in one single direction. The topology is expensive to maintain and is not reliable because removing one computer can disrupt your entire network.

In a mesh topology, a path is present from one computer to another computer in the network. The mesh topology is usually used in internet structure. The mesh topology can be complicated to construct because it has multiple connection between locations. For every computer that you have you will need at least one and a half connections for each one. This contributes to the expensive structure.

In choosing a network topology, understand that each one has its advantages and disadvantages. Research each one and see which one fits within your budget and which one fits your network layout. Also consider the amount of maintenance required in each topology. When setting up a network at home, consider a network topology that is simple and easy to maintain. You will also want a topology that is inexpensive to set up.

If you are choosing a topology for a business, you will want to consider a topology that is reliable and resistant to errors. Your customers will need a network that is free of downtime; therefore, be sure that your topology is one that withstands disruption.

TYPES OF NETWORKING TOPOLOGIES

BUS TOPOLOGY

A bus topology is a method of transmission on networks that uses a common vehicle for transmissions and thus it is categorized as shared communication. Imagine a bus picking up various people from one stop and dropping of people as it travels and then picking a few more. That is what happens in a bus network exactly.

A bus network uses a multi-drop transmission medium, all node on the network share a common bus and thus share communication. This allows only one device to transmit at a time. A distributed access protocol determines which station is to transmit. Data frames contain source and destination addresses, where each station monitors the bus and copies frames addressed to itself.

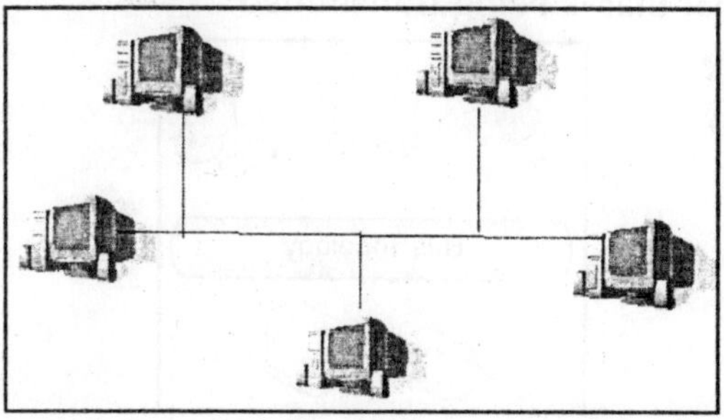

A bus topology connects each computer (nodes) to a single segment trunk (a communication line, typically coax cable, that is referred to as the 'bus'. The signal travels from one end of the bus to the other. A terminator is required at each to absorb the signal so as it does not reflect back across the bus. A media access method called CSMA/MA is used to handle the collision that occur when two signals placed on the wire at the same time.

The bus topology is passive. In other words, the computers on the bus simply 'listen' for a signal; they are not responsible for moving the signal along. However in a Bus topology only one device is allowed to transmit at a given point of time.

The DAP or the Distribute Access Protocol has the information about which station has to transmit the data. The data that is being transmitted have frames that will have the source name and the network address.

Function of Bus Topology

The bus topology connects each computer on the network into something called the segment trunk. A bus is usually referred to a cable that connects end to end and this is used to transmit the signals from one end to the other end. At every end a terminator is placed so that it understands in which direction the data is traveling and also the terminator is used to absorb the signals. If the terminator does not absorb the signal then the same signal is reflected back to the bus confusing the whole data flow. The bus is considered to be a passive network because the computers are largely dependant on the signal that is being transmitted.

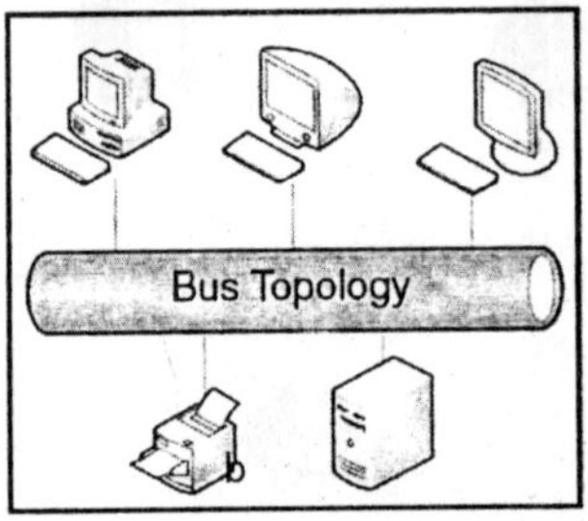

Advantages

The advantage of the Bus network is that if one computer fails in the network the others are still not affected and they continue to work. Bus network is very simple and easy to set up. If there is an urgent need to set up a network and perhaps be used on a short term basis then the Bus network is the best possibility. Bus networks use the least amount of cable to set up making it cost effective.

Limitations

In the bus network you will need a network connection in order to determine if the data is being transferred between two nodes. If the data transfer rate is high then the Bus network does not perform very well because the data travels in a stream and cannot be overloaded.

The bus network is a bit challenging when you have to troubleshoot the problems. Bus networks are not suitable as large networks as there are limitations to the number of nodes you can set up for one single cable. As the number of computers increase in the network the data transfer rate goes down accordingly and noticeably.

Conclusion

The bus networks in spite of its limitations is considered to be the easiest and the fastest network that can be set up compared to the other kinds of network. In bus networks there is a collision handling system which ensures that data travels without errors and data is delivered correctly.

There is a bus master on the network which ensures that data is flowing in the right direction and order. All the computers on the bus network however listen for the signals and they do not hold the responsibility to move the signal forward.

The signal carries forward on its own. So if one computer is not receiving any signals the signal still carries forward without stopping at the computer that has failed. These days bus networks are less common due to the advancement of networks and there are much lesser complicated networks that are easy to operate and efficient. However even these newer technologies derive their basics from older technologies like the Bus Topology.

RING TOPOLOGY

Definition

A ring topology is a network topology or circuit arrangement in which each network device is attached along the same signal path to two other devices, forming a path in the shape of a ring. Each device in the network that is also referred to as node handles every message that flows through the ring. Each node in the ring has a unique address. Since in a ring topology there is only one pathway between any two nodes, ring networks are generally disrupted by the failure of a single link.

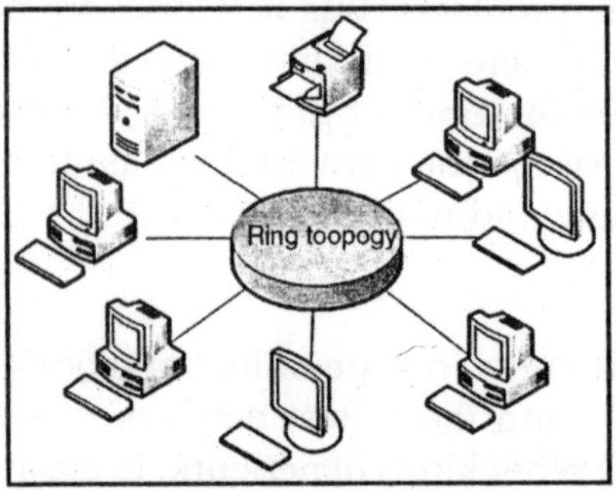

The redundant topologies are used to eliminate network downtime caused by a single point of failure. All networks need redundancy for enhanced reliability. Network reliability is achieved through reliable equipment and network designs that are tolerant to failures and faults.

The FDDI networks overcome the disruption in the network by sending data on a clockwise and a counter clockwise ring. In case there is a break in data flow,the data is wrapped back onto the complementary ring before it reaches the end of the cable thereby maintaining a path to every node within the complementary ring.

Ring network connects computers in a circle of point-to-point connections, with no central server, such as a series of desktop computers in an office. Each node handles its own applications and also shares resources over the entire network. If one node becomes inoperative, the other nodes are still able to maintain contact with one another. Such a network is best for decentralized systems in which no priorities are required

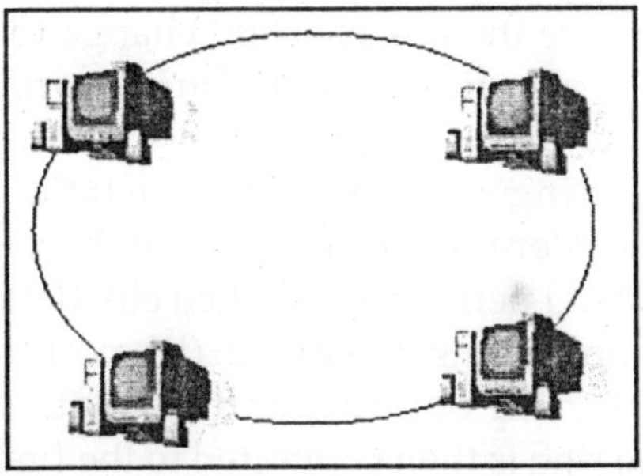

Under the network, a signal is transferred sequentially via a "token" fro one station to the next. When a station wants to transmit, it "grabs" the token, attaches data and an address to it, and then sends it around the ring. The token travels along the ring until it reaches the destination address. The receiving computer acknowledges receipt with a return message to the sender. The sender then releases the token for the token for use by another computer. Each station on the ring has equal access but only one station can talk at a time. To allow an orderly access to the ring, a single electronic token passes from one computer to the next around the ring as seen in (token ring). A computer can only transmit data when it capture the token.

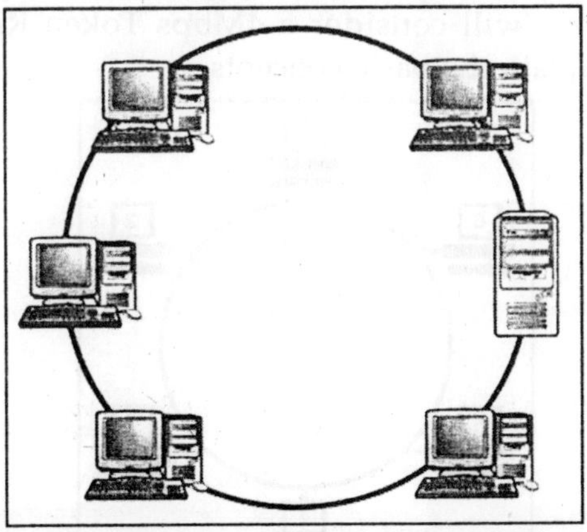

In a true ring topology, if a single computer or section of cable fails, there is an interruption in the signal. The entire

network becomes inaccessible. Network disruption can also occur when computers are added or removed from the network, making it an impractical network design in environments where there is constant change to the network. Ring networks are most commonly wired in a star configuration.

In a Token Ring network, a multistation access unit (MSAU) is equivalent to a hub or switch on an Ethernet network. The MSAU performs the token circulation internally. To create the complete ring, the ring in (RI) port on each MSAU is connected to the ring out (RO) port on another MSAU. The last MSAU in the ring is then connected to the first, to complete the ring.

TOKEN RING TOPOLOGY

Unlike Ethernet, Token Ring uses a ring topology whereby the data is sent from one machine to the next and so on around the ring until it ends up back where it started. It also uses a token passing protocol which means that a machine can only use the network when it has control of the Token, this ensures that there are no collisions because only one machine can use the network at any given time. Figure below shows the basic of a Token Ring Topology. Although 16Mbps is the standard ring speed these days (and Fast Token Ring is being developed) we will consider a 4Mbps Token Ring in this tutorial to explain the basic concepts.

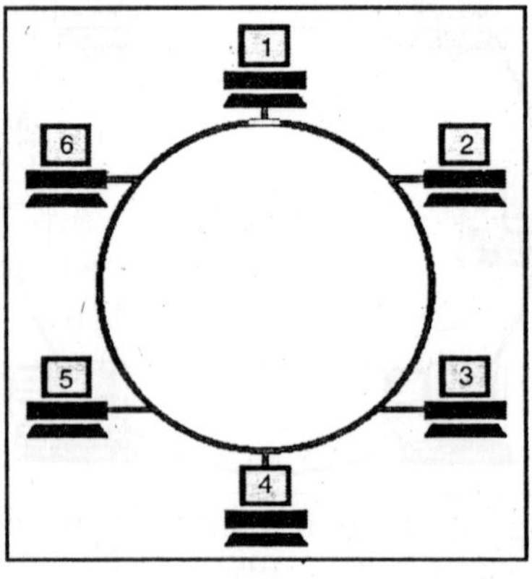

At the start, a free Token is circulating on the ring, this is a data frame which to all intents and purposes is an empty vessel for transporting data. To use the network, a machine first has to capture the free Token and replace the data with its own message. In the example above, machine wants to send some data to machine , so it first has to capture the free Token. It then writes its data and the recipient's address onto the Token. The packet of data is then sent to machine who reads the address, realizes it is not its own, so passes it on to machine Machine does the same and passes the Token on to machine . This time it is the correct address and so number reads the message. It cannot, however, release a free Token on to the ring, it must first send the message back to number with an acknowledgement to say that it has received the data (represented by the purple flashing screen).

The receipt is then sent to machine who checks the address, realizes that it is not its own and so forwards it on to the next machine in the ring, number .Machine does the same and forwards the data to number , who sent the original message. Machin erecognizes the address, reads the acknowledge-ment from number (represented by the purple flashing screen) and then releases the free Token back on to the ring ready for the next machine to use. That's the basics of Token Ring and it shows how data is sent, received and acknowledged, but Token Ring also has a built in management and recovery system which makes it very fault tolerant. Below is a brief outline of Token Ring's self maintenance system.

Token Ring Self Maintenance

When a Token Ring network starts up, the machines all take part in a negotiation to decide who will control the ring, or become the 'Active Monitor' to give it its proper title. This is won by the machine with the highest MAC address who is participating in the contention procedure, and all other machines become 'Standby Monitors'. The job of the Active Monitor is to make sure that none of the machines are causing problems on the network, and to re-establish the ring after a break or an error has occurred. The Active Monitor performs

Ring Polling every seven seconds and ring purges when there appears to be a problem. The ring polling allows all machines on the network to find out who is participating in the ring and to learn the address of their Nearest Active Upstream Neighbour (NAUN). Ring purges reset the ring after an interruption or loss of data is reported.

Each machine knows the address of its Nearest Active Upstream Neighbour. This is an important function in a Token Ring as it updates the information required to re-establish itself when machines enter or leave the ring. When a machine enters the ring it performs a lobe test to verify that its own connection is working properly, if it passes, it sends a voltage to the hub which operates a relay to insert it into the ring. If a problem occurs anywhere on the ring, the machine that is immediately after the fault will cease to receive signals. If this situation continues for a short period of time it initiates a recovery procedure which assumes that its NAUN is at fault, the outcome of this procedure either removes its neighbour from the ring or it removes itself.

Token Ring Operation Using a Hub

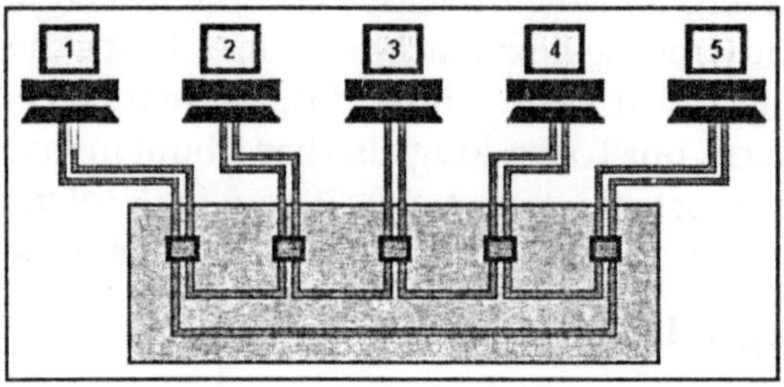

A Token Ring hub simply changes the topology from a physical ring to a star wired ring. The Token still circulates around the network and is still controlled in the same manner, however, using a hub or a switch greatly improves reliability because the hub can automatically bypass any ports that are disconnected or have a cabling fault.

Further advancements have been made in recent years with regard to Token Ring technology, such as early Token release and Token Ring switching but as this site is primarily concerned with cabling issues we will not go into any more detail here.

STAR TOPOLOGY

Star topology is the most commonly used physical technology in Ethernets LANS, when installed, the star topology resembles spokes I n a bicycle wheel. The star topology is made up of a central connection point that is a device such as a hub, switch, or router , where all the cabling segments meet. Each host in the network is connected to the central devices with its own cables although a physical star topology costs more to implement than the physical bus topology , the advantage of star topology make it worth the additional cost. Because each host it connected to the central device with its own cable, when that cable has a problem , only that host is affected, the rest of the network remains operational this benefit is extremely important and is why virtually every newly designed Ethernet a central connection point might be desirable for security or restricted access , but this is also a main disadvantage of a star topology .if the central device fails, the whole network become disconnected .when a star network is expanded to include an additional networking device that is connected for the main networking device, it is called an extended star topology.

Description

A star topology is designed with each node (file server, workstations, and peripherals) connected directly to a central network hub or concentrator as shown in figure below:

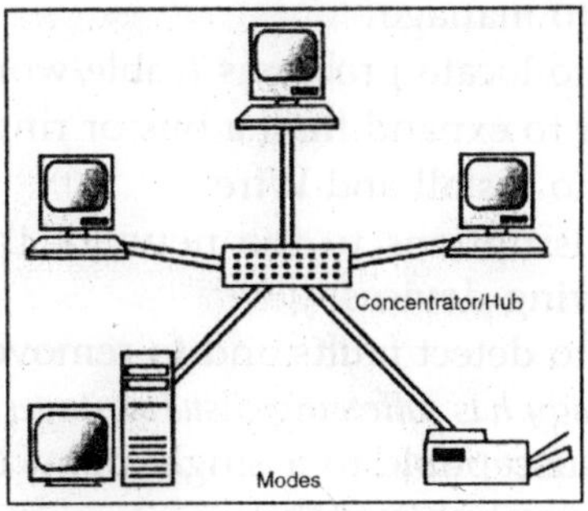

Data on a star network passes through the hub or concentrator before continuing to its destination. The hub or concentrator manages and controls all functions of the network.

It also acts as a repeater for the data flow. This configuration is common with twisted pair cable; however, it can also be used with coaxial cable or fibre optic cable.

Many businesses and home networks use the star topology. A star network features a central connection point called a "hub" that may be an actual hub or a switch as shown below:

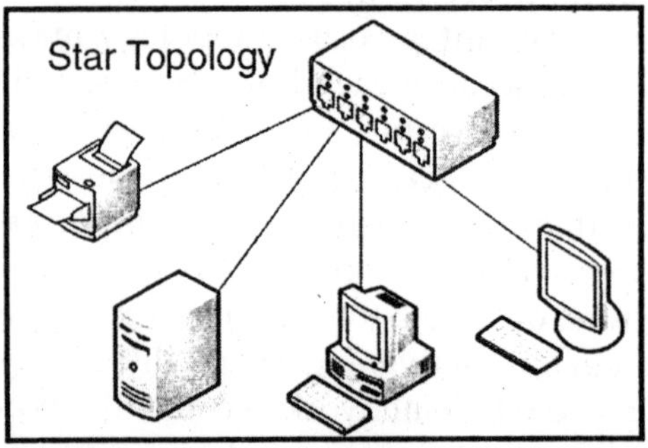

Devices typically connect to the hub with Unshielded Twisted Pair (UTP) Ethernet cables also known as RJ45 cables. Compared to the bus topology, a star network generally requires more cable, but a failure in any star network cable will only take down one computer's network access and not the entire LAN.

Star topology has the following advantages:

- Easy to manage
- Easy to locate problems (cable/workstations)
- Easier to expand than a bus or ring topology
- Easy to Install and Wire
- No disruptions to the network then connecting or removing devices.
- Easy to detect faults and to remove parts.

Star topology has following disadvantages:

- It is susceptible to a single point of failure be it the server or hub/switch

- With Increased devices and traffic can make the network slow
- Requires more Cable Length.
- If the hub or concentrator fails, nodes attached are disabled.
- More expensive than linear bus topologies because of the cost of the concentrators.

TREE TOPOLOGY

Among all the Network Topologies we can derive that the Tree Topology is a combination of the bus and the Star Topology. The tree like structure allows you to have many servers on the network and you can branch out the network in many ways.

This is particularly helpful for colleges, universities and schools so that each of the branches can identify the relevant systems in their own network and yet connect to the big network in some way.

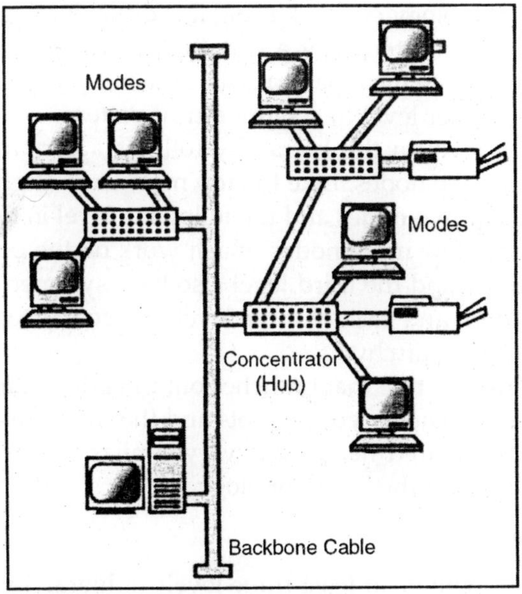

A Tree Structure suits best when the network is widely spread and vastly divided into many branches. Like any other topologies, the Tree Topology has its advantages and disadvantages. A Tree Network may not suit small networks and it may be a waste of cable to use it for small networks. Tree Topology has some limitations and the configuration should suit those limitations.

Benefits

A Tree Topology is supported by many network vendors ad even hardware vendors. A point to point connection is possible with Tree Networks. All the computers have access to the larger and their immediate networks. Best topology for branched out networks.

Limitations

In a Network Topology the length of the network depends on the type of cable that is being used. The Tree Topology network is entirely dependant on the trunk which is the main backbone of the network.

If that has to fail then the entire network would fail. Since the Tree Topology network is big it is difficult to configure and can get complicated after a certain point. The Tree Topology follows a hierarchical pattern where each level is connected to the next higher level in a symmetrical pattern.

Each level in the hierarchy follows a certain pattern in connecting the nodes. Like the top most level might have only one node or two nodes and the following level in the hierarchy might have few more nodes which work on the point to point connectivity and the third level also has asymmetrical node to node pattern and each of these levels are connected to the root level in the hierarchy.

Think of a tree that branches out in various directions and all these branches need the roots and the tree trunk to survive. A Tree Structured network is very similar to this and that is why it is called the Tree Topology.

Features

There will be at least three levels of hierarchy in the Tree Network Topology and they all work based on the root node.

The Tree Topology has two kinds of topology integral in it, the star and the linear way of connecting to nodes. The Tree Topology functions by taking into account the total number of nodes present in the network.

It does not matter how many nodes are there on each level. Nodes can be added to any level of the hierarchy and there are no limitations a far as the total number of nodes do not exceed. The higher levels in the hierarchy are expected to perform more functions than the lower levels in the network.

Advantages of a Tree Topology

- Point-to-point wiring for individual segments.
- Supported by several hardware and software venders.

Disadvantages of a Tree Topology

- Overall length of each segment is limited by the type of cabling used.
- If the backbone line breaks, the entire segment goes down.
- More difficult to configure and wire than other topologies.

MESH TOPOLOGY

A type of network setup where each of the computers and network devices are interconnected with one another, allowing for most transmissions to be distributed, even if one of the connections go down.

This type of topology is not commonly used for most computer networks as it is difficult and expensive to have redundant connection to every computer. However, this type of topology is commonly used for wireless networks.

The mesh topology incorporates a unique network design in which each computer on the network connects to every other, creating a point-to-point connection between every device on the network. The purpose of the mesh design is to provide a high level of redundancy. If one network cable fails, the data always has an alternative path to get to its destination.

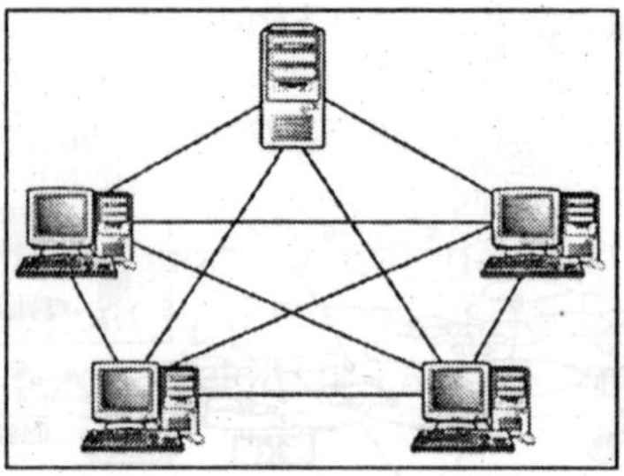

As seen in the above figure, the wiring for a mesh network can be very complicated. Further, the cabling costs associated with the mesh topology can be high, and troubleshooting a failed cable can be tricky.

Because of this, the mesh topology is rarely used. A variation on a true mesh topology is the hybrid mesh. It creates a redundant point-to-point network connection between only specific network devices.

Wireless Mesh Networks

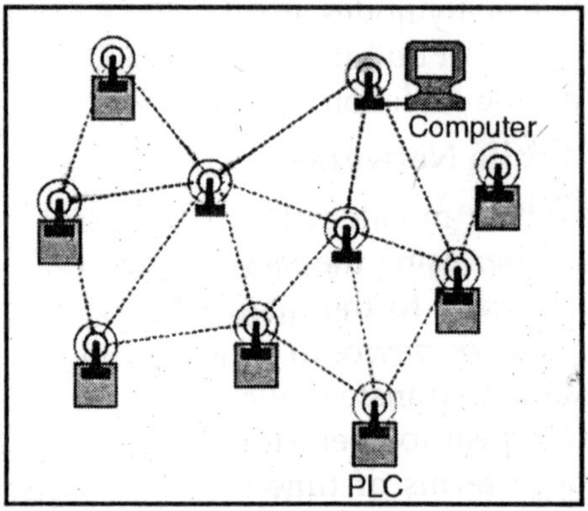

Wireless Mesh Networks work based on the radio frequencies and was originally developed by the army to be able to communicate. The reliability factor is high in any kind of Mesh Network.

There are three types of wireless Mesh Topologies:

- Fixed Wireless Connections
- Peer to Peer or Adhoc Networks
- Node to Node

Fixed Mesh Networks

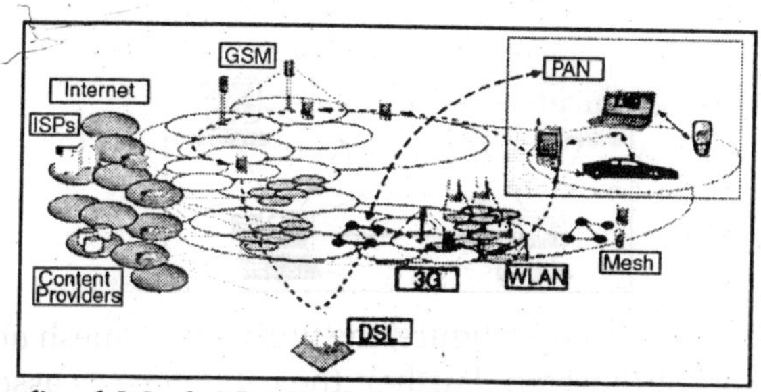

The fixed Mesh Networks will work only in the specified location and they are not mobile networks. They are meant to be used in a limited surrounding with boundaries. The location of nodes in affixed Mesh Network is all pre determined and they are not interchangeable.

The fixed Mesh Network does not work on line of sight like the other types of Mesh Networks. The total number of hops in a fixed Mesh Network is usually fixed and also short. There may not be many nodes as this kind of Mesh Networks exist within an office or building. More often than not the data travels ion a specific direction.

Peer to Peer Mobile Networks

In a peer to peer mobile network the individual devices connect to each other using the Mesh Network. The peer does not require connecting to the main node and they can still communicate from one device to another device by taking the shortest possible data transfer route. However many experts believe that in the peer to peer Mesh Networks the problems with scalability in terms of time taken for data transfer is questionable. The device has to know to transmit the data in the most optimal path and the entire data transfer or depends on this single factor. If the device is incapable then the whole purpose of using it in a peer to peer connection is lost.

EMAIL

DEFINITION

Email is simply the shortened form of electronic mail, a

protocol for receiving, sending and storing electronic messages. Email has gained popularity with the spread of the Internet. In many cases, email has become the preferred method of communication.

Though there is some degree of uncertainty as to when e-mail was invented, the father of the modern version is generally regarded to be American Ray Tomlinson. Before Tomlinson, messages could be sent between users but only those connected to the same computer. They could not be targeted to a particular individual.

Tomlinson devised a way to address email to certain users and thus was credited for one of the most important communication inventions in the 20th century. Tomlinson's idea was to identify the name of the user and the computer at which they were located. As a result, the basic formula for addressing an email was username@usercomputer. This standard has not changed over the years, other than the user computer now commonly being replaced by the name of an email provider. In many cases, this is the same as the user's Internet service provider.

The influence of email cannot be overstated. The United States Postal Service, for example, notes that it handles 212 billion pieces of mail per year. Many sources have nearly that many e-mails being sent back and forth every single day. In other words, email handles more than 300 times the amount of mail of the largest postal system in the world.

In many cases, users receive, send and store email based on one of two standards, SMTP or POP. SMTP stands for simple message transfer protocol. POP stands for Post Office Protocol. Though there is some amount of confusion over what these two protocols mean, the explanation is rather simple. POP is a protocol for storage of email. SMTP is a protocol for sending and receiving.

Index

M

N

O

P

R

S

T

U

V

W

Z